MUSIC

FOR THE

MOVIES

MUSIC

FOR THE

MOVIES

2ND EDITION
EXPANDED AND UPDATED

TONY THOMAS

SILMAN-JAMES PRESS   **LOS ANGELES**

First Edition

10 9 8 7 6 5 4 3 2 1

Library of Congress Cataloging-in-Publication Data

Thomas, Tony, 1927-
Music for the movies / Tony Thomas. — 2nd ed.
p. cm.
1. Motion picture music—History and criticism.
I. Title.
ML2075.T54 1997   781.5'42—dc21   97-27528

ISBN: 1-879505-37-1

Cover design by Wade Lageose, Art Hotel

Printed and bound in the United States of America

Silman-James Press
1181 Angelo Drive
Beverly Hills, CA 90210

To the memory of Miklos Rozsa

Contents

Introduction   *ix*

WHAT'S THE SCORE?   *1*
    Fred Karlin on the Mechanics of Scoring Pictures   *16*
    William Alwyn on the Aesthetics of Scoring Pictures   *31*

THE GOLDEN DAYS   *41*
    Herbert Stothart   *46*
    Victor Young   *50*
    John Green   *57*
    Alfred Newman   *65*

THE MITTEL-EUROPA STRAIN   *77*
    Dimitri Tiomkin   *78*
    Franz Waxman   *92*
    Bronislau Kaper   *103*
    Miklos Rozsa   *114*

THEMES FROM THE VIENNA WOODS   *137*
    Max Steiner   *141*
    Erich Wolfgang Korngold   *160*

THE PRICE OF EXCELLENCE   *185*
    Bernard Herrmann   *186*
    Hugo Friedhofer   *195*
    David Raksin   *210*

AMERICANA TO THE FORE   *221*

    George Antheil   *223*

    Virgil Thomson   *229*

    Aaron Copland   *2233*

    Alex North   *239*

    Elmer Bernstein   *249*

    George Duning   *262*

HENRY MANCINI AND OTHERS   *267*

    Leonard Rosenman   *277*

    Jerry Goldsmith   *284*

    Lalo Schifrin   *292*

MORE RECENTLY   *301*

    John Scott   *303*

    David Shire   *308*

    Bruce Broughton   *315*

    Basil Poledouris   *322*

INTRODUCTION

The first edition of *Music for the Movies* was written in 1971 and published two years later by A. S. Barnes and Company. My attempts to get a commitment from a publisher prior to writing it proved fruitless. In fact, I was warned by most of them that film music was a subject of limited interest and would be a hard sell. Barnes took a chance, however, and to both their surprise and mine, the book did quite well, eventually going into four printings. In 1979, Barnes published my second book on the same subject, *Film Score*.

Obviously, after more than twenty years since the first publication of *Music for the Movies*, some revision was needed: sadly, several of the composers I had written about had died, and an additional chapter was needed to cover the years since the first publication.

In the original introduction I gave my reasons for writing the book and, for the sake of new readers, perhaps I should repeat them. *Music for the Movies* is intended as an appreciation of the craft of film composition, albeit from a somewhat personal point of view. My fascination with film scoring began when I was eleven years old and I first saw *The Adventures of Robin Hood* and came out of the theater humming Erich Korngold's stirring main-title melody. My awareness of the score clearly is a result of growing up in a musical milieu. My father was a musician and I had, by that time, been studying piano for three years, regrettably to no avail. I had virtually no talent as a performer, but I did develop an appreciation of music, one that I was fortunate enough to make part of my livelihood. I became a radio announcer in Canada when I was twenty and was soon involved in music programming.

In 1959, as a writer-producer for the Canadian Broadcasting Corporation in Toronto, I took the first of many trips to Hollywood to gather taped interviews for various CBC productions, one of which was a weekly half-hour show on film music produced by Gerald Pratley. Aside from interviewing actors, directors and sundry film artists, I was in the happy position of conducting interviews with all the composers I had admired for so long. Of those dealt with in this book, I had meetings or correspondence with all but Victor Young, George Antheil, and Herbert Stothart. The quotations from Young came from research at the library of the Academy of Motion Picture Arts and Sciences in Los Angeles, those from Antheil from his widow, and those from Stothart from his son who bears the same name. All of the quoted comments from the other composers came from interviews I did with them or, in a few cases, from correspondence.

Music for the Movies is not intended as a definitive history of film music. It deals almost entirely with work done in Hollywood, and I'll leave others to write about the accomplishments of composers in Britain, Europe, Russia, and Japan. My aim is to create an overall appreciation of film scoring, but I must confess that my emphasis has been on those composers whose work I have most enjoyed. In a way, the book is an expression of my gratitude to them, not only for what they did in films but for whetting my appetite for music in general. Their work led me to explore all kinds of composition—and that's the best kind of music education because it's self-propelling.

WHAT'S
THE
SCORE?

During the production of *Lifeboat* at Twentieth Century-Fox in 1944, composer David Raksin was stopped by a friend in the studio commissary and told, perhaps a little too pointedly, that Alfred Hitchcock had decided against using any music in the film. Raksin, inured to snide comments on film music, mused for a moment and asked why and how that unusual decision had been reached. Said the friend, "Well, Hitchcock feels that since the entire action of the film takes place in a lifeboat on the open ocean, where would the music come from?" Replied Raksin, "Ask Mr. Hitchcock to explain where the cameras come from, and I'll tell him where the music comes from."

Amusing though it may be, this anecdote puts its finger on a sore spot—the general lack of understanding about the role of music in films. It is a role that is not fully understood even within the film industry itself, possibly because music is the most abstract of the film arts. It is also the most abused and the most exploited. Famous producers and directors have been heard to say that if pictures were better made, they wouldn't need music, to which the composers reply that good pictures are made by talent, not the lack of music.

Film composers operate on strange terms. A good score can't save a bad film, nor will a bad score kill a good picture. There is a certain stigma attached to film music that is partly warranted due to the large amount of cliché-ridden material written over the years. Ironically, the general level of film music is not the responsibility of composers alone since they are essentially creating a "work for hire"—i.e., they work for the producer. Unfortunately, far too many producers have tin ears while craving only the most obviously commercial music for their films. They are rather like the man who would march into Tiffany's and say, "Show me what you have in chrome."

A chilling example of musical ignorance at a high level occurred during the production of *The Battle of Britain*. Sir William Walton was hired to score the film, a logical choice in view of his skill and the fact that his soaring music for *Spitfire/First of the Few* in 1942 is a highlight in the annals of film music. After Walton's score for *The Battle of Britain* had been recorded, the tapes were flown to New York. There an official at United Artists, who deserves the distinction of being anonymous, listened and said, "The music stinks, get somebody else." Another composer, Ron Goodwin, who had written an agreeable score for *Those Magnificent Men in Their Flying Machines*, was brought in and wrote a competent, straightforward score. Goodwin, an undeniably tuneful composer, was probably somewhat embarrassed over the Walton matter, but a job is a job—particularly when the job is scoring a multi-million-dollar picture. On hearing about this dumping of his friend Walton's score, Sir Laurence Olivier made it known to the producers that he would have his name removed from the credits unless some part of the Walton score was retained. This would have been an ugly bit of publicity since Olivier's role as Air Marshall Dowding was the most crucial one in the film. The producers decided to keep Sir William's scoring for the five-minute segment of the film in which a montage of aerial dog-fights are presented almost like a surrealist ballet. This beautifully photographed sequence, dramatically and eerily scored by Walton, is easily the highlight of a generally disappointing film. Olivier's action, which he never allowed to be publicized in order not to embarrass Sir William, was a rare stand for an actor to take. Walton had scored Olivier's *Henry V, Hamlet,* and *Richard III,* so Olivier had every reason to know what imaginative, inventive scoring by a skillful composer can do for a film.

Film is a kind of discourse among its various parts, each at its best when doing something that none of the others can do as well. In this respect, music comes to bear when helping to define the meaning of the film by stimulating and guiding an emotional response to the visuals. Directly and pervasively appealing to the subconscious, music may also prepare the emotional climate of the other film components. It is this unique ability to influence the audience subconsciously that makes music truly valuable to the cinema. Moreover, music can complete the total picture to produce a kind of dramatic truth, when the visual element is not always capable of doing so.

Hopefully, idealistically, film will one day take its place beside musical theater as a free, unrestricted outlet for a composer's imagination. Ralph Vaughan Williams once said, "Film contains potentialities for the combination of the arts such as Wagner never dreamed of." In the meantime, the best film composers continue to wage guerrilla warfare, battling the disdain of the critics, the indifference of the public, the commercial pressures of the recording industry, and—worst of all—the lack of musical understanding of film producers and directors.

The art of combining moving pictures with musical tones is still a mysterious art. Describing its values and functions is rather like describing a beautiful woman—there's no way of doing it adequately, but one should not be condemned for trying. At its most functional level, film music serves as a cohesive agent, filling in empty spaces in the action or the dialogue—this is neutral, background music that must enliven and color scenes without drawing attention to itself.

The most important film music builds a sense of continuity that unites the visual elements. The obvious example of this is the cinematic montage, a cascade of varying shots that would be chaotic without some unifying musical thought.

Skillful scoring can accomplish the theatrical build-up of scenes by pinpointing various emotions and actions and then rounding them off with a sense of finality. In this respect, music becomes a definite storytelling device.

On a higher level, film music accomplishes two important things (how well depends on the composer): it creates atmosphere and colors the tone of the picture. Atmospheric music can be quite obviously geographical or historical. Placing the story in a certain locale at a certain time is a test of the composer's knowledge and imagination.

Coloring the tone and giving the picture its subtle extra dimension is the film music that separates the boy composers from the men composers. A competent composer is able to shade emotions, to lighten or darken moods, to heighten sensitivities, to imply, to suggest, to define character and refine personality, to help generate momentum or create tension, to warm the picture or cool it, and, most subtle of all, to allude to thoughts that are unspoken and situations that remain unseen. Such music plays upon the minds of the audience.

In the hands of clever composers, a true musical drama is created. Erich Korngold persuaded you that Errol Flynn was really Robin Hood, Max Steiner told you what it was like for a Southern aristocrat to lose the war and a way of life, Miklos Rozsa let you know how Ray Milland felt on a lost weekend, and Bernard Herrmann terrified you as some weirdo butchered Janet Leigh in the shower. If you believed that Dana Andrews really loved Laura, thank David Raksin; or if you shared Dana's mind wanderings as he sat in the nose of a wrecked B-36, tip your hat to Hugo Friedhofer. If your heart went out to Gary Cooper as he waited for those gunman at high noon, you might give a thought to Dimitri Tiomkin; and if you think Jennifer Jones really saw the Virgin Mary, then light a little candle to the memory of the late Alfred Newman. And Joan Fontaine was absolutely right when she felt Manderley was haunted, but it wasn't the spirit of Rebecca—it was Franz Waxman's music.

Endless discussion can be made about the need for music in films, but perhaps the most pertinent argument was made by Aaron Copland when he said, "I wish more audiences could have the experience of watching a movie without any music and then seeing it the second time with music added. I think that would give them a full sense of what music does for making the cold movie screen seem more humane, more touching, and more civilized." Copland's viewpoint is easy to illustrate by using *Our Town* (1940). His main theme, stated with only five notes, sums up the tone of Thornton Wilder's classic tale of family life in a small New England town.

What the acerbically witty pianist Oscar Levant once said about *King Kong* (1933)—"It sounds like a Max Steiner concert with pictures"—could surely be said about *Star Wars* (1977). John Williams' full-blooded, romantic, soaring, heroic score gives humanity to what are patently comic-book characters and gives their improbable adventures a vestige of probability. Williams has performed similar services many times. His music for *Dracula* (1979) gives the title character an erotic allure no previous version had ever touched upon. At the end of *E. T. the Extra-Terrestrial* (1982), as the strange-looking but lovable little creature says goodbye to his Earth chum and boards his spaceship to go home, it becomes almost impossible for the audience not to cry. What that audience may not realize is that they are not just responding to what they are seeing, but also to what Williams is doing to their emotions with his music.

The effectiveness of music in film is easily illustrated with John Williams' score for *Jaws* (1975). The opening reel of that fine film has a sequence where the camera moves through the murky underwater depths as ghostly plants sway back and forth. Without music it could be a shot from a Cousteau documentary—with Williams' ominous ostinato played on low celli it becomes a heart-arresting experience. That little bit of music tells us that these are terribly dangerous waters to be gliding through.

There are, of course, many examples of the efficacy of music scoring. In the desert sequences of *Lawrence of Arabia* (1962), Maurice Jarre's use of that strange electronic instrument, the Ondes Martenot, gives an almost surrealistic appeal to the solitude of the vast sand dunes, just as his use of percussion—and Jarre never lets us forget he was a percussionist before he was a composer—gives stature to the enigmatic T. E. Lawrence, as played by the enigmatic Peter O'Toole. In *Picnic* (1955), when William Holden spots Kim Novak and entices her to dance with him, George Duning's exquisite theme tells us precisely what Holden and Novak are feeling about each other. In *The Miracle Worker* (1962), Lawrence Rosenthal, with very light and subtle instrumentation, underlines the confusion of a blind-deaf-mute child and the compassion of a teacher who leads her into comprehension. In *The Elephant Man* (1980), John Morris performed a similar service, helping actor John Hurt communicate the poignancy of a gentle soul trapped in a hideously deformed body. These are composers who add that elusive comment that only music can make.

Film music is the *unseen* element in the movie experience and therefore the most difficult to discuss. It is the least tangible of all the many components involved in the most collaborative of all the arts. Two composers of equal talent might have quite different views on how to score the same film. Max Steiner's score for *Gone With the Wind* (1939) is one of the glories of that beloved picture. It captures the romance and the sadness and delineates all the many characters to tie the huge story together. However, another composer could have written a quite different score that might have been equally effective. All we can agree upon is that *Gone With the Wind* is a film that just had to have a music score.

Music can be a cohesive force in the making of a movie. A film is made up of many bits and pieces; music can tie them all together in a seemingly logical way. No one knows this better than a composer who has successfully scored films. Music is the art most removed from reality and most capable of penetrating the subconscience. Music makes a direct appeal to the emotions—its presence does not require any explanation. Music, especially in film, insinuates itself. Unfortunately there seem to be far too many film directors and producers who do not quite realize this.

Composers often complain that producers turn to them too late and then expect too much. This usually occurs with films that have not turned out well, and the composer is expected to save the bacon. Adolph Deutsch once commented: "A film musician is like a mortician—he can't bring the body back to life but he's expected to make it look better." Virgil Thomson had an even more trenchant view of the odd regard in which producers hold composers: "If the film is good, the composer is expected to subdue his talent. If the film is a poor one, the composer is supposed to perform a miracle."

Writing film music is unique in one respect—it is needed, and this is a situation that is found nowhere else in contemporary musical life. Possibly it is the closest circumstance we have to that of Johann Sebastian Bach, who similarly functioned as a provider of a steady, workaday flow of music for his church in Leipzig. Purists protest the thought of Bach or any great master writing for films, but it is likely that had they lived in the twentieth century, they might have been thus engaged.

The most valid criticism is that film music fails to live up to its vast potential. The truly interesting thing about composing for the screen is not so much what it is as what it can be. Erich Korngold put it this way:

> It isn't true that the cinema places a restraint on musical expression. Music is music, whether it is for the stage, the rostrum or the cinema. Form may change, the manner of writing may vary but the composer needs to make no concessions whatever to what he conceives to be his own musical ideology. The screen's uniqueness is a spur to the imagination, a challenge to resourcefulness. The cinema is a direct avenue to the ears and hearts of the great public, and all musicians should see the screen as a musical opportunity.

Korngold proved, as did Walton, Copland, and Prokofiev, that good composers write good music—movie or otherwise. Yet critics, both professional and amateur, are steadfastly snobbish about this area of composition. They seem willing to judge opera and the concert hall by its best examples and film scoring by its worst.

In the introduction to Clifford McCarty's book *Film Composers in America*, the late critic and impresario Lawrence Morton pointed out: "Good film scores may indeed be an overwhelmed minority, but they shine like good deeds in a naughty world." As McCarty's book made obvious, a complete list of all the scores written in Hollywood reveals much mediocrity. This is a sad realization because good scores are available at no greater cost than bad scores.

As is obvious to anyone with ears and any degree of musical sensitivity, many film scores barely merit discussion. They perform a function and are quickly forgotten. Fair enough. But what need be borne in mind in evaluating film music is that the majority of the creative arts—books, plays, poems, pieces of sculpture, music for the concert hall, and the opera house—also perform briefly and quickly vanish. What is needed is intelligent criticism.

Lawrence Morton put his finger on the real problem of film music:

It doesn't have to be good in order to perform its functional duties. Except in rare instances, it has nothing to do with art. It could, and one hopes for the day when it will. In the meantime, it has everything to do with commerce. Above all it must be successful—that is, it must do something for the picture, please whoever is paying for it, and, if possible, win an Oscar. The film producer does not exist who would not sacrifice even the greatest music if he believed that such a sacrifice would ensure the success of his film. This is something of an anomaly in an industry where first-rate achievement is permitted, even encouraged, in other departments—photography, for instance, or costume and set designing . . . certainly it has been proved that although film music does not have to be good in order to fulfill its function, good music actually performs that function far more satisfactorily than bad music. This truth must be constantly hammered at producers who hire hacks when artists are available. Criticism had been laggard in the performance of this job. Producers will rest content so long as movie critics, like the movie-going public itself, continue to exhibit their altogether remarkable insensitivity to all film music except popular songs, folk tunes, ballads, or familiar concert and opera classics; and so long as music critics continue to ignore film music completely.

Lawrence Morton was well qualified to criticize the critics and to be disappointed in both the public and the film producers. He was for some years the director of the Monday Evening Concerts in Los Angeles, and he was as aware of the range and quality as he was the quantity of the musical talent available to the film studios. Most of the best Hollywood musicians participated in these concerts, and their programs were among the most intellectual anywhere. The material ranged from rescued music of the Renaissance period to the most avant-garde of contemporary composition, and it was not uncommon to find Elmer Bernstein as the pianist in a rare Haydn trio or performing the music of Anton Webern. Everyone who heard these concerts was astounded to hear the disparaging comments about the quality of the musicianship involved in the making of films. It is amazing to find people who ordinarily shy away from generalizations leaping to embrace the obvious and tiresome canards about film music.

It is, of course, very easy to side with the composers and condemn the producers. However, the situation needs to be viewed in perspective since films are made because it is in someone's interest to make them. David Raksin sees the situation with a clear eye:

Hollywood is a business. It is not run for the edification or the enjoyment of people—it produces these things peripherally because it is to somebody's profit to do so. Those of us who work within this framework of profit-making are often engaged in trying, one way or another, to do something we think is art or artisanry—this place is full of people who are talented and highly skilled—but our films are made for the widest possible public, and they are therefore less specialized, less intellectual, and less satisfying in terms of everyday life. The popular taste doesn't need to have anything bad said about it by me. It's a fact of life, one of the more unfortunate facts and one of the real ones. This popular level of comprehension, of intelligence, of taste, is the level to which most films, to recoup their investment, must cater. Pictures are, in their way, a rather accurate reflection of the state of public mores.

It is difficult not to be nostalgic in discussing Hollywood. As an industry town, Hollywood is not, and can never be again, what it once was. The world has changed, the public and its tastes have changed, and methods of making films have changed. Many of the changes are for the better—it is faintly absurd to imagine all films made thirty or even fifty years ago to be more enjoyable than those made today. But there was a Golden Age in Hollywood and out of its very vastness came worthy works. The big studios, for all their faults, were able to hire the best available talent, and sometimes the talent was tough enough to overcome the taste of the people for which it labored. An examination of the history of Hollywood leaves one with the odd thought that many of the finest pictures must have been made in spite of the front-office executives rather than because of them.

The opposite proved the case in the music departments; those music directors who were men of genuine talent and taste were often left to rule their bailiwicks without interference. Alfred Newman, for example, as head of music for Twentieth Century-Fox, had the complete confidence of studio boss Darryl F. Zanuck and made his own decisions when hiring players, arrangers, and composers, but with the break-up of the major studios the music situation changed. Composers, like actors, writers, and directors, became free-lancers represented by agents. This independence of talent resulted, in the main, in better and more interesting films but not necessarily better and more interesting music scores.

Two factors have contributed to what may, with some protestation, be considered a decline in the standards of film composition. One is the virtual disappearance of music directors—heads of departments—men like Alfred Newman at Fox, John Green at MGM, Morris Stoloff at Columbia. Recalls Elmer Bernstein:

> I never even met the film's director on the first few films I scored. I was totally responsible to the music directors; and that was good, because the music directors took responsibility for the spotting of the picture and were right there to the end of the dub. If there was something wrong with the score, it was the music director who took the flak and who stood between the composer and the producer. The composer was therefore in a much more comfortable position because he was dealing with a colleague, someone who could read music.

That situation has not existed for years. Now composers find themselves dealing with directors and producers who not only know little about music but who seem to understand little about the relationship of the music to the films—other than to hope that a good theme song might be a hit recording and therefore become as highly effective and relatively inexpensive means of promoting the picture.

The second factor is the recording business, which is not a factor to scoff at. It is the recording industry and its marriage with radio that has altered musical culture in America. With the emergence of rock-and-roll in the mid-fifties, tastes began to change. Publishers and record producers catered to teenagers as never before, and within a decade, many of America's most celebrated song writers—men like Irving Berlin, Harold Arlen, Hoagy Carmichael, Harry Warren, and Arthur Schwartz—found themselves virtually shunted to the sidelines. Royalties from their old songs continued to pour in, largely due to Muzak, but no one seemed interested in anything new from them.

Something similar happened in Hollywood. More and more film scores emerged with pop-orientated music, often using rock or folk musicians on the soundtrack. The folly of that method gradually became apparent and within a few years it ceased. But the sixties proved barren years for some former giants of film scoring—Miklos Rozsa, for example, went for five years without being asked to score a film.

Whether the score is pop-oriented or traditionally orchestral is not the point, however. Any type of music might work in a film as long as it is compatible with the nature of the film—it need not flirt with emotions as most old scores did, nor ignore emotions as many contemporary scores do—but when a producer substitutes irrelevant music for interpretative music, he lessens one of film's most sensitive elements. The criteria for a good score remains constant: does the music complement the film, does it enlarge the film's emotional scope, does it help give the film cohesion . . . does music mean anything?

To help explain the art and craft of writing a film score, I turned to two composers. One is a contemporary American composer, Fred Karlin, and the other a deceased Englishman, William Alwyn, with whom I once had the pleasure of corresponding.

Fred Karlin pinpoints the beginning of his interest in music to the day he walked into a Chicago movie theater and saw *Young Man With a Horn*, a 1950 film starring Kirk Douglas as a character based upon the legendary jazz trumpeter Bix Beiderbecke. "Harry James did the actual playing of the instrument, and it turned out to be a major experience in my life. It convinced me that I had to play the trumpet." Karlin's parents bought him a horn, and he played it through his final year of high school and the following four years at Amherst College. It was while at Amherst that he had another change-of-life experience. He was deeply moved by a concert performance of Paul Hindemith's symphonic poem *Mathis der Maler*. Until then, he had been an honors student in literature, but after hearing the Hindemith he persuaded the Amherst music department to let him switch from literature to music. By writing a string quartet, he convinced them he was serious.

After graduating from Amherst with a degree in composition, Karlin returned to Chicago, where he found employment writing jazz arrangements. By 1958 he had become the house trumpeter at the popular Chicago music spot, Jazz Ltd., all the while continuing to study music. That same year he moved to New York. Within two years Karlin was writing arrangements for Radio City Music Hall (commissioned by Ray Wright, the theater's chief arranger), and at the same time he was working on arrangements for Benny Goodman's jazz group. As he moved more and more into the world of commercial music, he maintained his interest in more serious music by studying conducting with the esteemed Hungarian conductor-composer Tibor Serly, famed for his collaboration with Béla Bartók. In 1966, producer Alan Pakula and director Robert Mulligan decided he was the man they wanted to score their New York-based film *Up the Down Staircase*, beginning for Karlin a film career that has continued nonstop. Following the Pakula-Mulligan film with scores for movies as varied as the comedy *Yours, Mine and Ours* (1968), and the Film-Noir Western *The Stalking Moon* (1969), his résumé now lists some 120 theatrical and television films. He won an Oscar for his music for the song "For All We Know," written for *Lovers and Other Strangers* (1970), and an Emmy for scoring the TV film *The Autobiography of Miss Jane Pittman* (1974).

In 1988, Karlin designed an eight-evening film-composing workshop for ASCAP, which includes a scoring session with a forty-piece orchestra. Karlin donates his time to the annual ASCAP/Fred Karlin Film Scoring Workshop, which is free to its participants and has attracted talented young professionals from around the world. He also teaches at the University of Southern California as part of Buddy Baker's Film and Television Scoring program and is the author of two books: *On the Track: A Guide to Contemporary Film Scoring*, which he co-authored by Rayburn Wright (Schirmer Books, 1990), and *Listening to Movies: The Film Lovers Guide to Film Music* (Schirmer Books, 1994). The following was written expressly for this book.

Fred Karlin on the Mechanics of Scoring Pictures

The technical aspects of film scoring have changed dramatically during the past sixty years. In 1933 (the year Max Steiner scored *King Kong* for RKO), timings were taken with a handheld stopwatch as the film was projected in a small screening room. With that primitive technique, inaccuracy was almost a certainty, and the composers made adjustments on the scoring stage to correct the inevitable errors in synchronization. By the end of that decade Moviola editing machines were in common usage, making accurate timings relatively easy. The bulky green Moviola, with its nerveracking clatter and tinny yet piercing sound, necessitated the backbreaking manipulation of twenty-four or more thousand-foot reels of film and mag stripe (sound film). Yet Moviolas became the foundation of film music synchronization, enabling the music editor to prepare elaborate timing sheets for each cue in the score by reading the footage counters (and, later, real-time counters as well) attached to the machines. These timing sheets include an indication of all

Fred Karlin (photo by Lester Cohen, courtesy of ASCAP)

editorial cuts in the film, all actions of any significance (including emotional reactions such as the beginning of a smile), relevant sound effects (gun shots, off-screen shouts, and so on), the beginning and end of all dialogue phrases—all calculated to the hundredth of a second. Well-prepared timings sheets can remind composers of the nuances of the drama, and their use, along with frequent studio screenings, became the common work method for the next forty-five years or so. Only a few film composers used Moviolas (as I did), but we all used the timings sheets.

Now, however, some composers have no interest in—and often no need for—a music editor's typed-out timing sheets. With their computers locked into sync with videotape copies of the film, their music can be as synchronous as they wish, and they can be confident of one hundred percent accuracy on the scoring stage. After inputting the timings of a cue into special computer programs along with a target tempo, these programs will help select the precise tempo (and variations of that tempo as necessary) that will "hit" whatever significant moments in the action that the composer may desire for each sequence. These programs will even create sketch paper for a cue with all the timings and notes about dialogue and action printed above the relevant blank bars. You can see that although many composers still do use timings calculations as an aid in locating and recalling the specifics of a given scene, computer power has to a considerable extent replaced traditional timings breakdowns. Adjusting to this reality, many music editors now prepare their timings information within one of these specially designed film music programs and send a computer disc of the finished timings to the composer, who can then work with this information on his or her own computer as the score evolves.

What a dramatic change. When I scored my first film (*Up the Down Staircase*) in 1967, I lived in New York. There were no music editors there at that time—the film editors did whatever was required and the composers did the rest. I knew about click tracks (using a steady metronomic tempo while composing and recording), and had enough of a grasp of the basic mathematics of film synchronization to take timings on my Moviola and do the calculations myself. At that time, metronomic reference tempos were created by the music editor, who mailed me a complete set of "click loops" from Hollywood, with tempos ranging from very slow (48 beats per minute) to fairly fast (240 beats per minute). These loops were short pieces of 35mm mag stripe (sound film) with a specific tempo punched into the film (for example, every tenth frame, or every 10^1/$_8$ frame). As the film loop circled around one of the Moviola's sound heads, a steady click was produced as the prepared click on the loop traveled across the sound head every tenth frame or whatever the tempo might be. Digital metronomes and computer-generated clicks, however, have long since replaced the old click loops.

Although the technology has developed, the basic step-by-step process of scoring a film has remained very straightforward: read the script; screen a rough cut; spot the final cut of the film with the filmmakers and editors to determine the best places for music to begin and end; write a theme or two, and play these for the filmmakers to be sure everyone agrees on the concept and primary musical material; write the score over a period of four or six weeks, and demonstrate as much of it as the filmmakers desire; have it orchestrated (or, occasionally, orchestrate it yourself); record the score; and mix the score onto the soundtrack along with the dialogue and sound effects at the dubbing sessions. Over the years, however, this procedure has evolved somewhat.

Sometimes the director has a very clear idea of where he or she wants music, in which case the composer may not be able to contribute much to the spotting sessions. More often, however, there are possibilities for collaboration between the filmmakers and the composer, with the film editor and music editor present to add their points of view as well. With the universal usage of "flatbed" editing machines, many filmmakers prefer to spot in the editor's room using the editing machine, rather than projecting the film in a screening room. In either case, the film is played scene by scene, and rerun as necessary in order to select precise frames at which each music cue will start and end. The music editor then prepares all timings sheets within the next few days, designed to satisfy the composer's specifications.

After developing an overall idea or concept for the entire score and creating some thematic materials that express this concept, most composers in the nineties find themselves discussing their ideas with the director, who most often has a clear vision of what he or she believes the score should be for this particular film. Although filmmakers often like to talk about these ideas, they are more and more likely to demonstrate them with classical and pop music, and music from other film scores. By putting cues from a score such as Hans Zimmer's *Rain Man* directly onto the soundtrack while the film is still in rough cut, a director can be quite specific about tastes and expectations. He or she can be articulate by suggesting to the composer that a certain sequence or, in fact, the entire score, should be performed on electronic keyboards, using various plucked sounds that don't emphasize the film's emotions; the director can be even more communicative by adding to this directive, "Something like the score for *Rain Man*"; or he or she can be unmistakably clear about his or her wishes by synchronizing a particular moment in that score with a specific scene in the film.

The music used in this way is selected by the director, the film editor, or the music editor (but always approved by the director), and is known as "temp" music—that is, temporary music. If the composer is urged to replicate not only the emotional qualities of the temp music, but also its textural elements and even, in some cases, its melodic contour, the resultant music often sounds uncomfortably like its role model. Some composers and music editors prefer to use the composer's own previously recorded music for temp tracks. Composers' opinions differ with regard to the usefulness of temp music; however, most agree not only that it is an effective communication device, but also one with which all film composers must learn to live.

Another side of this situation had become significant in the evolution of the film scoring process: composers in the nineties usually are asked to demonstrate much, if not all, of their score for the director. This is almost always done by preparing fairly elaborate electronic versions of each cue so that the director may hear an electronic sketch of the score played with the picture. Stephen Spielberg asked for electronic sketches for *The Color Purple* in 1985, at which time the available electronic resources were comparatively limited. By synchronizing recorded electronic versions of each cue with the appropriate scene, he was able to experience the dramatic impact of each cue and ask for revisions until he was satisfied. At that time, these electronic sketches were referred to as "Polaroids." Although the term hasn't entered the mainstream of the filmmaking vernacular to any extent, the practice has now become widespread in proportion to the technical potential for better-sounding demonstration recordings. Filmmakers now expect a composer to offer these electronic demonstrations. This process has served as an invitation for the director to become much more involved in the actual creation of the music. The director is able to listen to an electronic demo and say, "What about an oboe there, rather than a flute?" Although this may seem overly involved—some would say meddlesome—consider how useful it is for the director to be able to suggest with self-assurance, "We need more tension at this moment," or "Let's play this scene a bit darker." Hearing these directives on a scoring stage with eighty musicians waiting to record can be a harrowing experience for a composer. In the days before electronic demonstrations, the director's changes often resulted in rescoring entire cues during a future scoring session—an exhausting and frequently costly necessity. (This can, and does, still happen, of course.)

The advantage of this system of give and take is that both the composers and the filmmakers are able to respond emotionally to the music as they watch the film, thereby increasing the odds that the score will have a strong dramatic connection with the film's essence. Whether a score plays with or against the film's emotional texture, this inherent or established connection is the most significant role played by music for the movies. During the composing of a score, this connection is reinforced by the composer through association. When we first hear John Williams' shark motif in *Jaws*, we are forewarned of something frightening. From the moment we first hear that same music as we see the shark, we associate that theme with both the shark and the feeling of terror it stimulates. The connection is created and subsequently works on the viewer's emotions throughout the remainder of the film. Sometimes such elements in the film as historical period, geographic location, ethnic backgrounds, or personality characteristics influence the music, which in turn creates deeper connections with the film and its characters. As the composer scores a film, these and other factors are considered in-depth.

On a practical level, the process of composing the score is one of refining an overall plan as the score begins to assume a life of its own, while continually considering the amount of time remaining and the amount of music to be written. Schedules usually allow from four to six weeks for the completion of a score. If only ten days remain until the scoring sessions, and there are thirty minutes of music still to be done, you know you must compose approximately three minutes a day for ten days to complete your score. Even assuming that the sketches will be given to someone to orchestrate (as they almost always are for feature films), most composers find this a demanding schedule, especially if it continues for extended periods of time. Nevertheless, this kind of workload is not unusual, and schedules are sometimes much more intense. Directors continue to edit films right down to the last possible moment (which may be the day a particular scene is scored by a ninety-piece orchestra). In such cases, the music editors, orchestrators, music librarian, and music copyists coordinate their efforts to guarantee that there will be music on the stands when the conductor raises his or her arm for the first downbeat of each scoring session.

Composers work differently with their orchestrators, and have different expectations. Some composers' sketches are virtually complete reductions of a fully realized orchestration, requiring no creative additions whatsoever, while other sketches rely more on the orchestrator's ability to complete and bring to life the composer's intentions. Henry Mancini's sketches are an example of the former; orchestrators obviously don't like to discuss examples of the latter. Sometimes an electronic demo becomes the sketch—nothing is written out, or the electronic sketch is printed by a computer notation program. It is not unusual to see two to four names listed as orchestrators on the end credits of a movie, depending on the composing schedule and length of the score. James Newton Howard, along with two orchestrators (Brad Dechter and Chris Boardman), orchestrated Howard's score for *The Fugitive*, and Randy Edelman and Greig McRitchie orchestrated Edelman's score for *Dragon: The Bruce Lee Story*. When schedules get tight, the list lengthens. *On Robin Hood: Prince of Thieves*, Michael Kamen worked with sixteen or more orchestrators, a necessary abundance in order to finish his lengthy symphonic score in a few short weeks.

Recording the score is usually exhilarating for the filmmakers and composers. Nothing can compare to the thrill of hearing well-recorded music played brilliantly and monitored through playback speakers that can deliver the full-frequency impact of the 1906 San Francisco earthquake. And since there is the likelihood that portions of the score may in time be overwhelmed by sound effects of similar dimension, the score will never sound better. On the scoring stage, the music editor oversees the score's synchronization with the film, noting any places in a cue that might be out of sync and suggesting adjustments as necessary. The recording engineer (mixer) records the score on a multitrack digital machine, assigning various instruments and instrumental sections for the orchestra to separate tracks to be mixed later. When budgets are tight, analog multitrack or even discrete three-track or stereo formats may be used.

Other specialists are on the scoring stage to back up the composer—a music copyist in case corrections need to be written out during the session; the music contractor (who has supervised the hiring of the freelance orchestra) to keep track of the mandatory ten-minute breaks, monitor orchestra deportment, and handle any last-minute crisis; the orchestrators, who may suggest subtle (or even drastic) changes in the orchestration (one of the orchestrators also often acts as liaison for the composer in the recording booth in order to adjust balances and timbres as necessary); and a host of stage managers and recording technicians to keep everything moving along efficiently.

Even with all this good planning and organizational backup, things can and do go wrong. Machines have broken down often enough for the industry to coin the term "downtime" to define the recording studio's responsibility due to equipment malfunctions. Downtime can be extremely costly with 100 musicians waiting for the red recording light. There are other pitfalls on the scoring stage as well. Wrong notes on the musicians' parts, although commonplace, are frequently corrected without question by the superb Hollywood musicians. Missing bars (or even missing parts) and incorrect transpositions are fixed on the spot while the meter runs. (Professional proofreaders are often employed prior to scoring sessions to prevent such problems.) Incorrect tempos (usually caught and corrected by astute music editors) can destroy a cue's sync until a correction restores perfection. And a director's frequent trips to the podium for extended conversations with the composer can completely devastate even the best-planned recording schedule, necessitating overtime at best, or even another session to finish scoring the film. Through it all, the facility of those who record film music is so astonishing that these scoring sessions are typically amazing displays of musicianship and finesse. On the average, two to three minutes of music per fifty-minute hour is recorded for theatrically released films (and frequently more for television).

After the recorded score is mixed down to as few as two stereo tracks or as many as eighteen or more mono and stereo tracks, the music is mixed with the dialogue and sound effects at dubbing sessions. These sessions take place on dubbing stages, which are really screening rooms (or even small theaters) equipped with state-of-the-art sound-mixing consoles and equipment. The film editor prepares the dialogue tracks (including separate tracks with rerecorded or "looped" lines); the sound effects editors prepare many reels of sound film with separate sound effects elements; and the music editor prepares reels of music edited to synchronize with the film. If the music is delivered to the dubbing stage on multitrack tape, then the tape has a sync pulse recorded onto a separate track to ensure that the music will stay in sync with the film.

Dubbing a major feature film can take weeks, during which the composer may appear now and then, and generally be available for advice and assistance. It is at this time that the final volume and recorded sound of the score is determined—a time when many composers hear their work diminish in significance and impact as bigger-than-life sound effects prevail, particularly during action sequences. Although films released in stereo tend to have more "space" for music, the final mix of a film's sound elements invariably influences the overall effectiveness of the score and its ability to contribute to the emotional impact of a film. Often a director's philosophy on sound will affect his or her use and balance of the sound elements. Basically, though, with consistent improvements in the quality of film sound and theatrical sound systems, movie music is sounding better than ever.

Studios still preview movies before they are released, much as they did during the thirties. Editorial changes may be made, scored scenes may be trimmed or extended, and music may therefore be cut or added as well. It is not unusual for composers to rescore scenes edited after previews to accommodate new timings. If scenes are added, as in the case of Alan J. Pakula's *The Pelican Brief* (music by James Horner), then these new scenes may also need scoring. If a soundtrack album is being released, then the composer will usually produce the album, selecting the music to be used, designing any combination of cues edited together to create longer pieces of music for better listening independent of the film, and determining the album sequence. Composers remix their scores for records, using the master multitrack tapes from the scoring sessions.

Although the process of scoring a film may seem to be straightforward, composers deal with creative questions and make significant decisions that have enormous impact on the score and consequently the film itself. The actual aesthetic choices a composer makes—hundreds each day—involving the nature of the harmonic language; the use of influences such as ethnicity, geographic location, historical period, the characters' personalities and social backgrounds; the function of music in the drama at any given moment; these and many other subjective and philosophical issues are the real essence of a film composer's creative contribution. The aesthetics, so to speak, as opposed to the mechanics.

—F.K.

• • • • •

What about the aesthetics, the artistry involved in inventing music to supplement movies? Most composers have expressed their views on this fascinating form of composition but few more eloquently than William Alwyn, a distinguished Englishman who managed to balance his output between the concert hall and the cinema. Alwyn, who died in 1985 at age eighty, was a major force in British music. He taught composition at the Royal Academy of Music in London from 1925 to 1955 (he was himself a graduate), served as Chairman of the Composers' Guild, wrote many articles for music magazines, wrote poetry, and painted. He also composed eighty film scores.

Alwyn, who was born in Northampton, became intrigued with the cinema and its music while still a schoolboy. He was taught flute by a man who worked in a factory during the day and played piano at a movie theater in the evenings. Eventually, as the theater expanded the accompaniment to a small orchestra, young Alwyn was hired to play the flute and rapidly came to know a vast repertory of standard concert pieces, such as the overtures "Zampa" and "Poet and Peasant," plus catalogue items written especially for the screen. As Alwyn described it, the catalogue was designed to meet any known human situation. Each session was frantic as the musicians strove to keep up with the large number of pieces, while maintaining the immediacy that was required. Pieces of sheet music were whipped on and off music stands with lightning speed. It was the pianist-leader who bound the enterprise together with ad-libbed modulations and improvised chords. For young Alwyn it was a most basic education in the craft of supplying films with music. Some years later he had further experience performing in movie theaters as a musician in London, but by that time the craft was much more sophisticated, with prepared scores and efficient timing devices.

The list of Alwyn compositions, aside from his film work, is a long one and includes five symphonies, several concertos for various solo instruments and orchestra, many concert pieces and a great deal of chamber music. He began his film career in 1936 by scoring a modest picture entitled *The Future's in the Air*, following it over the next few years with a number of documentaries and films for the British government. He did not really hit his stride as a major film composer until the war years, particularly with *Desert Victory* (1943), *The Way Ahead* (1944), and *The True Glory* (1945), each one a mixture of documentary and drama about the war. His scoring of these films was free of the bombast that characterized most war pictures of the era.

Following the war, *The Rake's Progress* (1946), which did much to propel Rex Harrison's popularity, contained some witty music, including calypso melodies for a South American sequence. The same year he wrote a masterful score for Carol Reed's stark drama *Odd Man Out*, set in Northern Ireland and starring James Mason as an IRA agitator who is wounded during a raid and spends the remaining hours of his life trying to elude the police by shuttling between those who help him and those who would turn him in. The score perfectly matches the bleak settings, the anxiety, and yet underscores the tenderness of the dying fugitive and the girl who loves him and dies with him. It is interesting that Alwyn has written effective music for two other films about the Irish: *Captain Boycott* (1947), a historical adventure, and *Shake Hands With the Devil* (1959). The latter is a darkly realistic account of the IRA in Dublin and stars James Cagney as a dedicated revolutionary. Alwyn's fine score was issued on record, one of the very few of his many distinguished compositions for the British screen to be made available in such form.

Alwyn also scored *The Rocking Horse Winner* (1949), an unusual drama about a boy who fantasizes while riding his rocking horse and actually predicts winners at a local race track, thereby helping ease his family's need for money, but with tragic results. The score is highly important, adding an undercurrent of tension. Other interesting scores by Alwyn include *The Card* (1952, titled *The Promoter* for U.S. release), one of the most charming of the Alec Guinness comedies; *The Million Pound Note* (1953), with Gregory Peck in the Mark Twain satire; *The Seekers*, a costume adventure set in New Zealand and incorporating Maori music; and *A Night to Remember* (1958), an excellent account of the sinking of the Titanic. Alwyn also wrote the music for two classic swashbuckler films: *The Crimson Pirate* (1952), with Burt Lancaster, and *The Master of Ballantrae* (1953), one of the last and best of Errol Flynn's costume adventures.

William Alwyn's final film score was *The Running Man* in 1963. By that time what had happened in Hollywood—the increased use of pop music in movies—also happened in London. (In Hollywood, the symphonic score made a gradual comeback, thanks largely to John Williams' spectacular success with *Star Wars* in 1977.) And then, the British film industry, which had enjoyed a period of expanded activity that began with World War II and something of a steady box-office boom thereafter, started to fade away in the sixties and has never recovered, a fact that is truly tragic. Although never approaching the output of Hollywood, studios like Ealing and Rank produced a steady stream of good films and employed most of the top composers. While composers Constant Lambert, Anthony Collins, Benjamin Frankel, Richard Addinsell, Malcolm Arnold and most conspicuously William Alwyn were all gainfully and regularly employed, occasionally even serious composers like Sir William Walton, Sir Arthur Bliss, Ralph Vaughan Williams, and Sir Arnold Bax were invited to score films. But by the sixties, television had become the primary source of entertainment in Great Britain and cinemas closed by the hundreds. As British film out-

William Alwyn on the Aesthetics of Scoring Pictures

The art of film music is a specialized branch of the wider art of the film. Because it is a specialized art, the purpose for which it exists and the separate functions it fulfills are sometimes misunderstood. The musician himself is inclined to confuse it with descriptive music, which is called program music in the concert hall. Oddly enough, direct description plays a relatively small part in film music.

Composing for the film demands from the composer a purely dramatic approach to music and provides a welcome additional outlet for his theatrical instincts, other than opera, ballet, or incidental music for the stage. Perhaps that is why it has attracted composers of the caliber of Walton, Bliss, the late Dr. Vaughan Williams (who composed his first film score at the age of sixty-nine and, as with everything he did, brought to film music his ever-youthful spirit),

William Alwyn

Aaron Copland, Georges Auric, Shostakovich (who learned his technique in the cinema and, by 1937, had already composed a number
of important Russian feature films), Honneger (again, a pioneer of
film music), and Prokofiev, to mention only a few.

It also requires from the composer a considerable degree of versatility. His technique must be such that it is adequate to any situation—comic or tragic—and any style, Shakespearean or Wild
Western. Versatility is sometimes regarded as a debatable asset in a
composer. Contemporary criticism is inclined to question the abil-

ity of a creative artist to be versatile. The composer must be channeled and docketed. But versatility does not mean an abandonment of individuality. An individual style can remain inviolate although it rings all the changes on comedy, tragedy, period, color, and form.

It should be established at once that the functions of the symphonist, the opera composer, and the writer of ballet music or of the score for a cinematic film are distinct, specialized, and various; and each demands a different critical approach from the intelligent listener.

The conscientious composer brings to absolute music, or serious music if you like, an utterly different approach from that which he adopts for the film. In absolute music he is concerned with the technical problems of formal design and construction. Even an essentially atmospheric work such as Debussy's *La Mer* is more dependent on its exquisite sense of line, phrase, and climax rather than on the sea, which is its inspiration, and more concerned with evocation rather than description.

One of the first lessons a composer learns is that music can do most things; but it cannot describe, except by verbal or visual implication. It is a constant association of visual ideas with music which unhesitatingly makes us think of the sea when Mendelssohn's "Fingal's Cave" is played. This piece could quite as easily have been associated with forest murmurs. Again, Debussy's piano piece "Jardins Sous la Pluie" would still function as music if he had called it less poetically, but equally appropriately, "Hail on a Hot Tin Roof."

I myself had the amusing experience of hearing some music of mine, aptly I thought, composed to accompany a film about butterflies, just as aptly, some years after, fitted to a film about elephants (without my permission, of course)!

The points I hope I have made, then, are that film music forms an entirely specialized function, distinct from any other musical function; and that far from being descriptive music, this is the one thing it is worst fitted for, and for which it is most rarely used in film. (I am, of course, speaking of good films, films that are intelligently made.)

As a film composer, I come to the film as a specialist, one of a team of specialists, of technicians concerned with this complex conglomeration of visuals, sound effects, music, and dialogue which go to make the completed contemporary sound film. I, myself, have a very clear idea of what I can achieve and what I should be asked to achieve.

"Film Music: Sound or Silence?" could well be my theme. It seems both provocative and paradoxical, but to me, at least, it makes good sense. Sound can only make its effect by contrast with silence. As a hill to a valley, fortissimo can only be relative to pianissimo. Music depends for its maximum effect on the absence of music.

Mozart, I think it was, once made the profound remark that the most important thing in music was no music at all. This most important paradox seems to be in danger of being forgotten in the very medium where it is all-important. The continuous stream of background music which mars so many present-day films negates the intelligent approach of the composer to the soundtrack. He cannot make his effect if music is laid on with a trowel. The continuous flow of musical sound begins by merely irritating, and then the ear tends to ignore it. If you go to a factory, to make yourself heard above the din of machinery you must first of all shout, but after a time the incessant noise becomes a mere background to normal conversation.

After his visit to America about two years ago, I asked Sir William Walton what was his main impression. "Oh," he said, "music never stops. In the hotel, at the drugstore, even at the dentist's, music is always being churned out, relentlessly and unceasingly." Unfortunately, this is becoming true of other countries as well as America.

The public has become conditioned to a continual background of musical sound in everyday life, but will still expect it as a background to its entertainment. It is with regret and foreboding one sees this encroaching upon the film score. This attitude cuts at the very roots of film music as an art. Without silence the composer loses his most effective weapon. It is a point to which the director must be increasingly alive and in which the composer is only too willing to cooperate. I do feel that far too much of my ingenuity is spent nowadays in persuading the filmmaker to keep music out of the film rather than to put it in.

"Silence is golden"; without it, film music can make little impact. The circus and variety-hall turns exist on such contrasts. Who can fail to be shocked into awed admiration when the performer reaches his most impressive act? The band abruptly stops. As the artist totters precariously on the top of his trapeze, he performs the incredible with the aid of silence—followed by a gunfire "roll" on the side drum. You top this with a triumphant fanfare and musical drama is enacted before your very eyes.

This is film music in all its pristine simplicity—the dramatic function of music as understood by playwrights from Shakespeare to Shaw, the theatrical use of music, which is the very origin and foundation of music in film. Indeed, film music stems from the theater and not, as often imagined, from the background of piano music which accompanied the silent film. Although some of the methods involved in silent-film accompaniment were carried on when the changeover began, particularly in the accompaniments to some documentary films and travel films. I am not referring to the imaginative treatment of sound in documentary films such as *Night Mail* or Rotha's *World of Plenty*, but to those routine films which are used to fill up a feature program.

Film music is essentially dramatic music, not descriptive music. Music functions to point the dramatic atmosphere of the film and add one more emotional plane to an attack which is already being made on the visual sense.

Music in films has the remarkable faculty for portraying something which is happening in the actor's mind, and not what you see in his face or in his actions. In the old silent film the actor had to rely on exaggerated gestures, the art of mime to express his emotions. In the sound film he can behave naturally with the aid of words; the "method" can come into its own; but he can also remain silent and poker-faced while music expresses for him the emotion which is to be shared by his audience.

This is an entirely new weapon in the film director's armory. With imagination he can shoot on two planes. I remember using a different version of this technique in *October Man*. The central character (John Mills) is suspected of murder. In all the bustle of C.I.D. questioning and investigation, he is utterly detached and thinking only of the girl he has just left. You, as an audience, realize this, not because of anything he says, but because you can hear remotely and intensely, high up on a solo violin, the persistent sound of a tune that you have already learned earlier on in the picture to associate with the girl.

Music can operate on a plane completely contrary to the visuals. There is still a wide field for experiment in this. One of the fascinations of composing for the cinema is that it is a young art, and to pioneer in any aspect of it is rewarding and stimulating to the creative artist.

Another function of film music, more obvious because of familiarity, is its use to secure dramatic tension. This has now become the commonplace of the television thriller, but usually you are only too conscious of it because little attempt is made to use it with subtlety. Generally it is the blatant use of the circus performer's drumroll. But to me it loses its effect when it becomes a cliché, and I know that I am being cheated emotionally by an extraneous device.

The whole art of the cinema is in its planning. It is coordination of a team, director, producer, designer, cameraman, musician, and actor all working together and interlocking to obtain a dramatic whole in which no single aspect is predominate. This applies particularly to the music. It should be sensed and not predominant; predominant but only sensed.

I am always a little worried if somebody says to me, "I liked your score for such and such a picture." It makes me wonder whether I have stepped outside my brief, which is to provide music which is as indigenous to the film as the camera angles and the film sets.

—W.A.

• • • • •

Films have always needed music, particularly in the early days of the silent screen to overcome the lack of the spoken word, as well as to help cover the sound of the projector, which, prior to the building of cinemas with separate projection booths, sat in company with the customers. The plush city theaters usually provided orchestras, but the lot of film accompaniment fell to the lowly pianist, who was almost always left to his own devices to improvise music to cover the full gamut of emotions and situations. It's safe to assume that the effect in most cases must have been little better than dreadful.

The man who conceived the film music cue sheet was Max Winkler, who was not a composer or even a musician, but a clerk in the music publishing house of Carl Fischer in New York. Winkler worked with the many conductors and pianists who came into Fischer's asking for advice on appropriate music to play for pictures. Winkler was the perfect music clerk—his mind was a catalog of thousands of pieces of music of every kind, and he was a man bright enough to spot a golden opportunity. In his autobiography, *A Penny from Heaven*, published in 1951, he tells of spending a sleepless night thinking about how to organize the array of music for films before hitting upon an idea. Winkler got up, went to a table, and wrote the cue sheet illustrated below.

MUSIC CUE SHEET
for
THE MAGIC VALLEY

Selected and compiled by M. Winkler

Cue 1. Opening—play Minuet No. 2 in G by Beethoven for ninety seconds until title on screen "Follow me, Dear."

Cue 2. Play—Dramatic Andante by Vely for two minutes and ten seconds. Note: play soft during the scene where mother enters. Play Cue No. 2 until scene of hero leaving room.

Cue 3. Play—Love Theme by Lorenz—for one minute and twenty seconds. Note: play soft and slow during conversations until title on screen "There they go."

Cue 4. Play—Stampede by Simon for fifty-five seconds. Note: play fast and decrease or increase speed of gallop in accordance with action on the screen.

The film for which Winkler prepared this cue sheet was imaginary, but the music selections were drawn from the vast listing in his mind, music he had known from years of contact. His next move was to approach the Universal Film Company in New York and explain to them that he could compile such a cue sheet for every one of their films. In this manner, the films could have their music arranged before they arrived in the theaters. Universal immediately saw the value of the plan. They put Winkler to the test by showing him sixteen film subjects in one screening and challenging him to think of appropriate music—a slapstick comedy, a Western, a love story, a newsreel, a travelogue, etc. They gave him a desk, a stopwatch, a pile of paper, and some pencils. For each picture, Winkler straightaway came up with a musical listing and a new career was born.

Max Winkler's cue sheets were soon turning up on the music stands of every movie theater in America. He formed his own company and supplied music and cue sheets for the films of Douglas Fairbanks, William S. Hart, Mabel Normand, and the studios of Fox, Vitagraph, and Goldwyn. Winkler hired composers to write music for films, not the prominent concert and theatrical composers of the day, but highly proficient hacks who specialized in supplying music for silent films. It was an age of musical abundance, with the theater managers and conductors specifying that they didn't want any repetition. Ironically, the music of these now-obscure and forgotten composers might have been heard by more people than the music of many of the great masters combined.

Max Winkler's catalog listed all the compositions by categories—action, animal, church, sinister, chase, sad, mysterious, majestic, furious, etc. His methods were quickly copied by others because, despite his staff of busy composers, he still could not turn out music in sufficient volume to meet the demand. In his book, Winkler charmingly admits, "We turned to crime. We began to dismember the great masters. We murdered the works of Beethoven, Mozart, Grieg, J.S. Bach, Verdi, Bizet, Tchaikovsky, and Wagner—

everything that wasn't protected by copyright from our pilfering. Today I look in shame and awe at the printed copies of these mutilated masterpieces. I hope this belated confession will grant me forgiveness for what I have done."

Throughout the twenties, Winkler and other music publishers prospered as never before or since. But the tower of plenty toppled with the coming of sound in films. It was a sweeping change that meant disaster for many thousands of movie-theater musicians. Supplying enormous amounts of music for silent films suddenly became a thing of the past. Winkler sold seventy tons of printed music to a paper mill for fifteen cents a hundred pounds. He had reconciled himself to becoming a minor operator in the publishing business when the film companies realized that they still needed music for film. They turned to him, and other publishers who had specialized in providing music for films, for the rights to his catalog. But as Winkler wrote, "I knew it couldn't last long. The film companies were paying millions of dollars to publishers and composers for the use of published music. They soon found it more profitable to hire composers to write original music and to organize their own publishing houses. My catalog was again heading for the junk pile, this time for good."

With that statement from Max Winkler lies the kernel of what would be a new musical situation—the gathering in Hollywood of men who would create and develop musical compositions for motion pictures.

THE GOLDEN DAYS

The heyday of Hollywood is long gone, and with it the huge, affluent, hyperactive studio music departments with their composers, music directors, arrangers, orchestrators, and staff orchestras. Despite the excesses and the egregiousness of the vast mishmash of epic title music, sentimental love themes, and action agitatos, there was much that was interesting and admirable. The snobs sneered and the critics enjoyed their cavil, but the fact remains that the musical activity of Hollywood was the most powerful educational force music had ever known. Only the insensate could fail to be affected by the continual exposure to such a variety of music, no matter how subliminal the effect might be. The purists could decry the authenticity of pictures made about the lives of Frederic Chopin and Franz Liszt, but no fair-minded person could deny the musical craftsmanship of the pictures. But what no Hollywood musician has ever been able to overcome is the solid barrier of prejudice that surrounds the community. André Previn, who began his incredibly varied career as a sixteen-year-old arranger for MGM, says:

> No matter where I went to conduct, my reputation seemed tarnished by Hollywood glitter. To have written a Broadway show is okay, even admirable; having played a lot of jazz is okay, but less admirable. But somehow, having worked in Hollywood is like being a well-known whore. The maligning comes from people who have never lived there, because if they had they would have found a musical community of the deepest culture and the most remarkable musicians.

A much less appreciative estimate of the Hollywood music departments came from the many composers who tried to break in but couldn't. In truth, the departments were much like closed shops. They were managed by musicians who were largely products of the entertainment business rather than the concert halls, and they doubtlessly felt somewhat ill at ease in the company of composers whose tastes and intents were beyond their own. Musically conservative at heart, the music directors were responsible to studio chieftains whose own concepts on the use of music in films were severely circumspect; hence, very few avant-garde composers made the Hollywood grade in the "gravy days."

In defense of the "old line" music directors, it must be realized that they were operating slick, well-organized departments, handling a great deal of product on tight schedules. To those composers of serious contemporary music who did get a chance to score films, it was quickly apparent that the ability to write music was not enough. The mechanical intricacies of scoring—the acute timing, the mixing of music with sound and dialogue, the dubbing, the synchronization—were not within every composer's ability or interest.

A classic example of the failure to adapt concerns Richard Strauss and a German film version of his opera *Der Rosenkavalier*. Strauss insisted on conducting the score himself; he was a master conductor and he saw no reason to delegate the job to a film conductor. The great composer changed his mind after hours of frustrating attempts to conduct the score where he repeatedly missed cues and couldn't follow the time marking on the screen. Confused and irritated, Strauss handed the baton to the studio conductor and walked out.

Several famous European composers migrated to California to escape the political climate of the Nazi era. Among them was Arnold Schoenberg, who spent the remainder of his life in Los Angeles, where he was avidly sought after as a teacher by many of the movie composers. Schoenberg showed no interest in film music, although his fame was such that a few producers thought it might be wise to get his name on a picture. One of them was the young, shrewd and successful Irving Thalberg. In 1937, Thalberg asked Schoenberg to come to MGM to discuss the scoring of *The Good Earth*. He was told by the producer that this film version of the Pearl Buck book was one of the studio's most artistic efforts and presented a rare opportunity for a composer. Thalberg described one scene: "There's a terrific storm going on—the wheat fields are swaying in the wind, and suddenly the earth begins to tremble. Then, in the earthquake, the girl gives birth to a baby. What an opportunity for music." Schoenberg looked at him incredulously, "With so much going on, what do you need music for?" Thalberg was puzzled by this apparent lack of interest. He then asked Schoenberg, "What would be your terms in working for us?" Replied the composer, "I will write music and then you will make a motion picture to correspond with it." Neither Thalberg nor any other producer approached Schoenberg again.

Among the elites who wrote an occasional Hollywood film score were Alexandre Tansman, Ernst Toch, Darius Milhaud, and Mario Castelnuovo-Tedesco, although a listing of the films on which they worked reveals the surprising fact that none of their assignments were for films of much distinction. Milhaud, who had written several interesting film scores in France, spent the war years as head of the music department of Mills College in California and scored only one picture, a dull thing called *The Affairs of Bel-Ami*. Castelnuovo-Tedesco, an Italian master who tutored film composers on the side, wrote scores for a string of Columbia Bs like *The Black Parachute* and *Night Editor*. Whether this was purely bad luck or plotting on the part of the other composers is open to conjecture.

Igor Stravinsky showed a little interest but no understanding of the process after Columbia hired him to score *Commandos Strike at Dawn* (1942). At the initial discussion of the film, the plot was outlined to Stravinsky—Norway during the war, the underground resistance of the Norwegian patriots, the raids of British commandos, etc. Stravinsky said he found all this fascinating. Some weeks later he called and said the score was ready, which surprised the producer because the film wasn't. However, the studio arranged for a performance of what Stravinsky had written, and then explained that although the music was admirable, it would not fit the film. Stravinsky lost the job but not the music; with a little adaptation it became *Four Norwegian Moods*, an admired concert work.

World-renowned composers usually came to the attention of the Hollywood brass through the machinations of other parties. Ben Hecht, a busy scriptwriter in the late thirties, with his friend George Antheil tried hard to land Ernst Krenek a position when he arrived in California in 1937. Krenek, unlike many of the expatriates of the film colony, was not Jewish, he simply detested the Nazis and refused to continue living in Germany. His musical reputation had been solidified by the success of his opera *Jonny Spielt Auf*, perhaps the most successful new opera of the thirties. Hecht and Antheil went to Sam Goldwyn to persuade him to offer a position to Krenek. Goldwyn said he had never heard of the composer. Antheil explained that *Jonny Spielt Auf* was a "smash hit" all over Europe. Goldwyn still showed no interest. Hecht now decided to stretch a point, "Of course, you've heard of his *Der Rosenkavalier*?" Goldwyn agreed that the name sounded familiar. Antheil chimed in with, "His *La Bohème* is probably his biggest hit." With this, Goldwyn started to show some concern, but Hecht then casually tossed in, "No, George, I think *Il Trovatore* is his Number One smash." Goldwyn flew into a rage, "That son of a bitch. His publishers are suing me—just because we used a few lousy bars from his opera. You tell him to keep a long way from me." Krenek never worked for Goldwyn, in fact, he never worked for any film company, in part because film composition held no interest for him.

However, the real story of Hollywood music is not the occasional famous name but the men who made film music their specialty and developed it into a fascinating musical form despite the lack of appreciation of their employers and the public. Many are the hard-working, consistent, always-reliable composers not mentioned in this book. But the mere mentioning of them *en passant* would be an injustice. A hard-working, consistent, reliable man is never an "also" man. Let the reader assume that in reading about Herbert Stothart, Victor Young, John Green, and Alfred Newman that he is also reading about the similar experiences and contributions of other composers who were cogs in the swiftly spinning wheels of the film factories.

Herbert

Stothart

Herbert Stothart's position in the history of film music is quite special. He was one of the pioneers who faced the challenge at the beginning of the sound era and helped develop film music into a new art form. Stothart's film career spanned twenty years, all at MGM. Those were the years when MGM, with chieftain Louis B. Mayer, was considered the royal studio. (Mayer claimed that he had under his command more stars than in heaven.) Mayer's taste in music tended toward the conventional and the sentimental; he loved operetta and musical comedy, and delighted in producing the lush musicals of Jeanette MacDonald and Nelson Eddy. He admired the classic romances, resulting in successful productions of *The Barretts of Wimpole Street, Treasure Island, Romeo and Juliet, Anna Karenina, David Copperfield, Camille, A Tale of Two Cities, Marie Antoinette,* and *Pride and Prejudice.* What all of these films, as well as every musical of MacDonald and Eddy, have in common is Herbert Stothart.

Stothart was not a great dramatic composer, but he was a great music director and perfect for MGM in those so-called "golden years" when the major studios had recognizable styles. Part of the style was the sound, and the sound at MGM had a lot to do with

Herbert Stothart

Stothart. It was a somewhat gentler sound than the other studios, particularly in the scoring. Stothart devised what might be called a muted orchestral sound, especially with the use of strings. Those MGM classics are marked with Stothart violin passages delicately backing up pastorale and romantic scenes. By the time he scored *The White Cliffs of Dover* (1944) and *National Velvet* (1945), his style was as recognizable as the work of the best MGM cameramen. He had very definite ideas about the use of music in film:

> The composer, through experience, learns what elements generate certain moods. Anger can be generated by what I call red tones, which slightly clash in orchestration and therefore men-

tally irritate. A tranquil mood can be inspired by quiet, gently flowing melody. Alarm can be created by clashing harmonies; unrest by monotonous beat of tom-toms and by effects strange in musical principle, and hence, played to unaccustomed ears. Sonorous bells and deep tones of the organ inspired reverence. These are all matters of elemental psychology. By deciding what extent to use them, one gets the shades in between the basic classifications.

Stothart was born in Milwaukee, Wisconsin, in 1885, of Scottish and German parentage. His first contact with music was as a choirboy, and while in school, he became involved with staging musicals. At the University of Wisconsin he composed and conducted material for the university's theatrical group. One of their shows, *Manicure Shop*, was performed in a Chicago theater and enjoyed a good run. With that, Stothart decided he had found his life's work. After studying music in Germany he found a job as conductor with the touring company of the Rudolf Friml musical *High Jinks* in 1914. He toured with various companies for five years. Gradually he began to interpolate some of his own music into shows, to the point that producer Arthur Hammerstein decided to team Stothart with his young lyricist nephew Oscar to write an original musical. The resulting *Tickle Me* ran for sixty-six performances in New York and triggered a decade of success for him in musical theater. In 1924, Stothart was the conductor of the celebrated Friml musical *Rose Marie*, for which he actually wrote several songs. Most of the musicals he conducted thereafter included some of his own music.

Stothart's first contact with motion pictures came in 1928, when Arthur Hammerstein purchased the American rights to the Russian film *The End of St. Petersburg* and asked Stothart to score the musical accompaniment to screenings in his theaters. Stothart, who had never given much thought to film, now found himself in a whole new field. With the debut of sound-on-film, the Hollywood studio heads descended on Broadway to scoop up musical talent. Among those impressed with Stothart's scoring of the Russian film was Louis B. Mayer. He offered Stothart a five-year contract, which Stothart signed in May of 1929 and renewed until cancer ended his career in February of 1949.

The history of MGM would be different without Herbert Stothart's scoring of more than 100 of its films. He seemed to be exactly the right man for its product. Not only was he expert in musical comedy—his scoring and conducting of the MacDonald-Eddy pictures are distinct in film history—he was remarkably adept at using source material. His use of the Mexican folk song "La Cucaracha" in *Viva Villa!* (1934) made it famous. In *David Copperfield* (1935), he used English folk melodies, as he did in all the MGM costume films set in England. *Mutiny on the Bounty* (1935) utilized British nautical material. He often called upon the masters to color his scores, such as Delius in *The Yearling* (1947) and Tchaikovsky in *The Three Musketeers* (1948).

Stothart was first nominated for an Academy Award in 1935 for *Mutiny on the Bounty*, and then nominated every year between 1937 and 1945. He won an Oscar for his music direction of *The Wizard of Oz* (1939), which contained not only his arrangements of the Harold Arlen-E.Y. Harburg songs, but several highly effective passages of original composition, one example being the cyclone sequence that transports Dorothy from Kansas to the Land of Oz. By contemporary scoring standards, Herbert Stothart's style may seem somewhat quaint, but for the MGM pictures of the thirties and forties it was right on the mark.

Victor Young

Victor Young's twenty years in Hollywood spanned the Golden Age of the American sound film, the years of abundance, the years of fantastic productivity. These were the halcyon days when the major studios collectively released up to 500 features a year to feed the weekly movie-going habits of millions. Young arrived in 1936—he died in 1956. In between came an enormous volume of musical productivity: he either wrote or arranged or conducted or supervised the scoring of something like 350 films. That wasn't all. There were two other concurrent aspects to his musical life—writing and conducting music for many of the top radio programs of the period and working as a recording artist for Decca. Since he was also a man who enjoyed smoking cigars, drinking, gambling, and carousing with his friends, it was little wonder that he passed away at the too-young age of fifty-six.

The remarkable thing about Victor Young was not his immense output but his seemingly inexhaustible fund of melody. Music was very easy for him—he was a natural songwriter. To the casual observer, it seemed that all Young had to do was sit at the piano and let the melodies fall out of his sleeves. Many of the songs and themes from his pictures are still part of the pop music repertory: "Love Letters," "Stella by Starlight," "Sweet Sue," "Can't We Talk It Over,"

Victor Young (left) at Twentieth Century-Fox in 1955 while scoring *The Tall Men*. At right is vocal director Ken Darby, who wrote the lyrics for two songs used in the film.

"A Ghost of a Chance," "My Foolish Heart," "Golden Earrings," "When I Fall in Love," "Around the World in Eighty Days," etc.

Young was slick and facile, as well as gifted with musical expression, and might have served himself, and music, better had he worked less copiously and more intently. But apparently he was a man who found it hard to say no, so at the completion of every film, broadcast, or recording there was always another film, broadcast, or recording to which he had committed himself. Occasionally, when he was thoroughly intrigued by a film (such as *For Whom the Bell Tolls*), he would put extra effort into the composition and prove himself capable of deeper, more serious music, but it seemed to him that no matter the degree of effort, the response was always the same: "Vic, that's terrific." So, on and on he went.

Young was born of a Polish family in a tenement district of Chicago. His parents were musically inclined—his father was an operatic singer who sang in the chorus of the Sheehan Opera Company. Young began playing the violin at the age of six, after having shown a fascination with the instrument while still a toddler. After his mother died when he was ten, he and his sister were sent to live with their grandparents in Warsaw. His grandfather, a tailor, encouraged his love for music, and Young was enrolled as a student at the Imperial Conservatory in Warsaw. The most prominent of Young's instructors was Roman Statlovsky, who himself had been a pupil of Tchaikovsky. Statlovsky was doubtlessly the strongest influence on Young, whose own scoring, like that of Statlovsky and Tchaikovsky, was characterized by long melodic lines and the use of stringed instruments. Young graduated from the conservatory with honors and made his debut as a solo violinist with the Warsaw Philharmonic Orchestra. Within a year, the teenage violinist was presented with a Guanerius violin by the Philharmonic Society of Warsaw.

The First World War interrupted Young's career. In 1917, when he was seventeen, he was arrested and interned after a recital in Russia. He escaped with the aid of a Bolshevist officer who admired his playing, and Young made his way back to Warsaw, where he was arrested by the German military government. His ability with the violin once more saved him from greater discomfort; he was put on parole and ordered to remain in Warsaw until after the armistice had been signed. His primary goal now was to return to America, and in February of 1920, he arrived in New York. Following a year of barely making ends meet, Young made his America debut at Orchestra Hall in Chicago.

After his Chicago debut, Young received an offer from the vaudeville circuit, with a contract that would have put him on tour at $500 a week. He was about to sign when it was mentioned that his performances were not to include any classical music, so he tore up the contract. Young eked out a living with occasional recitals until 1922, when he proceeded to Los Angeles to join his fiancée, who had arranged an audition for him with impresario Sid Grauman. Grauman offered him the position of Concertmaster with his Million Dollar Theater Orchestra, and the fiancée soon became Mrs. Young. A year later, he accepted the position as Concertmaster of the Central Park Theater in Chicago, the anchor theater in the Balaban and Katz chain of movie theaters, all of which had orchestras.

By the mid-twenties he was the assistant musical director of the Balaban and Katz chain, which required him to arrange, and sometimes compose, the music to be played before and with the more ambitious of the silent films. In 1929, he began his radio career and two years later signed an exclusive contract with Brunswick for broadcasts and recordings. By 1935, Young was one of the best-known music directors in radio, and certainly the best-known arranger, conductor, and accompanist in the record business. Almost every artist who recorded for Decca during Young's lifetime was, at one time or other, backed by Victor Young and his Orchestra. In December of 1935, he was offered a contract by Paramount Pictures, and a few months later he arrived in Hollywood.

Victor Young's contribution to the art of film scoring was fairly conventional. He knew what was needed musically, and gave the pictures what enhanced them. However, he worked for Paramount at a time when nothing experimental or outlandish was wanted or tolerated. In retrospect, what distinguishes his music is his warmth of melody. Young couldn't contain this aspect of his nature. Even when scoring a thriller like *The Uninvited* (1944), a picture with a supernatural storyline, his love theme was so distinctly beautiful that multitudes of people began asking for a recording. Young refurbished the piece, and as "Stella by Starlight," it remains one of the loveliest themes to arise from a film score.

Young was a lusty man. When, in the last year of his life, he was told by his doctor that he would have to give up smoking and drinking, his reply was, "The hell with that." He was a humorous man, given to practical jokes, one of which is legend in Hollywood music circles. Young and Max Steiner were the closest of friends, and both lovers of poker and horse racing and other things. On one occasion Young drove from Paramount to have lunch with Steiner at Warner Bros. Arriving at the studio shortly before noon, Young wandered over to the music department, where he found Steiner rehearsing the main title to a new film—with the orchestra. Standing and listening to what was a typical but distinct Steiner theme, Young had an idea. Unseen by Steiner, he wrote the theme on a piece of paper, left the recording stage, and drove back to Paramount. Within a couple of hours, Young had made an orchestral sketch of what he had just heard, and the following morning he recorded the piece with his own orchestra. He then called Steiner and invited him up to his house that evening for a poker session. By the time Steiner and the other card-playing musicians arrived, Young had wired his record player to his radio. During the game, he switched on the radio, which triggered the record player, and out came the Steiner music. After about twenty seconds, Steiner's eyes came up from his cards and he started to tremble.

"Oh, my God."

"What's wrong, Max?" innocently asked Young.

Steiner shook his head, "I don't understand. That music. Is that something new?"

"Hell, no," said Young, "I listen to this program all the time—they've been playing it for years."

Steiner tried to pick up the game but his concentration was destroyed. Soon he said, "Vic, I'm not feeling too well, I'd better go."

Young could never explain why he became a movie composer, it was simply something that happened. He said:

> Why, indeed, would any trained musician let himself in for a career that calls for the exactitude of an Einstein, the diplomacy of Churchill, and the patience of a martyr? Yet I can think of no other medium that offers this challenge and excitement, provided that your interest is the universe and your knowledge of musical forms is gargantuan.

His appearance belied his music. Young was short, slim, and rather tough looking. He delighted in recalling an occasion when a director who wanted him to score a picture took him to discuss the matter with the producer, and the producer turned to the director and asked, "This man can compose music? He looks like a prizefighter to me." Young was often mistaken for a retired bantamweight, and he employed the nimble footwork of a light boxer in sparring with producers, studio executives, and recording engineers. In an industry noted for its "yes" men, Young was a "no" man. He also learned to be devious. He was once told by a producer: "This picture should be scored in the style of Hindemith." Said Young, "I assumed he had only recently heard his first Hindemith recording. I nodded in solemn agreement, and went home to work on a score, which he later marveled at and heralded as being exactly what he had in mind. There was nothing Hindemithian about it—the style was completely my own."

One of Victor Young's last scores—*Around the World in Eighty Days*—was perhaps his ultimate achievement. The Mike Todd picture was a *tour de force*, and its gaiety and visual interests were supported all the way by Young's tuneful music, and the main theme, with added lyric, became a hit song.

He died of a heart attack in Palm Springs on November 10, 1956. Nineteen of his film scores had been nominated for Academy Awards, but the following March he received his only Oscar, which was for *Around the World in Eighty Days*. He had died while scoring *China Gate*, and the music credit of that film reads: Music by Victor Young, extended by his old friend Max Steiner.

Victor Young was always encouraging to young composers who came to him for advice, one of whom was Henry Mancini:

Vic loved life in all forms. He was a man's man. There was no sham, he said it "like it was" all the time. He gave the impression of being a man you might not readily walk up to, but once you got over your own hang-ups, you'd find he was a gracious man. But he worked too hard, and I think he drove himself to an early grave.

John Green

John Green had the peculiar affliction of possibly being over-talented. Green wrote a number of songs that are among the hardiest perennials—"Body and Soul," "I Cover the Waterfront," "Out of Nowhere," etc. He music-directed some of Hollywood's best musicals, four of which (*Easter Parade, An American in Paris, West Side Story,* and *Oliver*) brought him Academy Awards. He composed dramatic scores and became a distinguished conductor of symphony orchestras. Unlike many other successful musicians, Green did not have an impoverished background. His output and his varied successes attest not only to talent but to ambition and a powerful ego.

Green's father was an affluent New York banker and builder. The Green family was musically and theatrically oriented, and their home was always open to the leading artists of the day. By the age of three Green was showing an unusual interest in music:

> I sustained my first physical injury at the age of four when I fell off a chair on which I was standing conducting the "Poet and Peasant" overture, in front of our Victrola. I sprained my little conducting arm, but not enough to impair later efforts or not enough for anyone to notice. My real impairment came in being a rich man's son, and that was the hurdle I had to jump. My father was very opinionated but fortunately also humorous. He did not encourage my musical ambition. He believed there was

room in the arts only for the great, and I clearly recall him telling me, "Son, there's no bum like a pretty good artist, and you're pretty good." However, I was not about to be discouraged. I was wise enough to go along with his theory that I should have a good liberal arts education and acquire some business skill. I attended Harvard and graduated from their school of Economics, which landed me a job as a purchase and sales clerk in a Wall Street bond house. But I had no intention of following a career in business, and after six months I quit to team up with lyricist Eddie Heyman.

Green had actually turned semi-professional while still at Harvard. He participated in all the school musical activities and shows as an arranger and performer, and in his last year he played with the highly esteemed Harvard Gold Coast Orchestra. Also during that year he wrote his first successful song, "Coquette." One of his jobs after quitting Wall Street was as a rehearsal pianist for Gertrude Lawrence, during which period he and Eddie Heyman wrote "Body and Soul" for her.

He said:

But film had always been a major interest of mine and when I got wind of an opening for a rehearsal pianist at Paramount's Astoria studio I grabbed it—at $50 a week. My first assignment was *The Big Pond* with Maurice Chevalier and songs by Sammy Fain, including "You Brought a New Kind of Love to Me." Robert Russell Bennett had been engaged to orchestrate the songs, but he fell ill. Frank Tours was the music director at the studio—a remarkable Englishman whose father had been the original conductor for Gilbert and Sullivan at the Savoy Theater. I asked him if I could have a crack at the job, and he took a chance—in fact, the very first song I orchestrated was "You Brought a New Kind of Love to Me." This was in the days when the orchestra

MGM music chieftain John Green (right) and his youngest
composer-conductor, eighteen-year-old André Previn in 1957.

was right on the shooting stage with the performers as they were
being filmed—the singing and the playing was simultaneous—
a clumsy, costly process.

Green arranged the music for twelve films during his two years
at Astoria, and between assignments conducted the orchestra at
Paramount's Brooklyn Theater, which he described as an invaluable experience for a young musician. His conducting was striking
enough to bring an offer from Victor Young, who was then the
music director for the Atwater-Kent radio series:

Victor—God love his memory—hired me as an orchestrator and gave me wonderful opportunities, which in turn led to other things. It got me jobs with some of the best bands playing in New York at that time, the chance for my music to be heard on radio, and it brought me to the attention of Broadway producers. I later wrote scores for some miserable flop musicals, with an occasional hit song, and I went to England to write and conduct a musical for Jack Buchanan—the first original musical broadcast by the BBC, *Big Business*.

The thirties were busy years for young Johnny Green. By 1942 he had been hired by Richard Rodgers as the music director for the last Rodgers and Hart show, *By Jupiter*. This would lead him back to the movies:

> Louis B. Mayer, Arthur Freed, and Judy Garland came to the show one evening, and as I came up from the orchestra pit I was met by Freed, who told me he and Mayer wanted to discuss something with me. They insisted I come to Hollywood. I wasn't that interested, I really wanted to stay in New York and do something about my poor batting average in the theater. In fact, one of my turkeys was playing at the time and kept from total disaster by only one number—"The Steam Is on the Beam." However, MGM had a way of twisting one's arm by adding ciphers to the offer, and I just couldn't turn it down.

November 1942 marked Green's arrival at MGM and the beginning of a long and profitable association with the studio. His forte was the arranging and conducting of musicals, and MGM was the leader in the field. Green had always been an excellent conductor, so he injected great vitality into the scoring of the lavish and colorful musical entertainments that delighted the world, not to mention the MGM stockholders. Occasionally, Green was able to accept a job from another studio—he wrote the songs for Deanna Durbin in *Something in the Wind* for Universal and the score of Danny Kaye's *The Inspector General* for Warner Bros. The score of the Kaye comedy clearly shows that if Green hadn't been so busy with musicals, he could have done equally well composing comedic and dramatic scores.

In 1950 John Green's career entered another phase. Louis B. Mayer called him in to discuss the job of heading up the whole music department. Recalled Green:

> Despite the great activity and the abundance of talent, it was a badly structured and badly managed department. Mayer knew this and he told me, "We want the greatest music department that there has ever been in this entire business—the greatest orchestra and the greatest staff, and we want it managed with the utmost order and system." I blanched and said, "Mr. Mayer, it's going to cost a lot of money to have that kind of a department." To which he looked me in the eye and replied, "Well, we've got a lot of money." That was that. It was the beginning of ten years in which I was virtually autonomous—I made the deals as well as the aesthetics. I was paid an awful lot of money. I like to think I was lured not so much by the power but the challenge to build the kind of department they wanted. However, looking back on it, I sometimes regret accepting the offer—it was ten years I could have spent composing, but there were also creature comforts I was shallow enough to be lured by.

The MGM Music Department under John Green was, indeed, an impressive force. Miklos Rozsa, Bronislau Kaper, Adolph Deutsch, and André Previn were the prestige composers, and for the musicals Green had a group of men who, in combination, are never likely to be equaled: George Stoll, Lennie Hayton, George Bassmann, Roger Edens, Conrad Salinger, and others. Green was also very much a working boss—he produced a series of short subjects under the general title The MGM Concert Hall, with himself conducting the MGM Symphony Orchestra, and for which he won one of his five Oscars. He also assigned himself the task of writing a monumental score for the expensive but disappointing epic *Raintree County* (1957).

During his reign he was responsible for commissioning the first twelve-tone film score, Leonard Rosenman's *The Cobweb* (1955), which he also conducted, and the first electronic score, for the cartoon *Robby the Robot*. Green decided that *Executive Suite* (1954) should have no score at all: "It's also the function of a music director to know where to be silent, and there's nothing music could have done for that picture except hurt it."

Green's biggest job as a music director was his work for *Oliver* (1968), and it is entirely due to Green that the music in that film is so vital and lively, so soaringly effective. Green worked on the picture for two years and recorded the score in London, where he pulled top instrumentalists from the five leading symphony orchestras. "I'm the world's worst snob about who plays under my stick, and I can tell you that leaving that particular orchestra was like leaving one's favorite child."

Green won a well-justified Oscar for his efforts on *Oliver*, something that seems to puzzle those who wonder why it didn't go to Lionel Bart, who wrote the stage original. Bart is not a composer; he has the enviable ability to think of melodies—other people write them down for him. The difference between a simple melodic line on a piece of paper and what was heard on the soundtrack of *Oliver* is John Green, the rich and vigorous creativity of his orchestrations and his conducting. Asked to comment on the success of the film, Green says, "It's enormously complicated and very simple—all of its elements belong to each other."

John Green was largely responsible for André Previn being hired by MGM. Previn, born in Berlin in 1929 and musically educated there and in Paris, came to Los Angeles in 1939. His talent was abundant even as a schoolboy, and as Green recalls:

When we hired André, he wasn't quite sixteen and he could only come to work after three o'clock. He was incredible. After about three years as an arranger we gave him his first score, *The Sun Comes Up* (1948), and from then on it was André Previn, *composer-conductor*. I hardly know what to say about André, his technique and his facility seem limitless. In scoring, he was so fast and accurate you wanted to kick him in envy. And it wasn't enough to compose brilliant scores like *Elmer Gantry* (1960) and *The Four Horsemen of the Apocalypse* (1962), he was also moonlighting as a pianist, both jazz and classical. Now, of course, he's developed into a first-class conductor, and I don't imagine he will return to the film world. He and I became good friends. I remember calling him on his thirtieth birthday at 7:30 in the morning, which is something you don't do to him because he's not an early riser. I called and said, "André, today you're thirty, and it's no longer a miracle you can play a C Major chord," and hung up. He was still laughing when I saw him for lunch. I was with André once when he was asked by an interviewer whether having to write music to a deadline, such as we must do in this business, was a good thing for a composer. I remember his answer because it was exactly what I or any of the other composers might have replied had such a clear accounting come to mind. He said, "I think we need the deadlines because we don't have the luxury of waiting for that elusive muse. Very often we're not too terribly interested in the project at hand—you can get tired of even a good film after you've seen it several times—and if some of us were left to our own devices, the score would never be recorded, or we would procrastinate to the point where they would get someone else." So you might bear that Previn reply in mind whenever you are tempted to think how wonderful it is to be a film composer.

In the opinion of John Green, there was nothing particularly new about the concept of marrying music to film:

> It's the continuation of theatrical tradition—Shakespeare's plays at the Globe Theater had musical accompaniment. As for the particular value of music on film, I think if you were to see a major film whose score you liked, and then saw the picture without the score, you would find one of the major elements—and by major I mean almost as important as the photography—missing.

John Green died in May of 1989, at age eighty-one, a year or so after a stroke had brought his very active musical life to an end. A man who enjoyed the limelight—he always conducted with a white carnation in his lapel (or a red one if the jacket was white)—he was a major figure in the Los Angeles musical world and he frequently conducted at the Hollywood Bowl. His eight years in command of the music department at MGM form his most important contribution to film music history, but if that should be forgotten, something else will keep his name alive, a song called "Body and Soul."

Alfred Newman

If the Golden Age of Hollywood music can be epitomized in the experience of just one man, he would have to be Alfred Newman. When Newman arrived in Hollywood in 1930, sound on film was in its fledgling period, and the use of music, other than for visual performance, was an uncharted road fogged with ignorance and uncertainty. Newman paved that road, not only as a composer but as a superlative conductor and music director, and later as the head of a major studio music department. He worked ferociously and prodigiously all through the Golden Age, and when he died in 1970 he knew that its deflation and demise had preceded him.

David Raksin, who worked as a composer under Newman at Twentieth Century-Fox from 1944 to 1950, says this about him:

> He was a totally remarkable musician with an amazing sense of theater and timing. He was also a taskmaster, he always wanted your best, and no one who ever worked for him for long ever gave him anything else. Al was a self-regenerating man—just when everyone thought he had said all he had to say about film music, he would surprise everyone and come up with a great score. He could also be self-deprecating, and he would occasionally refer to himself as a "hack musician." It's a strange thing, but if you have any kind of a gift, there seems to be—in some cases—an inner bargain with yourself not to use it. It's tough to write

music on demand, it doesn't always come when you want it, and Newman was a rather reluctant composer. I think he was more instinctive than profound musically, but what he did have was an unfailing sensitivity to the dramatic meaning of a film scene and the ability to translate that meaning into the language of music.

Alfred Newman was the eldest of ten children born into a working-class family in New Haven, Connecticut. His father was a produce dealer with little interest in music, but his mother liked music and realized her first-born was gifted with unusual talent. The boy responded to the sound of music and craved to play the piano. A piano would have been a major luxury for this family, but they prevailed upon a friend who had one to let the boy use it. Since they couldn't even afford bus fare, Newman walked ten miles to and from his daily practice session. His first teacher was a house painter who had once taken a few lessons, and charged twenty-five cents for his tutoring. By the time he was eight, Newman was playing in public and earning money from clubs and organizations in New Haven. This money was saved and used a year later to send him to New York to study with Sigismond Stojowski, one of the finest teachers of that time and, fortunately, a warm-hearted man who was generous enough to take the boy on at little expense.

Newman continued to earn money as a child pianist during his years with Stojowski. At the age of twelve, he was sponsored by Paderewski for a recital in New York, and there seems little doubt that Newman would have developed into a major concert pianist had not the financial circumstances of his family ruled out any further study.

He literally went to work in order to send money home. He accepted an offer from Gus Edwards, an impresario who specialized in young talent, to perform five shows a day at the Harlem Opera House. At thirteen, he undertook a vaudeville tour in which

Alfred Newman conducting *Tonight We Sing* at Fox in 1953,
with (left to right) Jan Peerce, Roberta Peters, and Ezio Pinza.

he performed while dressed as Little Lord Fauntleroy. While touring with various musical-comedy road companies he was allowed
to occasionally conduct the orchestra. At age seventeen, Alfred
Newman was hired as the conductor for *The George White Scandals*,
and for the next twelve years he was conductor for many of the
famous Broadway musicals of the twenties. In 1930, when Irving
Berlin was contracted to make a film of his *Reaching for the Moon*,
he insisted that Newman go to Hollywood as the music director,
and what was originally planned as a three-month visit became a
career that kept him in Hollywood for the remainder of his life.

When Newman arrived in Hollywood, he found that the Berlin film was not yet ready to be scored, so the head of the studio, Joseph M. Schenck, loaned him to Sam Goldwyn. Newman worked on five other films before scoring *Reaching for the Moon*. He found his musical-comedy experience invaluable in this new profession of arranging music for film. He also found a friend in Goldwyn, who not only used him steadily over the next decade but cheerfully recommended him to other producers. Newman was the only composer Goldwyn ever really knew or liked, and whenever he wanted advice on who to hire, he called Newman—even after Newman became head of music at Twentieth Century-Fox. In this way, Newman was of help to many composers.

The first Newman score to win wide attention was *Street Scene*, a 1931 film of life on New York's East Side. The main theme of that score, later adapted by Newman into an orchestral piece called "Sentimental Rhapsody," became a hardy perennial of the film music world and turned up in half a dozen other films over the years—films scored by composers working under Newman. Other Newman themes also became popular: one melody from *The Hurricane* took on a life of its own as "The Moon of Manakoora," and any musically inclined person who enjoyed *Wuthering Heights* could hardly have failed to leave the theater humming the haunting Cathy theme. The score of this film helped make it a masterpiece of romantic filmmaking.

The quality of Newman's compositions varied, probably because he took on too much work and composing was not a job he enjoyed, but the quality of his conducting never strayed from excellence. His ability to lead an orchestra was perhaps his outstanding talent. His timing and his nuances and his precision were near perfection. He once told me:

I'd much rather conduct than compose. Composing is a lonely business, really lonely. Conducting is gregarious, you work with anywhere from five to a hundred men, the lights are always on, and there's an excitement to being with talented musicians and making music. I studied composition as part of my musical training, but I never wanted to compose. I studied music because I wanted to be a good conductor.

Newman was the most honored of the Hollywood musicians—nine Oscars came his way, although only one was for composing, *The Song of Bernadette*. The others were for musicals, and he never made any secret that the awards were group efforts; he was simply representing a team of arrangers and orchestrators of whom he happened to be the boss. The first was *Alexander's Ragtime Band* (1938), followed by *Tin Pan Alley* (1940), *Mother Wore Tights* (1947), *With a Song in My Heart* (1952), *Call Me Madam* (1953), *Love is a Many Splendored Thing* (1955), *The King and I* (1956), and *Camelot* (1968). On his final trip to the Academy Awards stage, Newman showed all the excitement of a father wearily walking into a maternity ward to look at his ninth child.

Newman had written many distinctive scores before he picked up his Oscar for *Bernadette*—outstanding were *The Prisoner of Zenda* (reused in its entirety in the 1952 remake), *Wuthering Heights, How Green Was My Valley*, and *This Above All*—but *Bernadette* enabled those who were sufficiently interested to study the score closely because it was the first to be released as a commercial recording (an eight-side 78 rpm Decca album, later transferred to LP). It was also his first of several strongly religious scores, which revealed Newman himself to be a man of faith, something his manner tended to belie. He wrote especially well for the strings, which in these religious pictures had a strikingly spiritual quality. In *The Song of*

Bernadette, the musical highlight is the revelation scene, which gave Newman considerable problems:

> My first reaction to the scene was to "hear" it in terms of the great religious experiences that had previously been interpreted by Wagner in his Grail music and Schubert in his "Ave Maria," which is a terrifying standard to have to approach. I first wrote for the scene in this vein, but I wasn't happy with anything I did. It then occurred to me that I was wrong in thinking of the scene as a revelation of the Virgin Mary. I read back over Werfel's book and found that Bernadette had never claimed to have seen anything other than a "beautiful lady." I now wrote music I thought would describe this extraordinary experience of a young girl who was neither sophisticated enough nor knowledgeable enough to evaluate it as anything more than a lovely vision. With this in mind, I thought the music should not be pious or austere or even mystical, or suggest that the girl was on the first step to sainthood. She was at that point simply an innocent, pure-minded peasant girl, and I took my musical cues from the little gusts of wind and the rustling bushes that accompanied the vision, letting it all grow into a swelling harmony that would express the girl's emotional reaction. And it was important that it express *her* reaction, not *ours*.

Newman's style of composition was essentially operatic—lyrical, dramatic, and expressive—and his method of scoring was predominantly of mood rather than leitmotifs and music counterpointing the action of the film, which was basically the style invented and employed by Max Steiner. Newman and Steiner were the two major influences on film scoring in Hollywood in the years between the mid-thirties and mid-fifties. Any newcomer who could successfully study, understand, and utilize both styles found the magic formula.

Quite a few of the best Hollywood composers drifted into the business with no particular intention to remain, but because of the suitability of their talent, the copious opportunities, and the high pay, they stayed, never to return to their previous musical environments. This was a situation peculiar to the American film industry. The studios put their composers under exclusive contracts that required that they devote themselves full time to writing for the screen. In England and France, however, with the centralization of the various arts in the capital cities, a composer might go from the film studio to the theater stage to the concert hall to the ballet—all within a year. The British and French composers also were far less likely to be tied to long-running contracts at enormous salaries. Hollywood, with its film factories working at full tilt, was not interested in its artists moonlighting, no matter how admirable the cause.

Newman was a victim of this fate; that is, if a man who ends up earning $2000 a week plus royalties can be regarded as a victim. He had arrived in Hollywood with the right credentials: a classical education and a rich background of experience in the theater. There were no mysterious areas of music to him, so he could tackle anything. He also continued his study of music; all through his busy years on Broadway, he had studied with George Wedge, and when Schoenberg arrived in Los Angeles, Newman was one of his first pupils. Composing was not a passion with him, but a study of Newman's scores shows a deepening of his composition, although it cannot be denied that he was a most eclectic composer. Much of what Newman invented for the screen was widely copied.

Examples of the best of Newman would be the ghostly theme in the main title of *Twelve O'Clock High*; the darkly dramatic and driving title music to Henry King's highly artistic Western *The Gunfighter*; the entire score of the same director's *Captain from Castile*, especially the final, spectacular scene of the Conquistadores marching in victory (Newman's exciting march was a deft tribute to Erich Korngold, whom he greatly admired); the asylum scenes in *The Snake Pit*, particularly the horrifying electronic therapy sequence; the sad gentility of his theme for *Anne Frank*; the anguish of the music that accompanies Christ's carriage of the Cross in *The Robe*; the somber tone poem in *David and Bathsheba* that approximates the cadences of the Twenty-Third Psalm; the Easter Service and the Grand Ball sequence in *Anastasia*, and the moody uneasiness of the music for the title character; the exuberance and optimism of the main title of *How the West Was Won*; and the glorious Hallelujahs that were deleted from the score of *The Greatest Story Ever Told* by its producer.

Newman became the General Music Director of Twentieth Century-Fox in 1940 and held the post for twenty years. Darryl F. Zanuck was his boss, and Newman was lucky to be working for a man who trusted him completely. He was well-paid, although nothing could replace the time and effort the job demanded, and given a huge annual budget, which he spent lavishly. Despite his obvious success, he frequently expressed less than contentment with his work. He spoke for the whole colony of composers when he said, "I often wonder what could be achieved if we were given enough time to work on a film score." In the case of *The Egyptian*, there simply was not enough time. Bernard Herrmann was assigned this sumptuous, dull epic and initially given eight weeks to write two hours of symphonic music. The release date was then moved up by two and a half weeks, whereupon Herrmann appealed to Newman for help. The two men resolved the problem by dividing the scoring between them; it was the only time two major composers collaborated to produce one homogeneous score. And it was no ordinary score. Dealing with ancient Egypt, the music had to reflect an almost unknown culture, and support the rich exotic visuals. After an initial discussion of modes and scales, the two composers wrote for five weeks, sending their sketches back and forth but seeing each other only twice during the process. The score was also unique in that each composer conducted his own portion. Alfred Newman never wrote anything other than film scores, and let it be known that they were not the frustrations of a serious symphonist:

> If I want to write great music, I've no right to be working in a film studio. Good film music must always be inspired by the picture of which it is a part, not by the desire of a composer to express himself. The effect of music in films is largely one of association, the important thing being to evoke the proper mood and spirit. If you can't accept these terms—stay away from films.

Despite the realistic attitude toward his work, quite a lot of the Newman music lived beyond the films and became popular recordings. Rare is the film music buff who doesn't rhapsodize over his *Captain from Castile* score, or point to the quality of various passages in *The Robe*, with its scholarly usage of ancient Hebraic music. The sincerity of feeling in Newman's religious subjects is beyond reproach, and reveals an aspect of his nature otherwise never referred to.

The Diary of Anne Frank was yet another Newman score with spiritual character. Despite the severe setting of the story and its horrific denouement, the music avoids atonality or jagged modernisms by focusing on a certain wistfulness and old European charm. The Frank family, driven from Hamburg and sheltered in the attic of a friendly house in Amsterdam, lived through an unnatural, suspended period in which their only pleasures were reminiscences and listening to the radio, from which they might hear and enjoy a Strauss waltz. For the sensitive, imaginative young girl, it was a period of fancy; fortunately, the fancy of a happy soul who could write in her diary, "In spite of everything, I still believe people are good at heart." Newman visited the house in Amsterdam where the Frank family stayed. He wanted to feel the atmosphere before writing his music, and he said:

> It was a strange experience—standing in that room where Anne lived and from where she was eventually led away to die, I had a feeling mixed of exaltation and repugnance. George Stevens had decided that the film shouldn't be one of gloom, but that we should concentrate on the love and humor of these people. During my visit, I had lunch with Anne Frank's father, a charming man, and he wanted to know what my music would be like. I could only tell him in the abstract that what touched me most about the book was its spirituality, and that was what I wanted to say in the music. This seemed to please him. When it came to the actual scoring—I didn't try to illustrate, except in a few places, what was happening on the screen, so much as invoke in the music the remembrance of happier times, and the longings for the future—the longings of an oppressed people.

Alfred Newman was a compassionate man and that shone through much of his music. He masked his gentle nature with a certain gruffness, as if somewhat embarrassed to be known as a man concerned about humanity in general and his associates in particular. Ken Darby, who died in 1992, was the choral director on several films scored by Newman—*David and Bathsheba*, *The Robe*, *How the West Was Won*, *The Greatest Story Ever Told*—and most of the Rodgers and Hammerstein musicals. He cited as an example of Newman's sense of values that, while they were doing *Carousel*, the composer persuaded Darryl F. Zanuck to give Darby billing in the credit titles as his associate—on the same credit card as himself. Said Darby:

That kind of generous recognition was rare in the film industry, but when I said so in front of the crew, Newman mumbled gruffly: "To hell with *that*. Nobody gets credit they haven't earned." He concealed his kindness just as he concealed the mechanics of music. I remember during the scoring of *How the West Was Won* Alfred shaking his head and musing, "How in hell am I going to do anything original for another Indian chase?" and then going home and doing one. It was a series of brass punctuations in a complex scherzo, with the horses' hooves and Indian yells supplying the counterpoint. His whole score for this film is a beautiful fabric of original material woven with traditional melodies.

Ken Darby recalled *How the West Was Won* as the most pleasant assignment on which he and Newman collaborated and *The Greatest Story Ever Told* as the most miserable. Produced and directed by the brilliant but painfully meticulous filmmaker George Stevens at incredible cost, *The Greatest Story Ever Told* was a major disappointment at the box office. Newman had been particularly successful writing music for biblical pictures and Stevens insisted that he was the one man for the job. Flattering as it was, Newman would have been wise to reject the offer.

The Greatest Story Ever Told involved Newman for over a year, three times longer than called for in his contract. As time went by, the producer and the composer drifted apart in their views on the use of music in this lavish telling of the final years of Christ. Stevens insisted that portions of the Verdi *Requiem*, as well as the celebrated "Hallelujah Chorus" from Handel's *Messiah*, be incorporated into the score. Newman refused and it was Darby who conducted these sections of the score. Newman asked that his name be removed from the credits but Stevens refused. The veteran composer rightly guessed the critics would sneer, as indeed they did with such comments as "Newman attempts to glorify his own music by incorporating Verdi and Handel." As on many previous occasions, it was a case of blame being laid at the wrong door. Many years later, long after Newman had died, Darby took unused portions of Newman's choral music for *Greatest Story* and, combining them with passages from *The Robe*, put together a five-movement symphonic cantata titled *The Man from Galilee*.

As he passed the age of sixty, the demands of his exacting profession began to tell on Newman. Long hours and the strain of responsibility took a heavy toll, and he was never easy on himself. A heavy smoker, he wracked his lungs with coughing in his last years, and although he was in no way an alcoholic, Newman did love expensive Irish whiskey, which he drank straight. His principal pleasure was his home and his family, his wife and six children. Uncompromising in business dealings, severe and impatient with those he didn't like, Newman could appear a rough man. To those fortunate enough to be his friends, he was remarkably soft-hearted and kind.

When Newman died on February 17, 1970, it was, for many of us, the official parting knell of Hollywood's Golden Age.

THE MITTEL-EUROPA STRAIN

History is full of irony. It is, for example, ironic that the fury and horror of the Russian revolution and the Nazi regime in Germany actually benefited the culture of the United States. Legions of artists left the Soviet Union and Europe in the wave of historical cataclysms, and many found their way to America. Quite a few of them discovered profitable outlets for their talent in Hollywood.

In their prime, the major studios drew their talent from all over the world; wealth and power enabled them to hire the best. Three Europeans and one Russian with deep musical roots would have a profound bearing on the development of film music: Dimitri Tiomkin (Russian), Bronislau Kaper (Polish), Franz Waxman (German), and Miklos Rozsa (Hungarian). Perhaps none would have become a Hollywood figure without a shove from history.

Dimitri Tiomkin

Dimitri Tiomkin was born in the Ukraine but grew up in St. Petersburg, which he left in 1919 when he was twenty. Seven years previously, he had entered The St. Petersburg Conservatory of Music at a time when nothing in Russia was more highly esteemed than music. The director of the Conservatory, Alexander Glazounov, then at the height of his fame as a composer, was regarded as a minor God. Tiomkin's mother began teaching him the piano almost before he could walk, and his father, a distinguished doctor and assistant to Dr. Ehrlich (the discoverer of the Salvarsan cure for syphilis), agreed to the boy's becoming a musician in spite of his own distaste for music.

Tiomkin recalled Glazounov as a kindly professor who pretended to be stern. His taste was classically traditional but romantic in spirit. He frowned on modernism and didn't care much for the impressionistic style of Claude Debussy, who was currently in vogue. "His teaching was not severe, and I think his influence on me was that of a radiant personality. He did have one particular musical influence— he loved fugues and he drilled us in them all the time, and that's probably why I have sneaked so many fugues into my film scores."

Tiomkin studied composition at the Conservatory, but his major concern was the piano. His teacher was Felix Blumenthal, who

Dimitri Tiomkin

also taught Vladimir Horowitz and Simon Barere. Both Barere and
Tiomkin earned their first money as pianists in movie theaters in
St. Petersburg. Tiomkin remembered pounding away on a piano at
the side of the screen, trying to come up with music that was more
or less suited to what was on the screen. His knack for scoring showed
itself even then:

> There was one film in which a woman was being choked, and as
> her head rocked back and forth, mine did, too, and I made the
> kinds of grunts and groans she might have made in a sound pic-
> ture. The audience thought that was funny, so the manager told
> me to "keep it in," and I did it every night.

After the Russian revolution, with life grim and opportunities for concert pianists nil, Tiomkin proceeded to Berlin. He was sponsored by his father, who had left his mother some years previously and remarried, and whose pro-German sentiments and respected medical knowledge had ensconced him in the German capital. Never having much rapport with his father, Tiomkin decided to strike out on his own. It was an emotional decision, and an impractical one in view of his lack of funds. The parting between father and son was bitter, and the two never saw each other again.

By chance, Tiomkin came into contact with Michael Kariton, another Russian pianist in Berlin, a man who could survive under any circumstances. Kariton offered to share his accommodation with Tiomkin and encouraged the young man to continue his studies. With his help, Tiomkin was able to take lessons from Ferruccio Busoni. Busoni, an Olympian pianist-composer, was philosophical in his teaching of music, dealing with the architecture of harmony rather than pure technique. Looking back on his musical education, Tiomkin feels he was fortunate to have studied with two such different men. From Glazounov he had been imbued with the romantic spirit of music and from Busoni he had learned the discipline of form.

Berlin in the twenties was the center of symphonic music. Tiomkin lived there for three years and during that time made his debut as a concert pianist with the Berlin Philharmonic Orchestra. His pragmatic friend Kariton persuaded Tiomkin to form a duo-piano team with him, since duo pianists were then in fashion. The place to go, cried Kariton, was Paris. Actually, Paris at that time could have done with fewer Russians rather than more. The city was swamped with Russian exiles, many of them aristocrats, some of them opportunists, and a few of great talent. Stravinsky, Diaghilev, and the Ballet Russe were all contributing to the cultural life of Paris. Tiomkin and Kariton made their mark, enough to get an

American offer. In 1925, they arrived in New York booked on a vaudeville circuit. This perturbed the Russians, until they learned of the salary—$1000 a week for six months. The tour taught Tiomkin about showmanship and whetted his appetite for American music. Now he could add jazz and musical comedy to his Russian romanticism and German classicism. The future Hollywood composer was in embryo.

Shortly after his arrival in New York, Tiomkin met Albertina Rasch, the Austrian-born ballet dancer and choreographer, and after his first tour, they were married. Said by those who knew her to have been a spirited woman, she had some influence upon Tiomkin's career. She persuaded him to return to solo performing, and in 1928 he went to Paris to give the European première of George Gershwin's Piano Concerto in F. Back in America, Tiomkin played Carnegie Hall and embarked on another tour. He specialized in contemporary composers; occasionally he would play Gershwin but his program consisted mostly of Ravel, Poulenc, Auric, and Prokofiev.

As Tiomkin performed, his wife continued her career as a ballet impresario. The 1929 stock market crash hit the Tiomkins hard— theirs were luxury trades and luxuries were suddenly out. But Albertina was ever-enterprising—the concert halls and the opera houses may have turned dark, but the movie houses hadn't. Films were an inexpensive form of entertainment, therefore the last the public would have to give up. Sound brought a new era to Hollywood and the industry was booming. The producers were looking for musical ideas and Mrs. Tiomkin had one for them—short ballet sequences. The idea was accepted and the Tiomkins left for California. While his wife worked at MGM, Tiomkin gave recitals in Los Angeles.

Albertina quickly brought to the attention of her employers the fact that her famous pianist husband also wrote music. Tiomkin

Dimitri Tiomkin conducting music from *Land of the Pharaohs*.

had, in fact, been composing for years for his wife's ballet company and occasionally playing some of his pieces at his recitals. Publishers had shown no interest in the compositions, so Tiomkin put the pieces in a trunk. The trunk was raided repeatedly in years to come when he needed material for his films. One of the early compositions was a ballet piece called "Mars," which Tiomkin played for MGM and they subsequently paid $3000 for it. Flushed with success in a new endeavor, Tiomkin turned out more ballet music for MGM.

Dimitri Tiomkin's first original film score was written in 1931, for the Tolstoy story *Resurrection*. It seemed plausible to the producers to hire a Russian composer to write music for the rumblings of the Russian soul, but Tiomkin must have laid it on too thick because they didn't ask for more. He returned to the concert stage, but he was intrigued with film scoring.

In 1933 he heard that Paramount was making an extravagant version of *Alice in Wonderland* and hadn't yet decided on a composer. Tiomkin arranged a meeting and gave a successful sales pitch on his particular abilities to score a film of this nature. In truth, he was completely baffled by the film, the story, and the dialogue. English was a hurdle Tiomkin never cleared. The Jabberwocky nonsense verses floored him, and he would reduce everyone to laughter whenever he asked about them. In garbled English he would say something like, "How give line correct saying, 'Twinkle, twinkle, little star'?"

Alice in Wonderland was a flop, despite all its stars, possibly because they wore masks and couldn't be identified except by voice. The impact of his score was enough to establish his ability but not enough to bring a deluge of offers. Tiomkin scored a handful of minor films over the next few years, but his first real break came in 1937 when Frank Capra filmed *Lost Horizon*, a beautifully made picture. Tiomkin's music was suitably romantic and mystical for the adventures of Ronald Colman in Shangri-La.

The success of the film brought Tiomkin not only offers to score more films but a request to return to the concert stage. Fate would allow just one more concert, however. He played Rachmaninoff's Second Concerto with the Los Angeles Philharmonic, and the reception was strong enough to lead him to think of resuming his concert career. Not long after this, he was involved in an accident and broke his right arm, which never healed properly. Although his right hand was strong enough for normal piano playing, it was never again up to the arduous pyrotechnics of concert-hall performance. The accident decided Tiomkin's future; he now became a full-time movie composer.

Tiomkin never felt much nostalgia for his early years in Hollywood. The pay was none too good; nor the conditions. He claimed that the composer in that era was almost a prisoner in a cell with a projection booth, a small screen, and a piano of dubious quality. "Sometimes the producer, billowing clouds of cigar smoke, would drop in and the poor composer, feeling more suffocated than ever, would give a nervous run-through of all his themes. No wonder the producer didn't like what he heard." After his success in later years, Tiomkin would refuse to play his score on a piano. If the producer wanted to hear it, he had to supply a studio session and an orchestra.

Tiomkin was a composer who always said yes to a producer and then went ahead and did what he felt best. In public, he spoke well of the producers with whom he worked, but in private, his views were likely to be less than flattering. The conditions under which composers worked in the heyday of Hollywood were " . . . terrifying, fantastically stupid. On *Alice In Wonderland* I worked twenty hours a day for ten days, conducting and recording." Tiomkin's most eloquent complaint was against the policy of calling in a composer after the film has been completed and handing him a short recording schedule. The speed with which many famous scores were composed and recorded is incredible.

The practice most infuriating to Tiomkin was denying the composer a say in the dubbing—the mixing of the voice, sound and music tracks:

> We seem to live in the strange belief that noise and loudness is
> a kick for the audience. Some producers want the music played
> loud, especially the brasses. The audience gets a pain in the ear
> and curses the composer. I always fight against too much music.

The producer says, "Here we must have music," and I always ask, "Why?"

One of Tiomkin's most felicitous associations was with Frank Capra. Capra had been pleased with the music for *Lost Horizon* and wanted to use the composer again. He felt that since his own forte was Americana, Tiomkin needed to learn more about American music, so Capra gave him books containing New England hymns, Negro spirituals, work songs, cowboy ballads, etc. Tiomkin delved into the long-forgotten lyrics and melodies from the cotton fields, the lumber camps, the river boats, and the merchant marines. This knowledge of musical Americana proved of immense benefit to Tiomkin, for it enabled him to provide sympathetic music for Capra pictures like *You Can't Take It with You* (1938) and *Mr. Smith Goes to Washington* (1939), as well as a large number of Westerns.

The Tiomkin Westerns include such spacious epics as *Duel in the Sun* (1947), *Red River* (1948), *High Noon* (1952), *The Big Sky* (1952), *Gunfight at the OK Corral* (1957), *Rio Bravo* (1959), *The Alamo* (1960), and *The War Wagon* (1967). Frequently chided about being Russian, yet able to write music descriptive of the American West, Tiomkin, whose geniality hid a mind like a steel trap, upturned his hands and quipped, "A steppe is a steppe is a steppe.... The problems of the cowboy and the cossack are very similar. They share a love of nature and a love of animals. Their courage and their philosophical attitudes are similar, and the steppes of Russia are much like the prairies of America."

Duel in the Sun was a gargantuan Western made by David O. Selznick; apparently, his idea was to make it the *Gone With the Wind* of cowboy pictures. Everything about the film was overdone, but viewed in the right spirit, it remains an entertaining opus, excessive though it undoubtedly is. Selznick was a producer unusually involved in his music scores, even to the extent of telling a composer what instruments to use and where. For *Duel in the Sun* Selznick wanted a particularly sumptuous score, and had the unusual idea of approaching several of Hollywood's best composers to make this proposition: each composer would be put on salary for two weeks to score one specific scene. At the end of the period, Selznick would review the pieces and select one composer to score the entire film. The selected composer would, however, have the two weeks included in the price of the job. None of the composers approached would accept the proposition. One was Miklos Rozsa, who had provided the greatly admired score for Selznick's *Spellbound*. Rozsa told his agent, "I want you to say to Mr. Selznick, in precisely these words, that if he had never heard a note of my music, I would find his offer insulting. Inasmuch as he has heard it, I regard his manner as outrageous, and I never want to hear his name again." Selznick also made the mistake of putting the contest idea to Erich Korngold, who looked at his agent with mock fear in his eyes as he shook his head, "No. What if I win?"

Duel in the Sun was scored by Tiomkin. The music was rich, lavish, and thunderous, sweeping across the plains with hundreds of horsemen, and rising in agonies of passion as Gregory Peck and Jennifer Jones loved and slaughtered each other. Selznick outlined the kind of score he had in mind and gave Tiomkin a card on which he had listed four particular emotions he wanted in the music: jealousy, flirtation, sentiment, and orgiastic. As soon as Tiomkin had written his themes for these, Selznick wanted to hear them. Tiomkin had already planned on fully covering these obvious aspects of an obvious story, but sly diplomat that he was, he graciously agreed. The themes for jealousy, flirtation, and sentiment all measured up, but Selznick didn't like "orgiastic." He felt the theme was too pretty and needed to be more violent. Tiomkin accepted the criticism and went to write something else. Selznick's reaction to the second try was no more enthusiastic, "No, it still needs more rhythm. I want it to be throbbing and unbridled. This is a rough cowboy and a tempestuous girl." Tiomkin bristled, but was his policy to go three rounds with a producer before taking a stand. Again he retreated to seek another musical solution. This time he scored with plenty of orchestral palpitations. When he played this feverish rhapsody for Selznick, the producer was still unsatisfied. "Dimi, what we must have here is love-making music, and this isn't the way I make love." Tiomkin was outraged. He picked up his score and shook it at Selznick, and yelled, "Look, Selznick, I don't know how you make love, but this is how I make love." The humor of the situation got to Selznick, he began to laugh and agreed to drop the pursuit. Tiomkin's third try is the one on the soundtrack, in the scene by the old swimming hole as Greg takes Jennifer against her will.

It often happens with composers that the pieces that become famous are not necessarily those they like best. Tiomkin's own preferences among his scores are *Lost Horizon*, *The Moon and Sixpence* (1942), and *I Confess* (1953). The interesting point is the common denominator: the gentility of the music. The tone is quiet, and sometimes tender. Tiomkin has often been criticized for orchestrally bombastic scores that albeit have become popular.

Another untypical Tiomkin score of considerable interest is *Cyrano de Bergerac* (1951). The score is suggestive of Rameau, and perfect for the period. Since the story is one of comedic and romantic exaggeration, the music follows suit. The overture is in the early-eighteenth-century concerto grosso style, which is appropriate because the opening scene plays out on a theater stage. A blustering horn figure characterizes the nose that marches on stage a quarter of an hour before its owner, and this figure is used fugally for the street fight in which Cyrano battles a hundred men. Tiomkin used a ninety-piece orchestra, with a thirty-piece brass choir. The brass is heard to advantage in the military sections, especially as the Cadets of Gascoyne march into the tavern. A particularly good piece of scoring is the tavern scene in which Cyrano relates his victories, punctuated by taunts from Christian about his nose. A dissonant chord chimes with each mention of the word "nose," pointing up Cyrano's rising anger.

Although Dimitri Tiomkin was respectfully regarded as one of the handful of men who pioneered film scoring, he sometimes regretted he didn't arrive later, at a time when composers had more freedom:

> To achieve anything in those early days was a problem. I think it was Alfred Newman who said, "Everybody around the studio has two jobs—his own and music." To do anything different was almost impossible; for instance, the end of the film always had to be a rising crescendo. I sometimes would try for a quiet musical conclusion, a poetic ending, but no, it had to be loud and definite. The opening title music had to be full of joy and gladness. It was actually forbidden at MGM to use minor chords in the opening music for a picture, their reasoning being that "minor" meant sad and "major" denoted happiness. The conviction with which they said these things was incredible, and sometimes funny. Victor Young once told me, when he was working on some picture or another, that the producer called him in and ordered him, "I want you to have music in the major for the heroine, and music in the minor for the hero. Then, when the two are on the screen together I want the music to be both major and minor."

The quality of Tiomkin's more than 100 film scores varied noticeably, possibly more so than most of the other major Hollywood composers. Tiomkin was known as a shrewd businessman, and he was for some years the highest-paid man in the profession. His effort on a score often seemed geared to what he estimated the effort is worth. For example, he scored two large-scale films in 1964 for Samuel Bronston, *The Fall of the Roman Empire* and *Circus World*. The first is obviously a score on which he worked with enormous patience and interest, and the second is just as obviously a hastily put together pastiche of self-plagiarism. Tiomkin, unlike most film composers, enjoyed being a celebrity and living in the grand manner. He was bitterly disappointed at not winning an Oscar for the *Roman Empire* score; it would have been his fifth. His music for *High Noon* had brought him two, for the song and for the score, and the scores of *The High and the Mighty* (1954) and *The Old Man and the Sea* (1958) each won him the famed gold statuette. With each nomination, Tiomkin stepped up his usual publicity in order to increase his chances.

John Green described Tiomkin as a fully effective human being:

> Composing expresses his talent; the achievement of international fame fulfills his ego; successful negotiating gratifies his gamesmanship; the use of his epic dialect satisfies his comedic need; his gift for gracious hospitality gives him happiness. You have never been a guest until Tiomkin has been your host.

Tiomkin was often accused of being too commercial. If this is true, it has served the films as much as himself. *The High and the Mighty* and *Friendly Persuasion* (1956) would probably not have done as well at the box office minus their famous Tiomkin themes. *The Old Man and the Sea* was a failure that might have been even more of a bore without Tiomkin's full-blooded music, the closest thing yet to a symphonic poem from the screen. In the case of *High Noon*, the film was literally saved by Tiomkin's invention of a song that was a part of the narrative and a score that generated tension. The film had been written off as a flop by the studio, based on their try-outs, but the addition of Tiomkin's song helped turn the film into a classic. Unfortunately, the great success of that song started a trend—the use of title songs, whether they were needed or not. The trend was a godsend for songwriters, film publicists, and recording artists, but a plague to composers forced to include the song as a theme in the score. Very often the song, almost always written by someone else, denied the composer the use of the credit titles for his own statement.

Tiomkin endeared himself to the press and the public alike by making humorous quips about his profession, such as saying he only did it for the money. He denied this when interviewed seriously:

> It isn't true that I do it only for money. Writing film music lets me compose in as fine a style as I am capable of. I'm a classicist by nature, and if you examine my scores you will find fugues, rondos, and passacaglias. I'm no Beethoven, but I think if I had devoted myself to concert composition, I might have been a Rachmaninoff. I'm not in sympathy with the harsh, atonal music of today—it's enough to lacerate your ears. Perhaps that is why I have done well in films—it was music for the masses.

One of the biggest laughs ever recorded at the Academy Awards was brought about by Dimitri Tiomkin. In accepting his Oscar in 1955 for *The High and the Mighty*, he stepped to the microphone and said, "I would like to thank Beethoven, Brahms, Wagner, Strauss, Rimsky-Korsakov . . . " and that was as far as he got, the auditorium rocked with laughter. Many people had made snide remarks about movie composers filching from the classics, and here was one of the most famous of them apparently admitting it. Tiomkin, whose Gregory Ratoff accent made anything he said sound funny, claimed his intention was to be serious and salute the masters who had developed the art of music. He had to leave the stage before he could finish his speech because the laughter was so great and he was too confused to continue. Many people later congratulated him on his sense of humor—few of them were composers. Several Hollywood musicians attacked him for casting ridicule on the profession. But Tiomkin admitted that he gained more fame in that moment of unconscious humor than in forty years as a musician. Was the humor truly unconscious? With Tiomkin it is very, very difficult to know. He was a charming and calculating man.

Dimitri Tiomkin ended his Hollywood career in 1967 with yet another Western score, *The War Wagon*. He then went to England to score a film about Catherine the Great, *Great Catherine*. It did poor business in Europe and almost none in America. Tiomkin then returned to Russia to produce *Tchaikovsky*, conducting the mammoth orchestral score himself. It, too, did poorly and convinced him his movie career was over. After his wife died in 1967, he met Olivia Cynthia Patch, a refined young woman, and married her in 1972. It was in London seven years later that Tiomkin died, having led a life that itself might make a good movie.

Franz Waxman

One of the composers most horrified by Tiomkin's Oscar speech was Franz Waxman. Waxman was a serious composer and a serious man. His bearing was rather like that of the traditional concept of the German professor, and his humor did not embrace gibes about music. Shortly after the celebrated incident, Waxman singled out Tiomkin and excoriated him. Tiomkin listened patiently and then said, "I don't know why you're so annoyed, Franz, I don't hear any influences of these great composers in your music." This so confounded Waxman, all he could do was walk away.

Franz Waxman was among the handful who have composed truly superior music for the screen. His craftsmanship, taste, and understanding of the medium were almost beyond criticism. The subtlety of his scoring was often beyond the comprehension of the people for whom he worked and he suffered because of it. It's possible that even Waxman himself didn't appreciate his own ability as a film composer since his primary interest was the concert hall, and he tended to regard his life in films as secondary.

Franz Waxman was a musician for whom music was an all-consuming way of life. The study of his Los Angeles home was filled with books, scores, and records in huge quantities, not only on the shelves that covered every wall but on the piano, on the desk, and

Franz Waxman

on the chairs. Even the fireplace had been converted into a filing cabinet. The forty-seven volumes of the complete works of Bach stood out only because of the brilliance of their red bindings. It was quite clearly the den of a man with an insatiable curiosity about music, and it was a room into which his young son, John, would occasionally wander, look around, and say, "Dad, someday we're going to have to straighten out all this junk."

Waxman was very much a composer of the late romantic German school. His style was texturally rich and expressive in melodic lines. He could bend the style to suit the subject of the film; he could use dissonances when needed, but his private musical nature was never truly influenced by the neo-romanticism of composers like Hindemith and Schoenberg. Waxman was aware of all that had been done by these and other composers, but he was adamant in his own convictions about structure and the emotional content of music. Luckily, his convictions were backed with a profound gift for melody. Unluckily, Waxman sometimes took himself and his work too seriously and put an enormous effort into the scoring of films that deserved no such effort.

Waxman believed in strong melodic lines in film scoring:

> Concert music is full of secrets. Brahms, for example, reveals himself slowly and the meaning of his music comes only with study. Film music must make its point immediately because it is heard only once by an audience that is unprepared and didn't come to the theater to hear music anyway. I believe in strong themes that are easily recognizable and which can be repeated and varied according to the film's needs. But the variations must be expressive and not complicated.

Franz Waxman truly believed that film composition is an art form and examination of his scores backs up the belief and shows the development of his scoring talent over the years. This is not true of all film composers, many of whom reached a certain level and stayed there, sometimes profitably. His death from cancer in February of 1968, age sixty-two, eliminated a man at the height of his creativity.

Waxman was one of seven children born to a fairly well-to-do Jewish family in Upper Silesai, now a part of Poland. (The family name was Wachsmann, which the composer changed after he arrived in America.) Tragedy struck this family terribly: one of the Franz's brothers died in infancy, another was lost in action in the First World War, and another died in a concentration camp during the Second World War.

Neither the parents nor any of their other children were musical. Waxman's early fascination with the piano and any thought of a career in music was discouraged by his father, who insisted on placing the boy as a bank teller after he left school. But Waxman's study of music convinced him of his mission in life. At the age of seventeen, he enrolled in the Dresden Music Academy, where his progress was so rapid that he was soon transferred to the more prestigious Berlin Conservatory. He supported himself by playing the piano in night clubs in the evenings; this led to him being offered a job with a then-popular jazz orchestra, the Weintraub Syncopaters. Some of the music for the band was written by Friedrich Hollaender, who was soon to win fame writing songs for Marlene Dietrich and, later, as a movie composer. Hollaender was impressed with young Waxman's talent and introduced him to the daughter of Bruno Walter, who in turn introduced him to her father. Walter was also impressed and contributed to Waxman's musical education.

In 1930, Franz Waxman's life took a distinct turn when Friedrich Hollaender introduced him to German movie producer Erich Pommer and suggested to Pommer that Waxman would make an excellent film orchestrator. One of Waxman's first assignments was arranging and conducting Hollaender's score for *The Blue Angel*, the film that made an international star of Dietrich. Waxman made a good living as a film musician, and his ambition to compose was realized three years later when he scored *Liliom*, Fritz Lang's version of the Ferenc Molnar story. It would have been the beginning of a career as a German film composer had it not also coincided with the ascent of the Nazis. Early in 1934 Waxman was beaten on a Berlin street, which produced an immediate resolve to remove himself and his new bride to Paris.

The rise of Nazism had a profound effect on the German theater and the musical arts as well as the film industry. It decimated the talent. Many of the finest German musicians, actors, writers, directors, and producers were Jewish and fled Germany, and would now contribute to the development of the film industry in the studios of Paris, London, and Hollywood. With their departure, the German film industry—then highly regarded for its artistry—suffered a blow from which it never recovered. Erich Pommer accepted a contract from Twentieth Century-Fox, with his first assignment to produce a film version of the Jerome Kern-Oscar Hammerstein II stage musical *Music in the Air*. This seemed logical to the studio—Pommer was German and the story was set in Bavaria. Since the story was about a young composer, why not bring over young Franz Waxman to adapt the score? While Pommer was at it, he also decided to bring over a young German writer to adapt the screenplay—Waxman's friend, Billy Wilder. The film opened at Radio City Music Hall in December 1934, heralding a bright and promising new year for Herren Pommer, Waxman, and Wilder.

Among the Hollywood directors who had heard Waxman's score for *Liliom* was James Whale, then nearing production on *The Bride of Frankenstein* and looking for a composer who could give the film something better than the average "squeal and groan" horror score. He offered the job to Waxman, who accepted even though he had never before thought in terms of musical fear and mystery. What Waxman wrote set a new standard for scoring such films. The themes for the film became stock items for the Universal Studios music library and were later used in many Universal pictures, including the *Flash Gordon* serial.

The success of *The Bride of Frankenstein* score led to an offer for Waxman to head the music department at Universal. Over the next two years he supervised the scoring of some fifty Universal films and wrote the music for a dozen of them. Next came a lucrative seven-year contract as a composer for MGM. Composing, especially for a studio like MGM, was more to his liking than directing a music department. The studio got its money's worth out of Waxman with an average of eight scores a year.

The first Waxman score to win wide attention was *Rebecca* in 1940. David O. Selznick had used Waxman two years previously to score *The Young at Heart*, which brought the composer his first Oscar nomination. The score for *Rebecca* (produced by Selznick) was a perfect complement to the du Maurier story; it conveyed the innocence of the young girl played by Joan Fontaine, the sophistication of Laurence Olivier's Maxim, the icy Mrs. Danvers of Judith Anderson, the mystery of the dark mansion of Manderley, and the malevolent spirit of the dead ex-wife, Rebecca. Despite the excellence of the music, Selznick was not satisfied that the score was sufficiently romantic, and called on Max Steiner to spruce up a few scenes, even though the Steiner style varied from Waxman's.

Of the nine films scored by Waxman in 1941, two were outstanding—*Dr. Jekyll and Mr. Hyde* and *Suspicion*. The Spencer Tracy version of the Robert Louis Stevenson classic had great style and impressed Waxman deeply; he was struck by a certain religious significance in the story and believed the author had meant it as a moral lesson—the triumph of good over evil. Ingrid Bergman appeared as the floozie Hyde takes to and torments, and Waxman skillfully and chillingly used her song "You Should See Me Dance the Polka" in variations that underline her growing fear. Waxman was so taken with the Stevenson story that he worked for years after on an operatic version, but it was never completed.

Alfred Hitchcock's *Suspicion* was another love story with mysterious overtones. Joan Fontaine played a woman puzzled by the man with whom she was in love. The love theme needed to have qualities that would imply a certain strangeness, so Waxman used an electric violin to give the sense of unreality, and by combining the instrument with a clarinet and a vibraphone, he was able to suggest a weird atmosphere. Waxman was fascinated with the possibilities of new sounds in orchestration, and it is interesting to listen to what he does in the scene where Fontaine believes her lover has tried to murder her and she cries out for help. For the final scene, an automobile chase, Waxman bases his music on the sound of high-speed whirling wheels.

With his MGM contract completed, in 1943 Waxman accepted an offer from Warner Bros. at a time when their music department was considered the industry's foremost. Among the more interesting scores he composed during his five years at the studio were two Errol Flynn war pictures, neither typical of war films of the period. Both films were rather somber and restrained in their heroics. Lewis Milestone's *Edge of Darkness* allowed Waxman the use of a few Norwegian melodies, but what gave this score real strength were his often darkly orchestrated variations on "A Mighty Fortress Is Our God." *Objective Burma* (containing one of Flynn's most intelligent performances) is a masterpiece of scoring. Waxman conveys the strain paratroopers dropped behind the lines are under, their stealthy trail through the jungle, the foreign, exotic terrain they move through, and the single-minded purpose of their mission. The closing sequence, the weary troops laboriously climbing a hill, is scored by Waxman in a fugal passage that abruptly stops when they reach the top, leaving the soundtrack silent except for the howling of a wind over the desolate hill.

Waxman's first Academy Award came in 1950 for writing the

score for Billy Wilder's *Sunset Boulevard*, which brought Gloria Swanson back to the screen in the role of a famous movie star. Many assumed the role to be close to her own story. It wasn't at all. Swanson was a realistic woman, not given to dwelling on the delusions that afflicted the fictional Norma Desmond. Waxman said at the time, "To convey the state of her madness I used a shrill, insistent orchestration of the music around her, and let an emphasized violin voice her explanation of her pathetic behavior." The music underlines the pathos of the woman with irony and sympathy, especially in the final scene where she descends the grand staircase of her mansion, believing she is playing Salome in a film.

Waxman won another Oscar the following year with his score for George Steven's film of Theodore Dreiser's *An American Tragedy*, retitled *A Place in the Sun*. (Waxman was the first composer to win two Oscars in succession.) Stevens urged a delicate performance from the young and stunningly beautiful Elizabeth Taylor and from Montgomery Clift as the young man from the other side of the tracks who murders his drab, impregnated girlfriend (Shelley Winters) in order to pursue rich-girl Taylor. The Taylor theme is played by a saxophone; Waxman apparently auditioned nearly a hundred players to find one who could give the right inflection to the melody. He felt this was essential to make the audience aware of the nature of the girl. At one point the scoring becomes painful. As Clift sits in jail awaiting his execution, Waxman plays a theme that gradually lifts in key changes, as if denoting the stretching nerves of the man.

Stevens felt Waxman's music was too Teutonic, so he asked Victor Young, the head composer at Paramount, where the film was made, to rescore certain scenes in the picture. Young refused, and another Paramount composer was assigned the ignominious task. Two years later, Stevens asked Waxman to go over Young's score for *Shane*, to which Waxman summarily replied, "Definitely not." Waxman showed even more integrity when he resigned from the Academy of Motion Picture Arts and Sciences in 1954 as a protest because Alfred Newman's score for *The Robe* was not nominated for an award. Moral stands such as this have been precious few in the history of Hollywood.

Franz Waxman composed scores of depth and quality for two religious films, *The Silver Chalice* (1954) and *The Story of Ruth* (1960), neither of which deserved his painstaking care. No musically sensitive person could fail to appreciate the erudition and eloquence of these scores, or to be puzzled by why he should have put so much work into such tedious pictures.

Waxman worked hard on another film that was also largely a failure but which deserved a better reception from the public—*The Spirit of St. Louis* (1957). James Stewart, far too old for the part of young Charles Lindbergh, nonetheless performed with sincerity and obvious respect for Lindbergh. Billy Wilder, the director, realized the film needed a score that would support the loneliness and apprehension of a man flying the Atlantic alone, so he called upon his old friend. Waxman's music carries the burden; it literally accompanies the lonely aviator and speaks his mind and alludes to the danger of drowsiness, his fear of not being able to land the plane, and his prayers. Truly a landmark in film scoring.

The major motif in Waxman's score for *The Spirit of St. Louis* appears in his oratorio "Joshua," which he conducted at the Los Angeles Music Festival in 1961. Waxman's contribution to California's musical culture was greater than that of any other composer who lived and worked in the film capital. In 1947 he inaugurated the Los Angeles Music Festival, conducting its concerts and bringing great artists to perform in it. Walter Arlen wrote after Waxman's death:

His courage in creating and sustaining the Festival despite obstacles and odds is a matter of indisputable record. Over the years he gave equal billing to Schoenberg and Shostakovich, Berg and Britten, Mahler and Milhaud, Hindemith and Harris and Honegger, Webern and Walton, Strauss and Stravinsky, even in the face of apathy and malice. Without him, our city would have been musically poorer.

During the fifties Waxman began to attend various European music festivals and would occasionally serve as guest conductor of various orchestras. These trips, and his annual Los Angeles Music Festival, probably interested him more than film scoring. Yet there was no evidence of any decline in his film work; in fact, the quality seemed to rise. *Peyton Place* (1957) and *The Nun's Story* (1959), two vastly differing subjects, are proof that an artist works best when busy.

Peyton Place is that rare commodity, a film that is immensely better than the book on which it is based. Filmed on location in New England, the picture features the distinctly beautiful landscapes of that region, plus the setting of a small town. It's doubtful if any native American composer could describe the scenes with more feeling than Waxman. Interviewed about the score, he said:

> Music in this film had to be simple in its harmonies, it had to tell of the problems and feeling of young people—I felt the drama could take care of itself. It took between six and seven weeks to write and it was fairly easygoing, because I was impressed with the picture. Fortunately I was not pressured to write or use a title song, a ridiculous restriction, and except for an initial discussion with producer Jerry Wald and director Mark Robson as to concept, I was left alone—the ideal situation. I was enchanted by the New England landscapes, and in order to get an authentic feeling I studied music of the area and let it color my themes.

The Nun's Story is precisely what it should be—a truly spiritual picture enhanced by the quality of Waxman's score. Director Fred Zinnemann felt that the film needed no music, but Warner Bros., who didn't care much for the project and doubted that it would make any money, insisted that the film's austere subject could be made more appealing with the addition of music. Waxman spent half a year preparing and writing the score in Rome, where it was also recorded.

> It was a most enjoyable assignment—a fascinating depiction of religious life, quiet in character and archaic in feeling. My thematic material is derived mostly from Gregorian chants, which I found while doing research in the library of the Papal Institute of Religious Music in Rome. Oddly enough, I have used the twelve-tone scale only once in my film career and it was in this picture, for the sequence in the insane asylum.

Waxman was nominated for an Academy Award for *The Nun's Story*, but lost to Miklos Rozsa and another religious film, *Ben-Hur*. Waxman was not a commercially minded man and set little store by the awards that seemingly mean so much to movie folk. On the subject of *Ben-Hur*, he said that it deserved to win and "Rozsa is the best film composer anyway."

Waxman's last concert composition was his choral and orchestral work "The Song of Terezin," commissioned by the May Festival of Cincinnati and performed there in May of 1965. The work is based on a collection of poems called *I Never Saw Another Butterfly*, illustrated by some of the children who passed through the Terezin concentration camp near Prague. Tragically, the composer was diagnosed with cancer shortly after this première, and it would be a bitter loss to the world of music when he died in early 1968.

Bronislau Kaper

Clever composers can, if they so wish, use their music to shield themselves. Depending upon the extent of their talent, they can produce a style that may not be a true reflection of their inner selves. In the case of Bronislau Kaper, the warmth of his music is so genuine that it is, indeed, a true statement of the man. Kaper was, as any of his colleagues will testify, a man of sentiment and wit, and his best work in films was for pictures that he openly admitted he loved—*Lili*, *The Swan*, *Green Dolphin Street*, *The Glass Slipper*, and *The Brothers Karamazov*.

Kaper was a composer who loved music. This may seem an odd statement to those who assume all composers to be music lovers. This is a matter of degree—composers obviously like music, most of them enjoy it and take pleasure from their ability to create it, but rare are those who love it with a passion. To visit Kaper in his home was to share his delight in listening to anything from a Polish folksong to Berg's *Wozzeck*, or better still, to hear him play the piano. What the listener heard was a stream of beautiful melodies played by a Middle European of the "old school" who readily admitted to an occasional tear while watching heartrending scenes in the films that he scored.

Kaper's ability to convey human feeling in musical terms helped many an actor. Edward G. Robinson came up to him after a screening of *The Stranger* and said, "Bronny, I owe you something. My acting became so much better after they added the music." George Peppard said, "There's a long scene in *Home from the Hill* where the camera stays on me as I walk to a cemetery. People are always saying what a fine piece of acting it was. Actually, I didn't do anything but walk and stare ahead. All the acting was done by Kaper."

John Green worked closely with Kaper during the years when Green was in charge of MGM's music department, and he conducted many of Kaper's scores. Kaper, unlike most of the film composers, was not a conductor. Said Green:

I think he was an unequaled master of music that occurs simultaneously with dialogue. He had an uncanny gift for it—he had a built-in computer that somehow recorded the actual pitch and rhythm and variations of projection and the impact of spoken voices. I would study his scores prior to conducting them, and there might be a scene with peppery dialogue—fast, loud, high-pitched, rhythmically complicated dialogue. I would see the score he had written for the scene and it would be black with notes—there would be high multi-noted woodwind passages, and I would wonder how we could run all this under dialogue. Then Bronny and I would play the score on the piano and it worked. I was amazed at how he did it—the timing cue sheets couldn't possibly give him every little syllable. But he had it all in his head—the music would flit in and out and flow among this dialogue miraculously. I've never known another composer who could do that.

Kaper was the child of a non-musical family in Warsaw. To please his businessman father, Kaper completed a course in law, although he had no intention of following it as a profession. His interest in music began at the age of seven when a piano was brought into the family home, and it was discovered that the boy could play it, even though he had received no instruction. Within a year, he was showing off to his relatives by stopping in the middle of a piece, getting up and running around the piano, and then picking up immediately on the right note.

Along with his study of law, Kaper also studied piano and composition, and with both courses completed, he headed for Berlin. There, in the mid-twenties, he found a richly productive musical atmosphere. New and creative strides were being made in the theatrical and cinematic arts in Berlin; Kurt Weill was only one of many young artists making an impression in a city wide open to experimental artistry. Kaper quickly got a job writing songs for cabaret and used the money to further his musical education. His introduction to the film world came through a young German producer with a complicated name, so difficult to non-German ears that when he went to Hollywood a few years later he decided to call himself Sam Spiegel. The film was called *Honeymoon for Three*, and from then on, Kaper was a film music man. He spent six years working on films in Berlin before the rise of the Nazis in 1933, when he and his wife moved to Paris. The move was a hasty one, and the Kapers arrived with little more than their clothes.

> But luck was on our side. Luck, what a wonderful thing. One evening we decided to live it up, despite our lack of funds, and we went to an expensive café on the Champs-Elysées. As we sat, a man came up and greeted us. He was a film cutter I had worked with in Berlin. "We've been looking for you—we're doing a French version of one of our films and we need your music." So right away I got a job.

Kaper spent the next two years writing music for French films and had several hit songs. One of them, "Ninon," sounds similar to Johnny Mercer's "Dream," written years later, and in the summer of 1935 the Jan Kiepura recording of it was played on every European radio station. Louis B. Mayer happened to vacation in Europe that summer and seemingly heard the song everywhere he went. He invited the composer to meet him:

> I went to his suite at the Ritz Hotel in Paris and played a lot of music for him. He didn't say much but he nodded his head a lot. Then I noticed him hitting his left hand with the edge of his right, as if cutting something in two. I asked him what he was doing. "This means half your salary is against your royalties." With this understanding, I was hired.

Kaper arrived in Hollywood in 1936 and immediately began writing songs for MGM. His contract with that studio was renewed time and again over a thirty-year period. Within months of his arrival at MGM, Kaper had written a smash hit—the title song of *San Francisco*, which remains an American anthem. A year later, something equally American, "All God's Chillun Got Rhythm," with Harpo Marx acting as a pied piper to an enthusiastic black chorus in *A Day at the Races*. More typically, Kaper wrote the beautiful ballad "While My Lady Sleeps," sung by Nelson Eddy in *The Chocolate Soldier*.

Kaper was not allowed to score a film at MGM until four years after his arrival.

> In Europe, we had done everything—songs, score, arrangements, directing—but in Hollywood you weren't allowed more than one job. With my first MGM picture I supplied the connective passages. They were horrified. They had so much money to spend, they couldn't think of a man doing more than one job.

Later, when he began scoring, he ran into the problem in reverse—they wanted to bring in songwriters to add to his score.

Bronislau Kaper rehearsing his music for *Lili* with star Leslie Caron.

Kaper scored half a dozen films a year at MGM, mostly run-of-the-mill, glossy entertainments for which the studio became famous and wealthy. Occasionally he would get a picture that provoked an emotional response in him, such as *Gaslight* in 1944, " . . . because Ingrid Bergman has such a marvelous face, I looked at it and couldn't help but write music for it every time she spoke, I was moved." It did not escape the attention of the Hollywood community that beautiful women affected Kaper in this manner.

Green Dolphin Street (1947) was another film Kaper enjoyed scoring; its romantic nature again brought forth beautiful themes. The main theme, picked up some time later by Miles Davis, has become a staple in the jazz world, although its original inspiration was far removed from jazz. Another peculiarity of the score:

> There was an earthquake in the picture, and I decided to score the scene with music leading up to the eruption, stopping, and then starting the music after the subsiding. Amazingly, people are always telling me how much they liked my music for the earthquake. Also, with the earthquake in *San Francisco*, they say the same thing, although there wasn't a note of music in the sequence. I've had some of my biggest successes with the lack of music in earthquakes.

Kaper's scores ranged from intimate drawing-room comedies to epics. But what he obviously liked best were those vehicles that coincided with his own tastes, such as *Lili* (1953), and *The Swan* (1956). The score of *Lili* brought the composer an Academy Award, although he felt sure he wouldn't have got it had the score not contained the song "Hi Lili, Hi Lo."

> I like pictures like *Lili*, and another one with Leslie Caron, *The Glass Slipper*, because they contain songs and dances that are part of the storyline and they have to shoot to your music. This way, you are not carrying the burden of somebody else's mistakes. Usually, you come to a picture that is finished, and it's like inheriting cancer. The worst thing that can happen to a film composer is being asked to score a film that someone else has already scored. Sol Siegel asked me to score a miserable picture about the Spanish Civil War called *The Angel Wore Red*, with Ava Gardner and Dirk Bogarde. It had an Italian score, and with a few notable exceptions, the worst scoring is done in Italy—

stupid, arrogant, monotonous, tasteless. It's a terrible experience to follow a bad example, but in this case they wouldn't have released the film otherwise.

The Swan was right down Kaper's alley:

I love this period. Right at the start of the film you see the legend "1910—somewhere in the middle of Europe." I get terribly attached to some films and this was one. There were tears in my eyes at the end, and I knew I was going to write good music. The story was delicate and stylish and elegant, with Grace Kelly as the princess, beautiful but cool, Alec Guinness as the prince to whom she is betrothed, and Louis Jourdan as the tutor who falls in love with her. I had to treat the first part as a subtle pantomime, and not give away much of the romantic feeling. Then Jourdan tells her he loves her, and the music takes over, so to speak. The end scene is one of the most delightful I've ever scored: Guinness is talking to Kelly and telling her why she is like a swan, as Jourdan, still in love with her and knowing she feels something for him, leaves the palace forever. There was a beautiful sadness to it. The Molnar story had a "once upon a time" quality—almost a swan song for a bygone era.

Two expensive disappointments were scored by Bronislau Kaper, *Mutiny on the Bounty* (1962) and *Lord Jim* (1965). Kaper philosophizes that both films allowed for travel—to Tahiti and Cambodia—and for some fascinating musical research. Other films on which he labored hard but largely in vain are *The Red Badge of Courage* (1951) and *A Flea in Her Ear* (1969).

The Red Badge of Courage is an anomaly in the listing of Hollywood films. Produced by Gottfried Reinhardt and directed by John Huston, the film was a beautiful but unwanted child of MGM. Lillian Ross wrote *Picture* (1952), an entertaining and perceptive book about the internecine affairs in the making of what was obviously, except to the MGM top brass, an exceptional piece of cinematic art. Butchered by the studio in cutting it from almost two hours to a mere sixty-five minutes, the film still is the finest screen version of a Civil War story. Kaper was deeply touched by Stephen Crane's account of a young boy's reaction to warfare:

> The music had to tell his story, how he felt about the death of his friends, why he ran from battle, and how he overcame his cowardice. These soldiers were simplistic men, they were of the earth, and they were put in the ironic, ridiculous position of having to kill their own countrymen. When the boy's regiment win their first battle and they are happy about it, I felt I had to underscore the tragedy of it all. And when the boy later runs away, I had to communicate his fears—with spasmodic music, like a heartbeat. When the boy writes a letter home, I scored it with a banjo to get a funny sound to a sad situation—to point up the absurdity of men at war.

A Flea in Her Ear was a flop at the box office, which is a great pity because Kaper's score is utter delight. His music for this Feydeau farce is a nonstop tuneful romp, and gives substance to what is essentially frou-frou. The score tinkles with Gallic wit, flirtations and breeziness, bistro music, bedroom music, promenade music, a few graceful waltzes, and a sprightly march for the cavalry rescue of a young lady.

> The point with this film was its farcical quality. Almost vaudeville. There was no depth to the story or the characters and there wasn't meant to be. It was a surface exercise, and it seemed to me that the Offenbachian route was the way to go.

A film for which Kaper had an affinity was Richard Brooks's version of *The Brothers Karamazov*:

The story was one of the closest things to me. I wanted to score the version that was made when I was working in Berlin but other commitments kept me from it. This time I was determined it wouldn't get away from me. As a child I read the book and for weeks afterwards I couldn't talk to anyone. Doing *Karamazov*, I had to let the audience know how I felt about the story, and yet I had to do it in a language they would understand. The gypsy music of that Russian period was a useful coloration, but I wrote in a rather Prokofievian style because of the violence in the story. I feel the music must always be an emotional reaction. Many people commented on the rather startling dramatic music I used with the credit titles. Well, I didn't want them to think this was just another family picture.

Kaper also proved adept at scoring comedies, with *Auntie Mame* a prime example:

Comedy is difficult because of the emphasis on dialogue. You cannot waste time in a comedy, and that's a bit of a strain on the composer. You don't have long stretches of music to express yourself; with dramatic subjects you have time to build, but with a comedy, every note must count. With *Mame* the first temptation is to comment musically on her gay, vivacious manner, but you see that on the screen, you don't have to say it again. What I did was to try and show that beneath this frivolity was a woman of deep sentiment, with problems, and that she was genuinely concerned about her nephew. To have scored her comically would have cheapened the film. When something is very effective on the screen, you add little to the music.

The bromide about film music not being heard irritated Kaper less then most of his colleagues.

Let's put it this way: if you don't hear the music on any level of consciousness, then it has served no purpose. At certain moments in films, nobody knows the difference between what is visual and what is acoustical. It all comes together. It's like seeing and hearing lightning—it's one effect.

There are no rules to film scoring. Kaper often pointed out to producers that the film they wanted him to score actually needed so little music they had best hire an arranger to provide a few transitions. Other films call for almost constant scoring:

> But music can do bad things, it can punctuate wrong lines, and it can turn a warm scene into a cold one and vice versa. With dialogue, the most effective technique is the use of silence, to lull the audience with neutral music into a sense of half security and then stop when something really important is said—nothing is as loud in films as silence.

The real test of a composer is a long sequence that has no dialogue or sound, and being required to tell the story with music. Kaper did this brilliantly in the opening sequence of *Butterfield 8*. The film begins with Elizabeth Taylor alone in bed, getting up, brushing her teeth, and choosing what clothes to wear. The scene is simple, but the implications are not:

> I had to tell the audience that this is an unhappy, neurotic girl. To suggest her character and her intentions. This wasn't easy— Elizabeth Taylor in bed looks so gorgeous, why should she be unhappy? This is where music comes in, this is the value of the composer in filmmaking: to add something that isn't otherwise apparent. And if you can't add something, don't bother to write it. Music without a statement is not music.

After 1968, Bronislau Kaper's interest in films began to wane. (He wrote no more film music after *A Flea in Her Ear*.) The industry had changed and he was not about to change with it. His golden age, the quarter century he spent with MGM, had passed. However, Kaper did not retire from the musical life of Los Angeles. Ever the charming gentleman, he was active in social affairs surrounding concerts and recitals and was a close friend of almost every famous conductor and soloist, all of whom were guests in his home and all of whom insisted that he play the piano for them. Sadly, cancer brought it all to an end in April of 1983.

After forty years of writing music for films, Kaper did not feel that everything had been said and done:

> If you're excited by something, you'll come up with new ideas. How many women have you known in your life? Then along comes another and you love her. You've seen eyes before, legs before, but wait—there's something different about this one, something in the eyes, in the voice, a smile, an expression, something in the way she walks. It's the same with films—all you need are a few little things and off you go again. If I were bothered by the clichés of the past, I couldn't live. Not just music. Life is also full of clichés. Don't fall for them.

Miklos Rozsa

It's very likely that when the ranking of twentieth-century composers is finally complete, the name Miklos Rozsa will be near the top. Rozsa managed what few composers have—a distinguished and highly profitable career writing film music while also composing for the concert hall, and having that concert music frequently performed and recorded. His *Violin Concerto* and his *Theme, Variations and Finale* are among the most popular of contemporary compositions. With his penchant for musicology, an enviable gift for melody, and a distinctly individualistic "sound," Rozsa long ago established a niche for himself as a cultured, affluent man of the world. His mansion atop one of the Hollywood hills bespeaks a degree of success that is rare in the world of music—marble statues of ancient Rome, bronze artifacts, oriental rugs, Rembrandt etchings, and paintings from various periods by Dutch, Flemish, and Hungarian artists. It is not the home of the average musician.

Rozsa did not set out to become a film composer. It was a friend who brought him into the business at a time when, as he candidly says, "I knew nothing about film music, nor did I care." Rozsa was born in Budapest in April of 1907, to a mother who loved the piano and an industrialist father who not only cared little for music but doubted that a decent living could be made from it. He advised his son against making it his career, but the boy's talent for music

Miklos Rozsa

was obviously too large and his enthusiasm too passionate to be contained. Rozsa could read music before he could read words, and he began violin lessons at the age of five. Two years later he played a movement from a Mozart violin concerto. He was elected president of the Franz Liszt Society at his school and won the society's composition contest at the age of eighteen with a trio for flute, oboe, and cello. Rozsa left Budapest to attend the University of Leipzig, but within a year he decided to devote himself entirely to music and enrolled in that city's famed Conservatory of Music.

Rozsa's father wrote to Hermann Grabner, his son's teacher, and asked for an opinion of the boy's talent. Grabner replied that the boy showed rather amazing promise as a composer. Shortly afterwards, the esteemed music publishing firm of Breitkopf and Haertel put student Rozsa under contract. He was then twenty-one, and they are still his publishers. After his graduation in 1929, Rozsa stayed in Leipzig and acted as an assistant to Grabner, all the while composing a steady stream of music.

In 1931, after several of his chamber works were performed in Paris, Rozsa decided to make the French capital his home. The success of his *Theme, Variations and Finale, Opus 13* in 1934 established him as one of the outstanding young composers of the day. His ballet *Hungaria*, performed by Anton Dolin and Alicia Markova, took him to London in 1936. Rozsa had known French film director Jacques Feyder in Paris and, while in London, he received a call one evening inviting him for dinner at Feyder's hotel. He then took Feyder to see the ballet:

> Jacques seemed very impressed and insisted we go out afterwards and celebrate my success. Champagne was ordered at his behest—I knew he enjoyed drinking it, but I had never touched the stuff. As the champagne went down, my value as a com-

poser went up. By the end of the second bottle I was better, according to him, than Beethoven had ever been. He told me I was the greatest composer alive, and why wasn't I writing for films? I said I'd never thought about it, mostly because I didn't write fox-trots. He replied, "You're out of your mind. I don't want fox-trots, I want serious music." Said I, "In films?" Feyder then let it be known he had made up his mind I was to do the music for his new picture and that we were to meet for lunch the following day at the Green Park Hotel.

Rozsa's blithe ignorance of the film world continued to manifest itself at the luncheon:

> I met Jacques and his actress wife, Francoise Rosay, at one o'clock, and he said he was expecting another couple. We had a few cocktails and the time slipped by. My main interest was eating—I was hungry and more interested in the arrival of food than his guests. Around three o'clock they came in, an attractive German couple who were introduced as Mr. and Mrs. Sieber. She sat on my right, and Feyder was on my left. I noticed people looking at us but I couldn't understand why. Suddenly she turned to me and asked, "Is my song ready?" I must have looked blank, and I felt Feyder nudging me. I came out with something like, "No, but I'm working on it." She then said, "Mr. Feyder tells me you're going to write the music for our picture." I smiled idiotically. A little later I leaned over toward Feyder and whispered, "Who is she?" and he snarled back under his breath, "Marlene Dietrich, you damn fool."

The film in question was *Knight Without Armour*, starring Dietrich and Robert Donat, produced by Alexander Korda. Feyder told Korda he wanted Rozsa to do the score, to which Korda replied, "Who's Rozsa?" Feyder looked astonished, "He's the greatest friend of your brother Vincent. They practically live together." Korda was finally talked into using Rozsa, although it might not have been possible had the great producer realized that until the previous day, the composer had neither heard of him nor his brother. Capricious though the entry may have been, it launched one of the most productive careers in film composition as well as a firm association between Rozsa and Korda.

Rozsa confesses that at the outset he knew so little about film scoring he bought a book to find out how to do it:

> I also went to see many films and found the scores mostly appalling, especially in American films. Some of the better French pictures had scores by Honneger, Ibert, and Milhaud, and they served to inspire. But I had a lot to learn about film scoring, and I learned the hard way—by making mistakes.

Rozsa scored half a dozen pictures for Korda before he was assigned to write the music for the extravagant fantasy *The Thief of Baghdad* in 1939. The war broke out just a few weeks into production, and Korda was unable to get enough money together to finish the picture. United Artists offered to supply the necessary funds but only if the film was completed in Hollywood. Rozsa proceeded to Hollywood in the spring of 1940, where he turned out a richly melodic score, well suited to the romantic and exotic needs of the Arabian Nights story. The score would have landed Rozsa a job with any studio, but Korda retained his services for three more pictures he would now do in Hollywood, even though they were largely British topics. The first was *Lady Hamilton* (1940), with Laurence Olivier as Lord Nelson, and Olivier's new wife, Vivien Leigh, as Nelson's inamorata. Next, *Lydia* (1941), with Korda's famous wife, Merle Oberon, in the title role, and finally *The Jungle Book* (1942), starring Korda's Indian discovery, Sabu.

Miklos Rozsa at the 1982 Santa Fe Film Festival, being
given an award by emcee Tony Thomas.

The Jungle Book is a film that leans heavily on its music score.
Fortunately, the score was brilliant, packed with imaginative descriptions of jungle animals. Rozsa later adapted it into a concert
suite with narration, and twice recorded it—first with Sabu and
some years later with Leo Genn. Neither the text nor the quality of
the narration serves the music well. The film itself was condensed
from Kipling's two *Jungle Books*, focusing on Mowgli, the boy who
wanders off into the jungle and is reared by a family of wolves. Rozsa's
score is fully descriptive of the images and the mysterious depths

of the jungle. The scoring of the various animals is particularly deft and tuneful: the elephants are characterized by roaring trombones and tubas, wolves by glissando horns, Baloo the Bear by a chuckling contra-bassoon, Bagheera the Black Panther by slithering strings, the hyenas by gurgling alto saxophones, the monkeys by high, perky piccolos, and Shere Khan the Tiger by muted, low brass. The score is a delightful lesson in instrumentation for young people.

Miklos Rozsa's first contract with a Hollywood studio was with Paramount in 1943. Two of the scores he wrote for that studio are of particular interest, *Double Indemnity* (1944) and *The Lost Weekend* (1945). The first is lean and slightly dissonant, with few themes. Rozsa relates that the score was condemned by Paramount's musical director:

> I was asked to appear in his office, where he there explained that the music was very bad. He told me it belonged in Carnegie Hall. I thanked him, but he said he hadn't meant it as a compliment. He then asked why I hadn't written something attractive, to which I replied that Billy Wilder's film was about ugly people doing vicious things to each other. Anyway, he and I had to go to the première together. The film went over quite well, but I still had the feeling I was in the doghouse. My music director and I started to walk away when Buddy de Sylva, the head of the music department, yelled after us to come back. I felt like Marie Antoinette on her way to the guillotine and I'm sure the music director felt even worse. De Sylva then let it be known that he thought it was a wonderful score. He turned to the music director and said, "And you're to be congratulated for hiring him." With this, our music director beamed and said, "Buddy, I always get you the right man, don't I?"

The Lost Weekend, for which Ray Milland won an Oscar for his portrayal of a dipsomaniac, was another film needing more than a conventional score. The film fascinated Rozsa because it was an exercise in imagination to musically underline dementia praecox and the craving for alcohol. Of particular help in this score, and later in the score for *Spellbound*, was an electronic instrument called the Theremin, played by the performer moving his hands back and forth near its pair of antennae to generate electronic sound oscillations. Some wag described the Theremin as the wail of a thousand women, but Rozsa's choice of the instrument seemed perfect as the voice of a disturbed psyche. In *The Lost Weekend*, it helped Milland to get across his unspoken craving for a drink without having to mug the feeling. One scene is made horrific by the music: Milland in his dementia sees a mouse running across the floor, and a whining little violin characterizes the animal. Then a bat materializes and swoops to kill the mouse viciously with nerve-racking musical jolts. How terrified and unnerved Milland is by this imagined incident is clearly pointed up by the scoring.

Spellbound won Rozsa his first Academy Award. Heralded as a landmark in film music, the score contains a theme that remains one of the most popular themes ever to emerge from a soundtrack. Rozsa adapted it into his Spellbound Concerto, which has been recorded many times. The Theremin played its most vital role in this story of an amnesia victim who fears that he might be a murderer. Its eerie sound blended perfectly with Rozsa's haunting music and contributed mightily to the aural atmosphere of implied madness and mystery. Rozsa used the Theremin again in *The Red House* (1947), and then abandoned it, fearing it might otherwise become a trademark. "I didn't want it to be the equivalent of Dorothy Lamour's sarong."

Rozsa began another distinct stylistic phase in 1946 when he scored *The Killers*. Mark Hellinger's production of this and two other pictures—*Brute Force* (1947) and *The Naked City* (1948), his last work before his untimely death—brought a new kind of crime film to the screen: realistically brutal, unsentimental, and harsh. Rozsa's thickly textured scores for these pictures, full of sharp accents and terse rhythms and tension chords, is unlike any he had written for the screen previously or would write later.

The films that Rozsa scored during his three years at Universal include *Kiss the Blood Off My Hands* (1948) and *Criss Cross* (1949). Another of his films from this period, *A Double Life* (1947), with Ronald Colman's brilliant performance as a demented Shakespearean actor, brought Rozsa his second Oscar. Rozsa asked psychiatrists for information about the sounds the mentally sick are predisposed toward, and then used the knowledge in scoring Colman's scenes of paranoia. The scoring for these scenes contrasted sharply with the concerto grosso style for the theater sequences of Colman playing Othello.

In 1949, Miklos Rozsa accepted a long-term contract from MGM, whose music department was headed by John Green. The studio orchestra was first-rate, and the recently introduced LP recording process, with MGM's own label, promised a new era in Rozsa's career. His assignments were consistently interesting and soon led to his becoming a specialist in the scoring of historical subjects.

Rozsa's composing style has often been described as polyphonic, chromatic, and intricately textured. It is the music of an educated composer whose tastes are definitely those of early-twentieth-century Europe. There is a Rozsa "sound" easily recognizable both in his film scores and his concert works. Being Hungarian also works in his favor, for there is an inbuilt exotic quality to native Hungarian music.

We stand alone in a Slavic sea. Hungarian peasant music is unique, it has no connection with other musical cultures, just as the Hungarian language is unconnected with other languages.

Our gypsy music is especially valuable, as Brahms discovered long ago and as Bartók and Kodály made apparent with their marvelous treatments. There is a certain oriental color in the gypsy scale, and it is a very useful palette to have in one's heritage.

One of Rozsa's most famous concert works, his *Violin Concerto*, commissioned, performed, and recorded by Jascha Heifetz, was put to use as film music by Billy Wilder:

Wilder approached me at a party and said he loved my violin concerto, and that he had worn out his copy of the record and wondered if I had another one. I was as intrigued as much as flattered, but all he would say was, "I've got an idea." Some months later he called me into his office and revealed the idea: he had written a screenplay called *The Private Life of Sherlock Holmes*, and he had written it around my concerto, inspired by the fact that Holmes liked playing the fiddle. The theme of the first movement is somewhat nervous, and this apparently suggested to Wilder Holmes' addiction to cocaine. (I've scored music for dipsomaniacs, amnesiacs, and paranoids—now I have a drug addict to add to my list of dubious characters.) The theme of the second movement of the concerto brought a lady spy to Wilder's mind, and the turbulent third movement conjured up, for him, the Loch Ness monster. He said, "This is perfect monster music." I wasn't flattered, but he was right, it did work out quite well. I agreed to score the film for him, using the concerto. He seemed to think this would be easy because I wouldn't have to think up any new themes. Actually, it was very difficult. The concerto was not written with any images in mind, and the timings had to be altered to fit the film sequences. It would have been much easier to invent something fresh.

Rozsa's contribution to the art of film scoring was enormous, and the decline in the number of his assignments during the sixties was a sad comment on the decline in the artistic integrity of film-making during the decade. He lamented this decline but philosophized that the changing times found him somewhat reactionary and out of step with newer concepts in cinema.

Miklos Rozsa decided to end his film career in 1981 after scoring the Steve Martin comedy *Dead Men Don't Wear Plaid*. He had been in the film business forty-four years and written music for some ninety movies. If pressed to choose his favorite among them, he would name *Ben-Hur* (1959), which brought him his third Oscar and, in the opinion of many critics, is the mightiest of all film scores. Others might choose *El Cid* (1960), but whatever the choice, it is likely to be found on a recording. Selections from about two-thirds of his film titles have been recorded, and of his forty-five non-film compositions, almost all are available as recordings. Few contemporary composers are as well represented on record as Rozsa. The life of this extraordinary man ended on July 27, 1995, having reached his eighty-eighth birthday the previous April 19.

Film music, ideally, is an extension of what Wagner began, the idea of the all-encompassing work of art comprising acting, drama, and music. Within his particular framework, opera music was the most important ingredient. This is not so with film, but to understand just how powerful the contribution of music is to film, one has only to think of Rozsa's scores for historical film subjects and imagine their impact minus the score. The following, by the composer, is here presented to illustrate the interesting ways in which his musical decisions were made.

$\bullet \quad \bullet \quad \bullet \quad \bullet \quad \bullet$

Miklos Rozsa on Musical Archaeology in the Movies, or, The Pilgrim Fathers Meet the Knights of the Round Table along the Appian Way

Films with historical backgrounds always present interesting problems to the composer. There had been innumerable other historical pictures before *Quo Vadis*, and they were all alike in their negligent attitude toward the stylistic accuracy of their music. It is interesting to note what painstaking research is usually made to ascertain the year of publication of, let us say, "Yes, We Have No Bananas," if it is to be used in a film about the twenties, but no one seems to care much if the Christians in the first century sing "Onward Christian Soldiers" by Sir Arthur Sullivan, composed a mere 1800 years later. It is hard to believe, but I was asked to use "Adeste Fideles" for the nativity scene in *Ben-Hur*. My argument that it is a Medieval Latin hymn fell on deaf ears. Only when I threatened to leave the picture was I allowed to disregard this notion.

No one expects to hear sixteenth-century Minnesinger music in *Meistersinger*, ancient Greek music in *Electra*, or ancient Hebrew music in *Salome*. The orientalism in *Aida*, *Samson and Delilah*, or *Queen of Sheba* is only used as color, and they are full-blooded, romantic operas mirroring the style of the period of their creation with no attempt whatsoever to represent the true style of the period of their action. But motion-picture art is different. It is realistic and factual. It not only tries to capture the spirit of bygone eras but also tries to make believe that it projects before the eyes of the spectator the real thing. There are no painted backdrops, fake props, cardboard shields, and wooden swords as in an opera, but everything is realistic to the fullest limit, and if the public doesn't believe that the Christians were actually eaten by the lions, the film has failed in its object.

When *Quo Vadis* was assigned to me, I decided to be stylistically, absolutely correct. First, thorough research had to be done. Though my old studies of the music of antiquity came in handy, I was greatly aided by George Schneider, the MGM librarian, who produced every reference to the period that could be found in libraries throughout the world.

Our first job was to prepare the blueprints for the antique instruments that had to be made. We reconstructed these from Roman statues (in the Vatican and Naples museums), antique vases and bas-reliefs on columns and tombstones, giving exact measurements for all details. The actual instruments were then produced by Italian instrument makers, so a great array of lyres and cytharas (the chief instruments of the Romans), double pipes (aulos), curved horns (buccina), straight trumpets (salpynx or tuba), tambourines, drums, sistrums, clappers, and other percussion instruments were made with amazing likeness to the real ones.

Then the music which was to be performed on scene had to be prepared. To select music for an historical picture of the middle ages, for instance, would have been an easy task, as there is a wealth of material available. But this is not the case with Roman music from the year 64 A.D. In spite of the fact that a great amount of Roman literature, painting, architecture, and sculpture has survived, there is no actual record of any music of the classical times of Roman history. There is a lot of reference to music in literary works of the time, so we know what an important part music played in the life of the Romans. Seneca complains that orchestras and choruses grew to gigantic proportions, and often there were more singers and players in the theater than spectators. There were numerous schools of music, and daughters of the rich bourgeoisie had to learn to play the lyre just as they had to play the piano centuries later. The slaves of the aristocrats entertained constantly, and Seneca also complains that "at table, no one can talk for the music." All this proves that music was widely practiced and belonged to everyday life.

In *Quo Vadis* there were three distinguishable styles in which music had to be created. First, the music of the Romans, such as the songs of Nero and the slave girl Eunice, the sacrificial hymn of the Vestals, and the marches and fanfares. Secondly, the hymns of the Christians, and thirdly, the music performed by the slaves, which could be called the Roman Empire music. As nothing remains of Roman music, this had to be created by deduction. We know that the culture of the Romans was entirely borrowed from the Greeks. Greek civilization and religion dominated Roman life and Nero himself preferred to speak Greek rather than Latin, and in sculpture, painting, poetry, and pottery they copied Greek models. As Greek musicians and instruments were imported and Greek musical theory adopted, the music of the Romans cannot be separated from its Greek models and ideas. It was, therefore, not incorrect to reconstruct this music from Greek examples. About the music of the Greeks we know considerably more. We know their thorough and involved musical systems, we can read their musical notations and we also have about a dozen relics of actual music, preserved mostly on tombstones and old papyri. These were of the greatest value in this attempt at reconstruction.

As the music for *Quo Vadis* was intended for dramatic use and as entertainment for the lay public, one had to avoid the pitfall of producing only musicological oddities instead of music with a universal, emotional appeal. For the modern ear, instrumental music in unison has very little emotional appeal; therefore I had to find a way for an archaic-sounding harmonization which would give warmth, color, and emotional value to these melodies. The hymns of the early Christians also had to be reconstructed by deduction. Saint Ambrose's collection of liturgical music for the Catholic Church appeared about 400 years after our period, and I wanted to go back to the very source from which the Ambrosian plain chant and later the Gregorian hymnology blossomed. As the early Christians were partly Jews and partly Greeks, their liturgical music naturally originates from these sources. These two influences have been prevalent in the Gregorian hymns, which are the basis of the Roman Catholic Church music.

The third category of the music was that of the slaves, mostly Babylonians, Syrians, Egyptians, Persians, and other conquered nations of Oriental origin. There were fragments of the oldest melodies found in Sicily with Arabian influence, and others found in Cairo, which I utilized. The orchestration of the music performed on scene was another problem. None of the old instruments were available and, therefore, an archaic sound had to be created with our modern instruments. I used a small Scottish harp, the Clarsach, and this delicate instrument gave a remarkably true likeness to the sound of the lyre and antique harp. For military music: cornets mixed with trumpets and trombones gave the roughness of the early brass instruments. Bass flute and English horn replaced the sound of the aulos. Our modern percussion instruments come close to the antique ones, and therefore it was safe to use tambourines, jingles, drums of different shapes and sizes, and cymbals. Bowed stringed instruments, however, could not be used. These came into usage nearly a thousand years later. For music that was supposed to be performed by a large group of players, I took the liberty of using the string group of the orchestra playing pizzicato to reinforce the main body of the orchestra. Harps and guitars were also added to achieve the percussive quality. Melodic lines, however, were only given to the woodwinds and brass instruments to perform. A romantic, chromatic harmonization would have been out of place, and a simple modal harmonization seemed to me the closest to the character of this music.

I didn't realize it at the time, but *Quo Vadis* turned out to be the first of a dozen historical films, all of them set in different periods and all calling for various degrees of research. I had been type-cast three times before: as a composer specializing in Oriental fantasies, next as one dealing in dark psychological subjects, and then a composer of hard-hitting crime pictures. Now I became the man the producers cried for whenever vast historical epics took shape on the drawing boards, and with my next assignment I advanced a full eleven centuries.

With *Ivanhoe*, I became my own first disciple (I suppose also the only one) and followed the example which I set up in *Quo Vadis*. Having tried to recreate the music of the first century by using, after thorough research, musical fragments from the period, I did the same in *Ivanhoe* by going back to sources of the twelfth century. I found a somewhat similar situation in musical matters between the two films. As Roman music was largely influenced by the Greek, so the music of the Saxons came under the influence of the invading Normans. It is a well-known fact that people on a lower level of civilization readily absorb the culture of the invaders or neighboring countries which have a higher civilization, as a subconscious expression of their longing for the higher level of life. The sources of Saxon music are extremely few and far between, but there is a large amount of music available of the French troubadours and trouveres who brought their music to England with the invaders. The various themes in *Ivanhoe* are partly based on these sources and partly my own. Under the opening narration, I introduced a theme from a "Ballade" by Richard the Lionhearted; the Norman theme I developed from a Latin hymn ("Reis Glorios") by the troubadour Guiraut de Bornth. The love theme of Ivanhoe and Lady Rowena is a free adaptation of an old popular song from the north of France—the manuscript was found in a collection in the Royal Library of Brussels. For *Rebecca* I needed a Jewish theme, mirroring not only the tragedy of this lovely character of Sir Walter Scott's but also that of her persecuted people. Fragments of medieval Jewish musical motives suggested a theme to me; in short, my scoring of the film was colored and inspired by the material discovered in research.

The next film was also English, but one taking place five centuries after the era of the Norman conquest and one dealing with a completely different musical fabric. *Plymouth Adventure* is the story of the Mayflower's journey from Plymouth Harbor to Plymouth Rock in 1620. I now looked for a musical theme which the Pilgrim Fathers might have known, and which also expressed their indomitable spirit of religious, personal, and political freedom. The pilgrims had one book with music on board: Henry Ainsworth's *Psalter*, which was printed in Amsterdam in 1612. This book contained the melodies the pilgrims brought to America and sang in their new country. I decided to use as the theme of the Mayflower the "136th Psalm", a melody which is imbued with vigor and fervent faith. It has a very interesting history. One can trace it back to French Psalters of the early sixteenth century, and fragments of it (according to Waldo Seldon Pratt's book *Music of the Pilgrims*) can be found in early German chorales. It had been called the "Huguenot Marseillaise," as it has the pulsation of a battle song. It has an unusual rhythm and I found its text most appropriate. I therefore used it vocally with an orchestral accompaniment for the opening of the film: "Confess Jehovah thankfully, for He is good, for His mercy continueth forever." The theme attains its culmination in a sequence of the departure of the Mayflower, when the sails of the ship fill with wind to start a voyage into the unknown. To give an atmosphere of authenticity, I tried to build the other themes in the manner of the seventeenth-century lutenist composers whose music the Pilgrim Fathers knew and must have brought with them. I didn't use any contemporary material, as these themes had to fit closely the situations and characters of the narrative. Again, it was a matter of coloration and style.

MGM's filming of Shakespeare's *Julius Caesar* in 1953 gave me a problem of a different kind. If it had been merely a historical film about Caesar, I would have undoubtedly tried a reconstruction of first-century music. However, it was more than that. It is a Shakespearean tragedy and, with all its language, a true mirror of Elizabethan times—and it is principally this language which dictates its style. In Shakespeare's time, as they had few scruples about stylistic correctness, the music was undoubtedly their own—Elizabethan. Should I have composed in a Roman manner, it would have been wrong for Shakespeare; should I have tried to treat it as stage music for an Elizabethan drama in Elizabethan style, it would have been anachronistic from the historical point of view. I decided, therefore, to regard it as a universal drama, about the eternal problems of men and the timely problems about the fate of dictators, I wrote the same music I would have written for a modern stage presentation: interpretive incidental music, expressing my own musical language, for a modern audience, what Shakespeare expressed with his own language for his own audience. The example set by Mendelssohn with his music for *A Midsummer Night's Dream* was obvious, as he wrote his own, highly romantic nineteenth-century music, which now everybody accepts as authentic to this romantic play of Shakespeare.

Dramatic music for historical films cannot help but be stylized, as the very nature of dramatic music excludes the exact usage of period music, which in almost all cases is quite undramatic. By studying the melodic, rhythmic, and harmonic elements of the past, the composer can create a language that is appropriate to the subject while still being his own musical expression. Berlioz once said that he had to change his style for each dramatic subject he overtook.

This was true also in my own case with my next three historical films: *Young Bess* was the story of Elizabeth I as a child, and the musical problems were fairly straightforward. *Knights of the Round Table* was an action pageant set in fifth-century England, and here I had to fall back on imagination since hardly anything exists from that period. Far more interesting was *Diane*, the story of Diane de Poitiers and her love for King Henry II of France. Unfortunately, the film was a dismal flop, but I still like it from the musical point of view because it allowed an exploration of the Renaissance period. Sixteenth-century French music was very interesting, composers like Josquin Des Prez and Orlandus Lassus were prolific, and I enjoyed studying their scores and composing music in the style, using viola da gambas, recorders, harpsichords, and various medieval instruments. I must confess I like some of my music for this sadly neglected picture. The love theme was later published for string orchestra under the highly unsuitable title "Beauty and Grace." The title is not mine.

Hollywood has not exactly achieved world fame for the historical accuracy of its film biographies, but *Lust for Life* was a gratifying exception. It not only captured the dramatic highlights of Vincent Van Gogh's tragic life but also with painstaking research remained absolutely factual. Based on Irving Stone's book and written for the screen by Norman Corwin, the film was directed by a man who is an artist in his own right, Vincente Minnelli, and produced by the impeccably tasteful John Houseman. Kirk Douglas not only managed to look like Van Gogh but was entirely believable as the ecstatic and exalted Dutch painter. My problem, as always with historical subjects, was to find a suitable style, one which would form an homogeneous unity with the pictorial happenings of the photoplay. The music that Van Gogh knew and liked was the high romanticism of the Wagner-Liszt-Berlioz school and its numerous satellites in France and Germany. His early impressionistic and pointillistic style, however, corresponds musically with the impressionism of Debussy, although Van Gogh himself could not have known his music. There is a twenty-five year time lag between pictorial and musical impressionism. The first important impressionistic orchestral work is Debussy's *L'Après-midi d'un faune*, which had its first performance in 1894, four years after Van Gogh's death. However, the emotionalism of the musical fin de siècle, the daring harmonic and orchestral palette of Debussy, corresponds, to my mind, at least, with the early style of Van Gogh, and gives a point of departure for further development as his own style started to develop, too. Nothing was further from my mind than to imitate Debussy's style for *Lust for Life*, but the timbre of this score is that of France at the beginning of the century.

I thought my career scoring historical subjects had completed itself, but I was quite wrong; the mightiest assignment of them all now came my way, *Ben-Hur*, to be followed, one after the other, by *King of Kings*, *El Cid*, and *Sodom and Gomorrah*. Happily, Rome is my favorite city, my second home. I love Roman culture, and that was where we made *Ben-Hur*. It involved a year and a half of my life and the conditions were those under which all composers should work—in short, to be with the film from the very beginning and to be regarded as one of the team of storytellers. The film called for a vast musical canvas, surely one of the biggest in film history, with many themes and much interweaving. The drama, the personal conflicts and the pageantry, required music which grew out naturally from its atmosphere. Fortunately, I had extensively researched approximately the same historical era for *Quo Vadis*, and discovered fragments of Greek, Hebrew, and Oriental music, and being aware that almost no purely Roman music had survived, I decided to stick with my own Roman inventions. The script demanded about half a dozen marches, and it was with these I tried to get as close as possible to the sound of what my research had led me to believe Roman military music might have been.

But *Ben-Hur* was largely a religious story and the biggest problem was deciding on the music for Christ. Everyone wanted me to use the Theremin, to get that spellbinding, supernatural, and eerie sound. But you can't use electronics for the first century, so I opted for the pipe organ. Every time you see Christ in the film or hear about Him or feel His presence, you hear the pipe organ combined with divided high strings, usually playing harmonics. The most interesting challenge with this theme was the scene where Christ appears before the multitude to deliver the Sermon on the Mount. The script specified that at no time was Christ's voice to be heard, so it became the job of the music in this sequence to intimate the revered words of the Sermon.

No assignment in my life was tougher than the next one—*King of Kings*. It was made right after *Ben-Hur*, and I moved from the one film to the other. Not only was the period and subject material similar but several of the scenes were the same, although treated a little differently. I thought at the time, "This is too much." I couldn't write the same music, or at least I wasn't expected to. What helped was the change of geographical location—*King of Kings* was made in Spain and I worked in Madrid. This helped me to think a little differently. That, and the very great difference in the treatment of Christ, who was here the central figure. In previous films about Christ, He had not been heard; now He was both clearly heard and seen. Thus, the central theme of the score is that of "Christ the Redeemer." It usually appears accompanied by female voices sustaining soft harmonies. The Hebrew themes are fashioned after examples of ancient Babylonian and Yemenite melodies, and the Roman music is, again, my own interpretation. From the musicological point of view, it might not be perfectly authentic, but by using Greco-Roman modes and a spare and primitive harmonization, it tries to evoke in the listener the feeling and impression of antiquity.

Spain was also the setting of *El Cid*, and a thoroughly Spanish subject. Rodrigo Dias de Bivar, the noble Lord (Cid) whose story the picture tells, was an idealization of a Castilian knight of the eleventh century. Numerous stories and ballads tell of his chivalry and gallantry and his conquests, although one wonders if he was quite as magnificent as the legends would have it. I was fortunate enough to write the score in Spain, to absorb the atmosphere, and to be advised by the greatest authority on the Cid and the Spanish Middle Ages: Don Ramon Menendez Pidal. *The Cantigas*, a collection of nearly 250 melodies dating from the time of Alphonso the Wise, but undoubtedly containing material from earlier times, proved to be an inexhaustible source. The rich libraries of the monasteries of Montserrat and the Escorial also enlarged my insight into the music of medieval Spain. Stylistically, the score for *El Cid* was influenced by three sources: the medieval, the Moorish-Oriental, and the combination of these two elements, which resulted in the music of the Iberian Peninsula and what today we call Spanish.

Sodom and Gomorrah was an intriguing subject that developed into a very bad picture. It is the kind of experience composers dread, a huge effort that sinks with the ship. But from the musicological point of view, it was too fascinating to deny. Again, the opportunity to delve into the ancient past and possibly discover something different, something to help the composer describe the evil and perversion of the Cities of the Plain, the Helamite tribes, the love of Lot and Ildith, the sorrow of Lot as he turns away from the Pillar of Salt, and the exodus of his people from the cities. Could I turn my back on such a challenge? Clearly I couldn't—and once again, Idlsohn's *Music of the Yemenite and Babylonian Jews* provided me with themes as points of departure, with the choruses of the Jews all based on authentic material which goes back to Biblical times. It was a vast amount of work for a disappointing film. But anyone who takes it upon himself or herself to compose music for films does so on such terms. The important thing is that you are working, you are writing music.

THEMES FROM THE VIENNA WOODS

And then, of course, there were Max Steiner and Erich Wolfgang Korngold, two Viennese whose influence on film music were commensurate, at least in the minds of their admirers, with Thomas Edison's contribution to electric illumination.

It is entirely logical that two of Hollywood's most prominent composers should have been Viennese. Vienna, like Hollywood, was an artistic mecca, a gathering ground of the arts, a magnetic milieu full of talented, expressive, ambitious people. And anyone who had successfully functioned in Vienna might well survive in Hollywood because the atmosphere was much the same, an atmosphere of stimulation, redolent with creativity but pock-marked with conceit and deceit, conniving and manipulating, jealousies and rivalries.

Viennese musicians in the early years of this century received an exposure to music such as no other city could offer. Vienna, the capital of the Austro-Hungarian Empire, drew its talents from a fantastic musical hinterland. Not only could a Viennese musician draw upon an epic classical tradition and a flourishing musical theater, but he could cull his ideas from the folk songs and dances of Austria, Bohemia, Hungary, the Tyrol, and many other regions of Franz Josef's domain. A musical child growing up in Vienna in the years from the turn of the century to the outbreak of the First World War, as did Steiner and Korngold, would hear the groundswell of modernism pioneered by Schoenberg and his disciples. The world had never before and would never again offer such opportunities for musical education.

The Hollywood in which Steiner and Korngold worked also presented a situation of abundant opportunity that is never likely to be repeated. The two composers were the "stars" of the Warner Bros. music department, which deserves more than a mere mention in any book about the history of music in Hollywood.

The four Warner brothers had championed the use of sound in films; others had considered it but dismissed it as too much of a risk. By the late twenties, motion pictures had reached a level of artistry and sophistication that was acceptable to the public and profitable to the producers. It was argued that the films, accompanied by large orchestras, small orchestras, organists, and pianists (as per the magnitude of the house) didn't really need dialogue and sound effects. The brothers Warner were enterprising enough not to believe this line. Their first "talkie," *The Jazz Singer*, met with enthusiasm when it premièred on the evening of October 6, 1927, in New York, but it took a year for the industry to accept the fact that the silent era had ended. Some of the strongest resistance came from the music publishers who had built up profitable businesses supplying sheet music to nearly 20,000 movie theaters in the United States and Canada. The film tycoons resisted the spending of enormous sums of money for the equipment to record the soundtracks (first to disc, later to film), not to mention the cost to convert theaters and install sound systems.

But *The Jazz Singer* had opened the way, and there was no ignoring the new direction. The Wall Street financiers loaned several hundred million dollars to the Hollywood moguls to retool their plants, so 1929 became a sort of second California gold rush. Hundreds of musical people bought themselves tickets to Los Angeles; it seemed to them that the kind of movie most likely to flourish in this new era would be the musical. The Warner brothers had won their gamble and, hedging their bets, aligned themselves with three big music publishing houses—Witmark, Harms, and Remick. Other studios followed with other publishing houses, and American music moved one gigantic step closer to becoming Big Business.

Jack L. Warner, the youngest of the brothers, made a decision early in the game, "Films are fantasy—and fantasy needs music." For all his hard-nosed commercialism and often dubious taste, it is to his credit that he allowed the forming of a music department that was, for many years, the foremost of its kind. Eventually it would be equaled and perhaps surpassed, but for a dozen years or more, from the mid-thirties to the end of the forties, no studio paid more attention to the sound of music in its films than Warner Bros.

Warner Bros. had actually pioneered film music before the arrival of the "talkie." The first film with a fully synchronized musical score was Warner Bros.' *Don Juan*, starring John Barrymore, in 1926. The music was composed by William Axt and David Mendoza, and recorded by the New York Philharmonic under Henry Hadley. Axt had, the year before, written music for *The Big Parade* and *Ben-Hur*, both to be played by orchestras in the theaters. The success of his *Don Juan* score brought Axt the first studio contract given a composer, not from Warner Bros. but from MGM, for whom he wrote dozens more scores before his retirement in 1939. Warner Bros. quickly looked around for a musician to set up a music department for them. They decided upon Leo F. Forbstein, who was at that time (late 1928) conducting the orchestra at Grauman's Metropolitan Theater in Hollywood.

Forbstein was one of the best-known movie-theater conductors during the twenties; born in St. Louis, Missouri, he had led his own orchestra at the age of sixteen, while still a student, and he had built a reputation as a musician with a talent for organization. This is what Warner Bros. wanted, and Forbstein began 1929 as head of their music department, responsible for all their musical activities. He held this position for the remaining twenty years of his life. By the mid-thirties Warner Bros. was producing Hollywood's best musicals, starting with *42nd Street* and followed by a string of mammoth glittering vehicles, most of which were choreographed by Busby Berkeley. Forbstein was able to lay aside his baton and do what pleased him most—manage his growing musical bailiwick. It was Forbstein who persuaded Max Steiner to join Warner Bros., and it was Forbstein who signed Erich Korngold to a contract, the first composer of international reputation to be so contracted.

Max Steiner

Both Steiner and Korngold came from prominent Viennese families. Steiner was named after his famous grandfather, Maximilian Steiner, the impresario of the Theatre an der Wien. It was he who persuaded Johann Strauss, Jr., to write for the theater. Strauss, like his father, had done well as a composer of waltzes and little concert pieces, and as a conductor of his own orchestra, but he had steered clear of the stage, reasoning that apparently it had defeated even Schubert and Beethoven. Maximilian Steiner decided to change this; the first Viennese composer he persuaded to write for him was Franz von Suppe, whose operettas *The Beautiful Galatea*, *Light Cavalry*, *Boccaccio*, and *Poet and Peasant* all began their lives at the Theater an der Wien. Although these were inferior to the operettas of Jacques Offenbach (the French composer who developed the form), they did well purely on the merit of being Viennese and because of the anti-French sentiment generated by the Franco-Prussian War.

Johann Strauss, Jr., badgered by Steiner, decided to try his hand at operettas. His first was *Indigo and the Forty Thieves*, and with the highly popular composer conducting, it was an unqualified hit. Next came *Die Fledermaus*, and after it, the deluge. There was, however, an odd aftermath to this very successful Steiner-Strauss collaboration. When Strauss was fifty-two, his wife died. Six weeks later he became infatuated with Angelika Dietrich, a pretty but flighty girl

Max Steiner

thirty years his junior. All Vienna scoffed, but the handsome, middle-aged maestro married the girl and took her to live with him on his estate outside Vienna. The sound of creaking was soon heard in the marriage, and within a few months Angelika left Strauss and went back to what she truly enjoyed—the glitter of the Viennese salons and the admiration of many men. Ironically, the man she decided to move in with was her unhappy husband's old friend and benefactor, Maximilian Steiner, whose son, Gabor, fell in love with and married one of the beautiful chorus girls in his father's theater. From this union would emerge, on May 10, 1888, a son, their only child, whom they would call Maximilian Raoul Walter Steiner.

The Steiners were a prosperous business family. Gabor owned and managed a theater and dabbled in several other entertainment enterprises (he built the Riesenrad, the giant ferris wheel in Vienna's famous park, the Prater). His wife, Marie, inherited three of Vienna's leading restaurants from her family. Both parents encouraged the precocious musical talents of their son Maximilian. They sent him to the Vienna School of Technology, where he showed little interest in anything scholastic. But later, at the Imperial Academy of Music, he was brilliant and completed a four-year course in only one year, for which he was awarded a gold medal. His brilliance was aided by the affluence of his family, who could afford to send him to the best teachers available, including Robert Fuchs and Gustav Mahler. Having a father with a theater was also helpful.

Recalls Steiner:

He produced Offenbach and Gilbert and Sullivan and all the others. When I was twelve he let me conduct an American operetta, *The Belle of New York*, by Gustave Kerker. Kerker happened to be in Vienna at the time, and he asked my parents if he could take me back to America with him as a "boy wonder." My mother told him, "No, all musicians are stinkers." And then, as an afterthought about her own problems with her restaurants, "and that goes for all waiters."

Steiner made his first mark on the musical world when he was sixteen:

I wrote an operetta and called it *Beautiful Greek Girl*. I asked my father to stage it and he refused, saying he didn't think it was very good. He had a stage manager named Karl Tuschl, who had just left him to lease and manage the Orpheum Theater on the Josefstadt. So I took this thing of mine to Tuschl, and he thought it was worth doing, perhaps because it seemed like a good ploy to rival Gabor Steiner's theater with something written by his son. I conducted the opening night, and the production ended up running for a year. Out of that came offers to conduct other shows, a couple of which took me to Moscow and to Hamburg. In 1906 I accepted an offer from the British impresario George Edwards to go to London to conduct Lehar's *The Merry Widow*, and that was the start of eight years in England for me. I conducted all kinds of musicals at Daly's Theater, the Adelphi, the Hippodrome, the London Pavilion and the Blackpool Winter Garden. Then came the First World War and I was interned as an enemy alien. But artists are luckier than most other people, and through the Duke of Westminster, who seemed to be a fan of mine, I got my exit papers to go to America. However, my possessions and my money were impounded, and I arrived in New York in December of 1914 with $32 in my pocket.

Over the next fifteen years working in the American theater, Max Steiner built a solid reputation as an arranger and orchestrator of musical comedies, and as a conductor of stage shows of composers from Victor Herbert to Youmans, Kern and Gershwin. His last effort on Broadway was *Sons Of Guns*, which opened on November 26, 1929. Two years previously, Steiner had orchestrated and conducted Harry Tierney's *Rio Rita* on Broadway, and now that Tierney had contracted with RKO to do the film version, he asked the studio to hire Steiner. RKO's head of production, William Le Baron, went to the theater to see Steiner conduct and was impressed with the fact that Steiner's thirty-five musicians each played several instruments, making his elaborate orchestration sound even richer. Obviously, here was a man Hollywood could use. The next day, Le Baron had Steiner put his signature on a contract, and thus began the real career of Max Steiner, Dean of Film Music until his death in 1971.

Steiner arrived in Hollywood at a time when musicals were churned out as fast as they could be produced, but by the end of

Max Steiner

1930 the glut had spent itself. RKO laid off most of its musical staff, and Le Baron asked Steiner to run the department—and take a cut in salary. Using a ten-piece orchestra, library music, and the limit of a three-hour recording session per film, it was all Steiner could do to provide main and end titles, plus whatever "on screen" music was called for.

His first original composition for film was *Cimarron*:

At that time there were only about three or four composers in Hollywood, and the one they wanted for this picture was busy at Paramount. Le Baron said to me, "Could you knock out something for this picture? If we don't like it, we'll get someone else to redo it. Just give us enough for the preview." The picture was a big success; I didn't get any mention in the credits, but some of the reviewers asked who had written the music. I then realized I was on to something.

The real start for Steiner the film composer was *Symphony of Six Million* in 1932. David O. Selznick, then thirty and beginning his career as a producer, came to RKO intent on making quality productions. He had bought the Fannie Hurst book and hired Irene Dunne, Ricardo Cortez, and Gregory Ratoff to star in the film. Selznick was not satisfied with the result of the filming and approached Steiner:

David said, "Do you think you could put some music behind this thing? I think it might help it. Just do one reel—the scene where Ratoff dies." I did as he asked, and he liked it so much he told me to go ahead and do the rest. Music until then had not been used very much for underscoring—the producers were afraid the audience would ask, "Where's the music coming from?" unless they saw an orchestra or a radio or phonograph. But with this picture we proved scoring would work.

It was Steiner more than any other composer who pioneered the use of original composition for the background scoring for films, although in those early years at RKO, sheer volume of work prevented him from applying the technique to every film to which he was assigned. Mostly the scores consisted of a main title, perhaps a snippet or two during the film, and then the end title. Even within those limitations Steiner could make himself felt.

Katharine Hepburn's first film, *A Bill of Divorcement*, ends with John Barrymore and her sitting at a piano playing a Steiner miniature sonata, which leaves the audience feeling they have heard more music than they actually have. This is something at which Steiner quickly became a master—the careful placing of music. That, and an unusual talent for "catching" things musically—giving a musical fillip to a little piece of action or a human characteristic. He caught Leslie Howard's limp in *Of Human Bondage*: Leopold Stokowski told Steiner he thought this was a stroke of genius. Other people, Aaron Copland among them, considered it in questionable taste.

Either way, it was an arresting device and one that became a Steiner trademark in the use of music in film. At its best, this "mickey-mousing" could be very effective: a dog walking along a corridor in *Since You Went Away*; old prospector Walter Huston scrambling like a goat up a hillside in *The Treasure of the Sierra Madre*; Errol Flynn gently loping his horse across a parade ground in *They Died with Their Boots On*; or the harp-celesta counterpointing of the water dripping in Victor McLaglen's cell in *The Informer*. And any number of catchy tunes for comic characters.

The film score that brought Steiner to everyone's attention was *King Kong*:

> It was made for music. It was the kind of film that allowed you to do anything and everything, from weird chords and dissonances to pretty melodies. When the picture was completed, the studio

bosses were very skeptical about it and doubtful that the public would take to it. They thought the big gorilla looked unreal and too mechanical. In fact, they didn't want to waste any more money on it and told me to use old tracks. Merian C. Cooper, the producer, then came to me and asked me to score it to the best of my ability and that he would pay the cost of the orchestra.

Steiner took him at his word; he brought in an eighty-piece orchestra and ran up a bill of $50,000. But it was worth every penny because it is his score that literally makes that film work. As soon as the audience hears that three-note theme—those three massive, darkly orchestrated descending chords—it knows it is in for a fantastic experience. The score accents all the strangeness, mystery, and horror in the story; it limns the frightful, giant gorilla but also speaks for the streak of tenderness in the monster, the fascination and the compassion he feels for the terrified girl he picks up in his huge paw. The music is the voice of the doomed brute.

Steiner became the man the producers ran to when they were in trouble with their films, as if he were a doctor who could heal the afflictions of their children. When *Of Human Bondage* was previewed, it had no score and the producers were distressed to find the audiences laughing in the wrong places. Steiner was called in and asked to clarify the film with his music. When John Ford's *Lost Patrol* was previewed, all agreed that the film, admirably directed and acted, lacked a certain tension. It was felt more sympathy was needed in order for the audience to sense the plight of a band of soldiers, lost in the desert and being picked off by Arabs who were never seen. Steiner was again brought in to acoustically supply the suspense and "paint in" the Arabs.

Ford took no chances on his next film, *The Informer* (1935), and hired Steiner before he started production. He even sent his scriptwriter to talk to the composer, which, claims Steiner, is the only time in his film career he has conferred with a writer prior to filming. In this case, the filmmakers' extra care paid off because it brought them Academy Awards, including one for Steiner.

For most of his Hollywood career, Steiner was probably too busy to be concerned with any aspect of film other than music. The mere scanning of the list of his scores leaves one wondering how any man could have done so much. In addition to composing scores, Steiner also acted as the arranger-conductor on many RKO musicals. He was the music director on most of the Fred Astaire-Ginger Rogers pictures—*Flying Down to Rio*, *Roberta*, *Top Hat*, *The Gay Divorcee*, and *Follow the Fleet*, his last job for RKO. Steiner claims he left RKO because they refused to raise his salary, but a more feasible explanation would be the offers made by other studios.

By 1936, Selznick had set up his own production company, and the only composer he wanted was Steiner, who wrote the scores for three films Selznick produced in association with United Artists: *Little Lord Fauntleroy*, *The Garden of Allah*, and *A Star Is Born*. Steiner would probably have worked for Selznick exclusively but he was used to prodigious work schedules and Selznick didn't turn out films very quickly. When Steiner accepted a long-term contract from Warner Bros., it included the provision that he could work for Selznick when that producer needed him.

The first Steiner score for Warner Bros. was *The Charge of the Light Brigade* (1936), with Errol Flynn leading the noble Six Hundred. Over the years he would score fifteen of Flynn's pictures, mostly action stories, and although he did this kind of work most dexterously—supplying exciting passacaglias for fights and battles—he complained that this wasn't really the kind of movie he enjoyed. What he really liked were the Bette Davis romantic dramas (he did eighteen of them), and the actress said many years later, "Max understood more about drama than any of us."

It's doubtful if any composer in history worked harder than Max Steiner. In his first dozen years for Warner Bros. he averaged eight scores per year, and they were symphonic scores calling for forty and fifty minutes of music each. He would seldom look at a film more than two or three times; then with the aid of an assistant he would break down the sequences he felt needed music and map out the timings. In the case of sequences that needed split-second cues, he would have someone make an acute timing sheet. After making a piano sketch of the score he would go over it and mark in the instructions for orchestration. Only a man with a torrent of musical ideas could possibly have coped with the volume of work.

His peak year was 1939, when he worked on twelve films, including *Gone With the Wind,* the longest score then written. Selznick had spent two years putting his mighty package together and Steiner was the only composer he would consider, but the problem was Steiner's Warner Bros. workload. The scoring was discussed several times, but Selznick couldn't get Steiner to agree to a starting date. He then let it be known that he might consider Herbert Stothart as co-composer of the score. Stothart, the long-time MGM composer, dearly wanted the assignment, but once Steiner heard of the possibility of another composer being brought in, he doubled his efforts to clear himself for Selznick.

Writing the three-hour score for *Gone With the Wind* occupied Steiner for twelve weeks, although it was during that same period he wrote the "Symphonie Moderne" for *Four Wives,* and the incidental music for *Intermezzo.* There are sixteen main themes in the score and almost 300 separate musical segments. Steiner says he managed to live through these twelve weeks only with medical aid; a doctor came frequently to his home and gave him Benzedrine so that he could maintain a daily work routine of twenty hours at a stretch. He was greatly aided in this Herculean task by a team of five of Hollywood's best orchestrators: Hugo Friedhofer, Bernard Kaun, Adolph Deutsch, Maurice de Packh, and Heinz Roemheld, all of them composers and all capable of rounding out Steiner's ideas and devices. Obviously, the score would never have been written without these five men.

Steiner recalls the excitement of the preview at Riverside, California:

> Selznick and all his executives and aides were beside themselves with anxiety and elation. During the intermission I went out into the lobby, spotted David and some of his entourage, and went up to them. I asked them if they had noticed anything amiss in the first half. They looked at each other, puzzled. Selznick shook his head. I then pointed out to them that the entire eleventh reel was missing. None of them had noticed it. I had because I was waiting for my music.

Sadly, the score did not win the Oscar it deserved, although the film won eight. Bob Hope, the emcee, referred to that particular Academy Award show as "this Selznick benefit."

About producers and the studio chieftains, Steiner would shake his head:

> They're amazing people. They seem to think that if they pay you well, they own you. Even Leo Forbstein, who understood the problems of composers, became unreasonable after a few years of being an executive. When I was scoring one particular epic, I fell ill with intestinal flu. One evening, after several days in bed, Leo phoned and asked me if I could come in the following morning at nine and conduct a recording session. I explained that I was flat on my back, under sedation, and so weak I couldn't even get up to go to the bathroom. All he could say to this was, "Max, we gotta have you there." My doctor was with me, so I put him

on the phone and he told Leo how sick I was. Afterwards, the doctor handed the phone to me and I said to Leo, "It would cost me my life to get there at nine tomorrow morning." There was a long pause and then Leo asked, "Well, how about one o'clock?"

Steiner's favorite story of musical ignorance:

When I was at RKO, recording a session, one of their directors came in and asked me if I would record one of his compositions with the orchestra. In this business you never say no. He then gave me a single sheet of paper, on which was written the simplest, barest melodic line. He went off and I laid the thing aside. The same afternoon he came back and asked if it was ready. I said, "Look, this would have to be harmonized and orchestrated and . . . " Before I could say anything else, he chimed in with, "Come on, Maxie, you can do all that later, get the guys to play the piece now." But that's not as bad as some producer badgering you to write a score as fast as you can so he can take off on a trip. I remember one who did this, and I told him I couldn't possibly have the score completed in the next three days in order to record the following day, because it was a difficult score. He wanted to have a première the next week so that he could go to Europe. There was no way to do this and he had to delay his trip. At the première he came up to me and said, "What was so difficult about it—it sounded all right to me."

Steiner's career with Warner Bros. spanned almost thirty years and included the scores for nearly 150 films—an incredible output. Not unnaturally, there was a fair amount of self-plagiarism and repetition, especially toward the end, but the general level of craftsmanship and the consistent understanding of the musical needs of motion-picture storytelling added up to an astonishing total contribution. Four of the most outstanding scores, at least in the minds of Steiner buffs, are *Dodge City* (1939), *They Died with Their Boots On* (1941), *The Big Sleep* (1946), and *The Treasure of the Sierra Madre* (1948).

Steiner wrote scores for more than twenty large-scale Westerns, and *Dodge City* is a fair representative of that genre. Its title music tells the audience immediately that it's an epic of Western Americana, all about empire building and progress. The stately measured tones of the theme, with downward modulations à¡ la Puccini (*Tosca* on the range?), accelerate into upward-spiraling scherzos as a scene of a train and a stagecoach racing each other unfolds. When Flynn and his marvelous pair of sidekicks, Alan Hale and Guinn Williams, spot the train carrying their boss, Colonel Dodge, Flynn yells, "Let's pay our respects to the Colonel," and off they gallop, supported by a galloping orchestra. Later, when old Henry Travers looks over a map to figure out where his family might be in their wagon-train trek, he says, "I'd say they'd be at Broad Plain by now," and the music bursts into an expansive, lilting, loping melody that bespeaks the glorious visual of the wagons and horses and cattle making their way across a handsome landscape. Throughout the film, whether drama or comedy, the music picks up the picture and carries it. Dodge City is, after all, just an entertainment, with no attempt at being serious, accurate, or realistic.

They Died with Their Boots On was Warner Bros.' glamorized account of controversial George Armstrong Custer's career from his days at West Point to his death at the battle of the Little Bighorn. Again, it's entertainment. Flynn was at his best as the charming, impetuous, glory-loving Custer, with Olivia de Havilland giving her eighth and final performance opposite Flynn. Steiner's love theme for the two is exquisite, perhaps his love theme par excellence, and he uses it to almost painfully overscore Flynn and de

Havilland's final scene together, before Custer rides off into history, never to return. Since Custer himself had chosen the Irish jig "Gary Owen" as the regimental march for his U. S. Seventh Cavalry, it was reasonable to feature it in a film such as this. The infectious tune is splendidly treated by Steiner in a montage sequence following Custer's introduction to his officers at Fort Lincoln; he and a friend play the melody on the piano, then it is picked up by a small group of soldiers with fifes and drums, then by a bigger group and finally by the entire band on parade. Steiner also used it in an effective scene of the regiment riding along a crest in the early light of dawn, counterpointing it with the love theme.

But the real highlight of this score is the highlight of the film— the last stand of Custer and his men. Steiner pits his Indian theme against "Gary Owen" in furious, mounting key changes. This is an extraordinary composition, and the only way to appreciate its merit is to hear it away from the picture. It is easy to see why Steiner did not enjoy assignments such as this one; the visual is so commanding that the audience is hardly aware, except subliminally, that music is being employed.

Two of Humphrey Bogart's best films have Steiner scores. *The Big Sleep* is the ultimate private-eye story, with Bogie as Philip Marlowe, Raymond Chandler's tough, glib detective. Steiner ushers in the mystery and mayhem with heavy chordal passages accented with chimes. He gives Bogie a cheeky little theme; for Lauren Bacall, a wryly romantic one, with swirling music for chases in fog, orchestral flutters for suspense, and in that final showdown where Bogie routs the hoods, there are rising modulations punctuated by heavy chords. When the gunsmoke clears and Bogie and Baby look at each other in that sardonic but enticing way, you know they're meant for each other because there's a gorgeous Steiner theme telling you it can't be any other way.

The Treasure of the Sierra Madre is a rich, full score but one that does not please every film lover. Many say it overplays its role, while others say, justifiably, that it isn't Mexican music, it's Spanish. Criticisms aside, the score rates high on the lists of Steiner admirers, and in certain scenes it is beautifully effective. The main theme denotes the determination of the plodding prospectors bent on the finding of gold, with variations ranging from joyful to tragic. In the scene where bandits attack a train, Steiner builds excitement with massive orchestral figurations. A passage of particular power marks Fred Dobbs' (Bogart) fright following the shooting of Curtin (Tim Holt), and his panic when he finds the body has disappeared. Steiner almost holds up a mirror to Dobbs in these scenes. He also makes Dobbs' violent end even more painful as the magnificent Mexican actor Alfonso Bedoya, whose huge mouthful of teeth made him look like a shark when he grinned, comes across Dobbs while the exhausted man drinks at a waterhole. The quietly pulsating music underlines Dobbs' fears and the obvious intentions of the bandit to kill him. As Bedoya cuts Bogart down with his machete, musical stings match the strokes of the large blade and indicate the butchery. Yet another example of Steiner's "catching" an action.

In *Life with Father* (1947), Steiner also "caught" William Powell with a theme that delineated both the pomposity and the good-heartedness of the character. In *Adventures of Don Juan* (1949), he provided a cheeky six-note motif for Flynn that speaks like a trumpet call for the amorous cavalier. Steiner put his finger on the wackiness of *Arsenic and Old Lace* (1944) with a bizarre treatment of "There Is a Happy Land, Far, Far Away." Many times he helped Bette Davis put across her emotional, dramatic problems, notably in *Now Voyager* (1942), where she, as an ugly duckling, struggled to get away from a domineering mother and find happiness. That score brought Steiner his second Oscar, and was one of his favorite scores.

He and Davis also did well by each other in *Dark Victory* (1939), in which she played an heiress dying from a brain tumor. At the end, her eyesight almost gone, Davis makes her way from her garden to her bedroom, aided by a harrowing cello theme. The music lets the viewer know that this is her last trip.

Steiner, a soft-hearted man who pretended otherwise, was always effective with emotional scenes. In Selznick's *Since You Went Away* (1944), the film that brought Steiner his third Oscar, he poured out a stream of melodious themes for this wartime tribute to the American home front. Over-sweet and now terribly dated, the film contained one scene that was made to order for Steiner. At the railroad depot, Jennifer Jones sees her soldier (played by her then-husband, the ill-fated Robert Walker) off as he leaves for the war, never to return. The music underlines the poignancy of the situation and then, when the train begins to move and pick up momentum, so does the music as the girl runs along the platform, almost hysterical. The sequence is an emotional wallop of music, dialogue, and photographic effects. What made it even more touching, as Steiner must have known at the time, was that Jones and Walker were, in fact, at the end of their marriage and finding it painful to act together—especially as Jones was being courted by producer Selznick.

According to Steiner, film and music help each other in much the way a husband and wife help each other in a good marriage, but neither one can save the other. As for his method:

> There is no method. Some pictures require a lot of music, and some are so realistic that music would only interfere. Most of my films were entertainments—soap operas, storybook adventures, fantasies. If those films were made today, they would be made differently and I would score them differently. But my attitude would be the same—to give the film what it needs. And

with me, if the picture is good, the score stands a better chance
of being good.

While Steiner was always a melodist, he also knew how not to
use melody in film scoring. Sometimes a melody calls attention to
itself when it should not. Steiner used catchy themes to point up
the main characters in pictures, but he was also adept at doing something more subtle—writing neutral music with chordal progressions
and just enough melodic motion to make it sound normal but not
enough to compel attention. Steiner looked upon scoring more as
a craft than an art:

> The hardest thing in scoring is to know when to start and when
> to stop. The location of your music. Music can slow up an ac-
> tion that should not be slowed up and quicken a scene that
> shouldn't be. Knowing the difference is what makes a film com-
> poser. I've always tried to subordinate myself to the picture. A
> lot of composers make the mistake of thinking of film as a con-
> cert platform on which they can show off. This is not the place.
> Some composers get carried away with their own skill—they take
> a melody and embellish it with harmonies and counterpoints.
> It's hard enough to understand a simple melody behind dialogue,
> much less with all this baloney going on. If you get too decora-
> tive, you lose your appeal to the emotions. My theory is that the
> music should be felt rather than heard. They always used to say
> that a good score was one you didn't notice, and I always asked,
> "What the hell good is it if you don't notice it?"

On being complimented as the man who invented movie music:

> Nonsense. The idea originated with Richard Wagner. Listen to
> the incidental scoring behind the recitatives in his operas. If
> Wagner had lived in this century, he would have been the Number
> One film composer.

Asked to criticize contemporary music:

I have no criticism. I can't criticize what I don't understand.

Steiner's last film score was for *Two on a Guillotine* in 1965. A miserable, feeble film, its producer accused Steiner of "ruining it." To have ruined such a film could only have been regarded as an accomplishment. It was, however, a weak coda to a mighty career. Steiner would have liked to have continued scoring movies, but no other producers called upon him. He was by now in his late seventies and his eyesight had failed drastically, something he tried to hide even from his friends. A charming and amusing man, given to terrible puns and very earthy jokes, Steiner could not always conceal his bitterness about an industry that didn't seem to want him anymore. Occasionally, the bitterness was justified, as when Twentieth Century-Fox announced their intention of filming *The Day Custer Fell*, a project that they later dropped. Steiner called the studio to tell them he would be interested in scoring the film, and the young executive with whom he spoke asked if he had ever written any music for Westerns.

The Steiner birthday parties were always joyous occasions for his many friends. Steiner, who retained in old age the appeal, and sometimes the capriciousness, of a boy, owed his health and welfare to his understanding, patient, charming wife, Lee. At his eighty-second birthday party, May 10, 1970, Steiner bedecked himself in all his ribbons and medals and donned a Beethoven wig to greet his guests. Albert K. Bender, who organized the Steiner Music Society (an international league of admirers), responded, "Max, you look better than Beethoven." To which Steiner replied, "I should hope so—he's dead." The following year, the Steiner birthday party was attended by only a handful of close friends. Long ailing, the old composer was in too much pain to bear company. In his last months he suffered the agonies of cancer. Finally, on December 28, 1971, his heart stopped. When Max Steiner died, a link with Old Vienna ceased to be and yet another door on the Old Hollywood was closed.

Erich Wolfgang Korngold

The place of Erich Wolfgang Korngold in the history of film music is special, aside from the mainstream. He wrote only eighteen scores in twelve years and worked under ideal conditions. Korngold was the highest paid composer of his time; all of his assignments were for expensive, major productions, and he worked on a film only if it pleased him. Embraced as part of the creative production team, his advice on dramatic construction was often heeded. He was, in fact, a "fair-haired boy." While his scores may be superior to most others, it is unfair to compare him with composers who might have produced equally substantial scores had they worked under Korngold's conditions.

Korngold arrived in Hollywood in 1934 with a shining reputation. Hailed as a second Mozart, he had astounded the music world with his concert works and operas. As a teenage composer, pianist, and conductor, he had the most prominent composers of the day shaking their heads in disbelief. Richard Strauss said, "This firmness of style, this sovereignty of form, this individual expression, this harmonic structure—one shudders with awe to realize these compositions were written by a boy."

Erich Korngold receiving his Oscar for *The Adventures of Robin Hood* on
February 3, 1939 at the Los Angeles Biltmore Hotel.

When Korngold was ten, his father took him to Gustav Mahler
for a critical judgment. The boy played from memory a dramatic
cantata as Mahler walked up and down reading the score, his pace
quickening with growing excitement. At the end he looked at the
father and declared the boy a "genius" and made suggestions for
education.

A few years later, with a pair of one-act Korngold operas playing all over Europe, Puccini remarked, "The boy has so much talent he could easily give us some and still have enough left for himself." That Strauss, Mahler, and Puccini should feel this way about
the music of Erich Korngold was not surprising because they were
the three strongest influences upon it. An analysis of Korngold re-

veals a Straussian orchestral color, a Mahlerian feeling, and the melodic concepts of Puccini, all of them somehow melded and dominated by a strong Viennese character—plus Korngold's own personality.

That such a composer should find his way to Hollywood and write exceptional scores for film is not surprising. But it is also rather sad that such a talented composer would fall into a big, soft, comfortable trap and never really emerge to return to his former prominence. The Korngold story is indeed sadly ironic, rather like the Horatio Alger saga in reverse—beginning with spectacular success before subsiding into general success. His story also points to the furious acceleration of musical development in the twentieth century. While as a youth his music was regarded as daring and startlingly modern, by the time he died, it was considered somewhat old-fashioned.

Every artist is both aided and hindered by the era in which he lives. Korngold had the good fortune to be born into the stimulating musical environment of Vienna at the turn of the century, but the enormous misfortune of entering adulthood as the political climate of Europe was such that it put a virtual end to his career in the concert hall and the opera houses. He was thirty-seven when he made his debut in the film world. But for the Nazi regime he might have continued writing opera.

There were critics who claimed he had already reached his high-water mark, blossomed too soon, and spent himself. Who can be sure? Perhaps Korngold's true mission was to cultivate film scoring and expand its dimensions. Certainly he arrived at the ripest possible time. Warner Bros. needed a composer to score its well-produced, intelligent costume dramas. Korngold's concept of a film scenario was as another form of opera libretto, and it worked magnificently with subjects like *Anthony Adverse*, *The Adventures of Robin*

Erich Korngold with Alan Badel, who played Richard Wagner in *The Magic Fire*, for which Korngold was the music supervisor.

Hood, *The Constant Nymph*, *The Sea Hawk*, and *King's Row*. As the age of the filmed historical romance passed, so did Korngold's interest in film scoring. By 1947, at age fifty, the decision to divorce himself from the movies and return to serious music was made. However, the world had changed, and when he returned to Vienna, his Vienna had "gone with the wind," and he was unable to revitalize his former fame. Hollywood had been very good to him—and bad for him.

The musician most closely associated with Korngold was Hugo Friedhofer, who orchestrated all but one of his scores. Later, Friedhofer himself would become one of the industry's finest composers—but he was the only man Korngold fully trusted to orchestrate his music as he would have done himself, given the time. Says Friedhofer:

> I learned and grew from my association with Korngold. I find it hard to speak of him without feeling emotional. He was a warm, witty, humorous man, and he took his film scores as seriously as any other kind of composition. I know there is a tendency in some quarters to be rather derogatory about his music, but I don't think that anybody with any spark of feeling can listen to Korngold and not agree that here was a man who knew exactly what he wanted to say and said it beautifully. He was "all composer" and his work gave a new impetus to film scoring. To be honest about it—we were all influenced by him.

Erich Korngold was born May 29, 1897, in the city of Brno, then part of Austria but now Czechoslovakia. He was the second son of Dr. Julius and Josephine Witrofsky Korngold, both of affluent means. His older brother, Hans Robert, lived five years longer than Erich Wolfgang but, as the novelists might put it, never amounted to anything very much. The reason for this might be that his father centered all his pride and attention on his gifted younger son.

The father had given his sons the second names of Robert and Wolfgang, after Schumann and Mozart, his two favorite composers. There were times when Erich regretted his name. With his fame as the outstanding musical prodigy of the time, the father was often accused of having added the name Wolfgang later, to play up the obvious comparison with Mozart. This was a particularly stinging accusation because Dr. Julius Korngold happened to be Vienna's foremost music critic. He had taken the position of music critic with *Neue Freie Presse* in 1902 and held it until 1934, during which time he duplicated the esteem and respect of his celebrated predecessor, Eduard Hanslick. Thus, Dr. Korngold's pride was mixed with confusion and embarrassment. He could not conceal the boy's talent, nor could he promote it. He also knew that the boy's music would be played by musicians who were out to curry favor, and used as a weapon by other musicians who were not in favor.

Erich Korngold showed his precocity at an unbelievably early age. At three, he could beat time, and at five, he was playing four-hand piano pieces with his father. He could also pick out elaborate chords on the piano and reproduce any melody he heard. By the time he was seven, he was composing. He was put in the hands of teacher-composer Robert Fuchs, and at ten, on the advice of Mahler, he was sent to study with Alexander Zemlinsky. As Mahler saw it, there was no point in sending the boy to the conservatory, for his grasp of form and theory, his perfect pitch, and his facility with the piano obviated further study.

At the age of eleven, Korngold wrote his first major work, the ballet-pantomime *Der Schneemann* (*The Snowman*); first performed at the Vienna Court Opera in a command performance before Emperor Franz Josef, the work was subsequently staged in some forty Austrian and German houses. Other works followed; a trio written the following year was given its première with Bruno Walter as the pianist; then came a piano sonata, the *Seven Fairy Pictures*, and a large-scale *Sinfonietta*. All of them were widely performed, with some doubting them as the work of so young a boy and a few actually insinuated the music was really the composition of the father.

In the summer of 1910, Korngold, now all of thirteen and already a *cause célèbre*, vacationed with his family in the southern Tyrol. During this time he and his father visited various famous musicians who formed little summer musical colonies throughout this spectacular area. One of the neighbors was master pianist Artur Schnabel, with whom he formed a lifelong friendship. Years later when Korngold was ensconced in Hollywood, Schnabel would express amazement at this association of "such a composer in such a line of work." He was always convinced Korngold would "surely give it up," and that he was "unhappy making all that money."

In his excellent biography of Schnabel, Cesar Saerchinger referred to this first meeting of Korngold and Schnabel and the young composer's second piano sonata, which the pianist introduced to the public shortly afterward:

> There is no doubt that Korngold, at thirteen was not only a phenomenally gifted composer but that the sonata in question was a remarkable work, well worth performing. Speaking about it nearly forty years later, Schnabel called it "still a most amazing piece." Never afraid of doing the unusual, he decided to play the work in public, and did so during the following season in young Korngold's home town of Vienna, as well as in various other places. Aside from the objective estimate of its merit (which it got), one would have expected only favorable comment on Schnabel's gesture in the press. There appeared, however, several malicious innuendoes regarding his motives—in view of the fact that Korngold senior was at that time the most influential critic in Austria. The gossip that went around is best summarized by the imaginary conversation in which a colleague asks Schnabel whether Korngold's sonata is "rewarding," to which he replies: "No, but his father is." Schnabel paid no attention to the rumors and not only continued to play the work, but he and Flesch also played young Korngold's violin and piano sonata (written in 1912) at their regular recitals in Berlin.

According to his father, Erich Korngold was a normal child when not composing or playing the piano. He was tractable, cheerful, and well-behaved but almost trance-like at those moments when music came over him. The critics could find nothing childish in the compositions; they reviewed the pieces as being complicated, elaborate, and definitely pointed toward the future.

Korngold wrote his first opera, *The Ring of Polycrates*, when he was sixteen, and his second, *Violanta*, the following year. Both were performed all over Europe, with the latter reaching the New York Metropolitan. Both are one-act operas, the first comic, the second dramatic. *Violanta* caused comment due to its sensuous and rather erotic nature, qualities that perplexed even the young composer. When questioned about the opera, all he could do was shrug and assume that one doesn't have to experience love and passion to describe them.

In 1916, Korngold would have a chance to become more worldly—he was inducted into the Austrian Army. His two years of military service were in no way warlike. Seemingly, he didn't even have to perform much in the line of drill because he was always being called into the officer's mess to play the piano. At one point, his Colonel asked Korngold to write a march for the regiment. On hearing the piece, the Colonel expressed his delight but added, "Isn't it a little fast?" to which the composer replied, "Well, yes, but this is for the retreat." It was typical of the humor that marked Korngold and endeared him to his friends.

Among the staunchest of young Korngold's supporters was Bruno Walter, who, at various times and places, conducted all the Korngold operas. After the composer died in 1957, Walter reflected:

> The experience of hearing him play and sing for me the two one-act operas [*Polykrates* and *Violanta*] which I was going to perform at the Munich Opera House will remain unforgettable. One could have compared his interpretation of his works on the piano to the eruption of a musical dramatic volcano, if the lyric

episodes and graceful moments had not also found their insinu-
ating expression in his playing.

Korngold also had enemies—Vienna could be vicious as well
as charming—mostly musicians who disliked his father. Richard
Strauss had been one of his keenest encouragers and had conducted
several Korngold compositions, but Strauss's affection for the young
man cooled with time, probably because his famous librettist, Hugo
von Hofmannsthal, despised Dr. Julius Korngold, who was cruel in
his critiques of the Hofmannsthal works. In a letter Hofmannsthal
wrote to Strauss dated May 5, 1927, he wrote:

> As soon as you have had a little while to settle down, I shall be
> delighted to tell you the story of the comic opera or musical
> comedy with which we are going to challenge *Der Rosenkavalier*.
> We cannot, of course, expect our work, neither in words or mu-
> sic, to soar to the heights of the light opera now said to be com-
> ing from the pen of Erich Wolfgang. But then, it is no use ask-
> ing for the moon.

Korngold's first composition after leaving military service was
an incidental score for a production of Shakespeare's *Much Ado About
Nothing* at Vienna's famed Burg Theatre. The concert suite from
the score became a popular concert item, and several selections from
the score, notably the "Garden Scene" and the "Hornpipe," were
often played (and recorded) by violinists Fritz Kreisler, Mischa
Elman, and Jascha Heifetz.

Korngold's most famous work, the opera *Die Tote Stadt* (*The
Dead City*), was presented in 1920, and one assumes that most of its
writing must have been done during Korngold's two years in the
army. First presented in Hamburg during the three years Korngold
spent in that city as the conductor of its opera house, *The Dead City*

is set in Bruges and concerns a widower obsessed with the memory of his wife. He falls in love with a young dancer who greatly resembles the dead wife and, during a trance, he kills her. The melodic highlight of the opera is "Marietta's Lute Song," one of the most performed of all twentieth-century arias. The opera was an immediate and sustaining success all over Europe and was selected by the Metropolitan in New York as the vehicle for Maria Jeritza's American debut. The German soprano was very popular, and one of the operas in which she had made her name was Korngold's *Violanta*.

Korngold was also responsible for the Johann Strauss revival during the twenties. Passionately interested in the music of the Strauss dynasty, he exhumed a number of lost scores and reorchestrated them. Korngold staged his version of *A Night in Venice* in 1923, and two years later, *Cagliostro in Vienna*. He would later rescore several other Strauss works, as well as operettas by Offenbach and Leo Fall. In 1927 Korngold wrote what he considered his best work, the opera *The Miracle of Heliane*, although it never rivaled the popularity of *The Dead City*.

In 1929, Korngold began a long association with the great German impresario Max Reinhardt that would change the course of his life. Reinhardt cultivated Korngold's liking for the theater. Together they staged a number of musical plays, the most famous being their version of *Die Fledermaus*, which, with a completely reworked score, became *Rosalinda*. Korngold, using little-known Strauss music, put together an operetta called *Waltzes from Vienna*, which became popular as *The Great Waltz* in America. The next year came the similarly constructed *The Song of Love*. After the success of the Strauss vehicles, Reinhardt and Korngold did a similar treatment with the scattered music of Offenbach and staged it as *The Beautiful Helene*. In New York in 1944, Korngold further reworked the score and called it *Helen Goes to Troy*, which ran for several hundred performances under his baton. Korngold also conducted his score for *The Great Waltz* in long runs in Los Angeles in 1949 and 1953.

By the early 1930s, Erich Korngold was well-known, well-liked, and well-off. Part of his time was given to composing chamber music, part to the theater, part as a guest conductor, and the rest to anything that caught his fancy. At the age of thirty-three he was awarded the title of Professor Honoris Causa by the President of Austria, and began teaching classes in opera, composition, and conducting at the Music Academy of Vienna.

Max Reinhardt had come to terms with Warner Bros. for a film version of his own stage version of Shakespeare's *A Midsummer Night's Dream*. Warner Bros. apparently felt the need to produce a prestige film, and with true film-tycoon thinking (find the best and offer enough money), they picked the world's most estimable stage director—Reinhardt. When it was time to start filming, Reinhardt discovered himself saddled with a producer, Henry Blanke, and a co-director, the German-born William Dieterle. However, for his music score, Reinhardt wanted Korngold to take the famous Mendelssohn stage score for *A Midsummer Night's Dream* and adapt it for filming. This interested Korngold, and he accepted the generous offer and arrived in Los Angeles in late 1934 with his wife and two young sons.

A Midsummer Night's Dream involved Korngold for half a year. Warner Bros. gave Reinhardt the choice of all their players; he chose James Cagney as Bottom (the most striking performance in the film), Dick Powell as Lysander, and Mickey Rooney as Puck, and for Hermia he chose Olivia de Havilland, a nineteen-year-old beauty who had just played the part in the Hollywood Bowl production of the play. The film was a box-office failure, but over the years it has assumed something of the aura of a classic film, forever shown at film retrospectives and Shakespearean festivals.

Darkly shaded, dramatic, and fantastic, the film is most obviously Germanic in style, a rather odd treatment of a Shakespearean comedy. It is enormously aided by Korngold's scoring, which used all the Mendelssohn incidental music from the stage play and supplemented it with fragments from the "Songs Without Words" and Mendelssohn's Scottish and Italian Symphonies. Reinhardt wanted the film "underpainted by the music." To do this, Korngold had to apply the scoring in three different layers: first, by pre-recording some sections (e.g. the Scherzo and the Nocturne) and having the players perform to them; then, having the orchestra perform some sections of the score as the actors were being filmed; and finally, by conducting some of the actors in the rhythmic reading of their lines and adding the music later. No film score had ever been so elaborately executed, and it made a great impression within the industry.

The acute timing necessary in film scoring is one of its most difficult factors. Korngold's innate sense of timing was a constant source of amazement to the musicians and sound engineers with whom he worked. He had very little mechanical aptitude and would never employ the click-track where the conductor can hear the pre-determined timings of so many bars of music matched to so many frames of film. Even a stopwatch confused him. His stopwatch was his brain. When he was first being shown around the studio by Henry Blanke, Korngold asked him: "How long is one foot of film?" "Twelve inches," replied Blanke. "No, that's not what I meant. How long is it in time?" Blanke confessed that he had never before thought about it, but called over one of the technicians, who explained that film runs at twenty-four frames per second, with sixteen frames for every foot. Therefore, one foot would take two-thirds of a second. "Ah," cried Korngold, "exactly as long as the

first two measures of the Mendelssohn Scherzo," thereby inventing the timing method that he would use in all his scoring. He
never used timing sheets, cue marks, or earphones. If a sequence
called for forty-two and two-thirds seconds, he would write a piece
of music and conduct it so that it would fill forty-two and two-
thirds seconds.

After he finished *A Midsummer Night's Dream*, Korngold returned to Vienna to work on his new opera, *Die Kathrin*. Four
months later he returned to Hollywood, having accepted an offer
from Paramount to write a film operetta with lyricist Oscar
Hammerstein II. *Give Us This Night* starred Gladys Swarthout and
Jan Kiepura, and it turned out to be the least memorable of
Korngold's films. The highlight was a short opera as its finale, the
first opera written originally for the screen. But the film was so
trite and corny that it quickly sank from sight. (Years later, when
film product was badly needed for television, the program directors even had second thoughts about playing it on TV.) The lovely
Swarthout sang beautifully, but the atrociously hammy Kiepura sang
twice as much, twice as loud, and hogged the film. Korngold had
been attracted to the idea of the scenario as it had been described
to him—it took him years to master the English language—but he
knew nothing about the Hollywood penchant for rewriting scripts
during the production. Hammerstein recalled Korngold saying to
him, as the script went from hand to hand, "This thing gets worse
from week to week—by the time they film it, it will be useless." He
was right.

During the filming of *Give Us This Night*, Korngold was approached by Warner Bros. to score *Captain Blood*. Korngold said
he wasn't interested, especially in view of the picture he was currently doing. However, Warner Bros. kept after him with daily phone
calls and telegrams. Finally, he agreed to look at the film, and he

was enchanted with its quality. He liked its humor and its romance. After signing the contract, Warner Bros. told him he had three weeks to write the score. Korngold now discovered why even the best film composers need orchestrators. Three weeks was not quite enough, even working frantically, around the clock. Korngold told Friedhofer to use part of a Liszt tone poem for the duel between Errol Flynn and Basil Rathbone and the naval battle at the end.

The film was a great success and the score reflected all the vitality and spirit of the adventurous story; it ushered in Flynn as the foremost movie swashbuckler, and was the first of seven Flynn films scored by Korngold. With another fifteen of his films scored by Max Steiner, Flynn became the best musically supported actor in film history.

With *Captain Blood* a certified blockbuster at the box office, Warner Bros. pressed Korngold to sign a contract on any terms he wanted. He refused, but he did agree to score a few brief passages to *Green Pastures* (1936), a film that was otherwise scored with a choir singing Negro spirituals. He was charmed by this story of the Bible as seen through the eyes of black children in the American South. Korngold scored "The Creation" and "The Flood" and a few other fleeting spots. He asked that his name not be included in the credit titles lest it draw attention away from the excellent work done by choirmaster Hall Johnson. He was impressed by this erudite black musician who spoke several languages, including German, and Korngold frequently invited him to dine with him at The Green Room, the restaurant at Warner Bros. He couldn't understand why Johnson politely declined the offers until, while having lunch with producer Hal Wallis, it was explained to him that none of the cast of *Green Pastures* was allowed in The Green Room because blacks were not, at that time, admitted—not even the star of the picture, Rex Ingram, who was playing "De Lawd." The black actors ate at the cafeteria on the lot. On being told this, Korngold got up to leave. "Where are you going?" asked the surprised Wallis. Replied the composer in a loud voice, "I'm going down to the cafeteria to eat with God."

Korngold still showed little interest in film music, but Warner Bros. persuaded him to look at their *Anthony Adverse*. Once more, the composer was hooked by the appeal of an epic romance—Hervey Allen's lavish novel set in mid-eighteenth-century Italy, the Alps, and France. This, to Korngold, seemed like an opera. In fact, he could only come to terms with a film if it struck him in this manner. The score of *Anthony Adverse* is very much an opera minus singing; it forms an almost nonstop sound fabric behind the picture, threaded with more themes than any other film score, and was, for those who cared to listen, the most extensive composition developed for a film until then.

It won Korngold an Academy Award. With this and much other acclaim, Korngold's interest for film scoring increased, although he still feared becoming known as a "film composer" and continued to turn down the contracts that were offered him. He did, however, agree to score two more pictures, both with Errol Flynn—*The Prince and the Pauper* and *Another Dawn*, the former a charming treatment of the Mark Twain yarn, the latter a dreary soap opera.

While scoring *Anthony Adverse* Korngold came upon a technique that was later adapted by other composers—pitching the music just under the pitch of the voices and surging into pauses in the dialogue. Korngold was also the first film composer to write long lines of continuous music, great chunks that contained the ebb and flow of the film's mood and action. The key, of course, is Korngold's conception of film as a form of opera. Once, in conversation with Hugo Friedhofer, Korngold said he thought the second act of Puccini's *Tosca* was the best bit of opera he knew, and he added

"Come to think of it, *Tosca* is the best film score ever written." That view is a clear indication of Korngold's film style.

Any discussion of Erich Korngold among those who knew him in Hollywood always draws forth reminiscences about his sense of humor. While he was working at Paramount, there was an arranger at the studio named Sigmund Krumgold. Each one's mail was always going to the other. Spotting Krumgold in the commissary, Korngold went up to him and asked, "Siggy, are you getting any of my letters?" Krumgold admitted that a few pieces had come his way. With a dramatic flourish, Korngold said, "Well, I hope to God they're more interesting than yours," and walked away. While at Warner Bros. he was always being asked for his opinion on musical matters. Leo Forbstein got him to come into a screening room one day to look at a newly completed sequence from one of their gargantuan musicals with hundreds of chorus girls performing elaborate, geometric routines and a huge orchestra playing a complicated, lengthy arrangement. When it was over, Forbstein, obviously proud, asked for Korngold's assessment. He said, "Leo, it's fantastic, colossal, stupendous." Then he leaned a little closer to Forbstein and added, "But it isn't very good."

In late 1937, Korngold returned to Vienna for the staging of *Die Kathrin*. By now, the political climate of Europe was one of growing trauma, and he found it difficult to muster his forces and arrange for the première, which was delayed several times and, finally, forbidden by the Nazis. Korngold was not a political person and seemed oblivious to what was happening, possibly because his was an affluent, happy, almost "dream" world in which everything had always worked well for him. But he was now persuaded by friends that he should consider leaving Austria until the situation was resolved. This, coupled with the advice of a doctor that his ailing youngest son needed a warm climate, persuaded Korngold to return to California. He bought a house in the Toluca Lake district of North Hollywood, less than a quarter of a mile from the Warner Bros. studios, so that he could walk to work. He had decided to accept more assignments from Warner Bros. if they would meet his terms, i.e., he would have carte blanche in scoring a film and the music could not be tampered with, and further, that the music would remain his property and not that of the studio. Warner Bros. was so anxious to get his name on a contract that they allowed him any condition.

The first thing they wanted him to do was score *The Adventures of Robin Hood*, the most expensive production that had so far been done. Korngold looked at it and declined. He thought it was beautiful but felt that he could not do it justice in the short time they allowed for the score to be completed. He wrote out a formal letter of refusal and delivered it to Warner Bros. On February 12, 1938, Leo Forbstein arrived at the Korngold home to try to persuade the composer to take the job. He was still uninterested but something else happened that day that helped change his mind—Austrian Chancellor Schuschnigg met with Hitler at Berchtesgaden, and agreed to the union of Austria and Germany. Korngold was deeply attached to Vienna and the news depressed him. He began to talk with Forbstein about *Robin Hood* and agreed to write the score provided he could do it on a week-to-week basis and drop out if he wasn't pleased with the way the job progressed. Forbstein realized that his mission had been a success. Seven weeks later the score was married to the soundtrack for what is most probably the pluperfect example to that time of the blending of film image and music.

The Adventures of Robin Hood is about as good a film of its type as has yet been made. Its script and direction, its costumes and sets, its action and pacing leave little to be desired. The casting is near perfection. Flynn is at the peak of his appeal as Robin, with Olivia de Havilland exquisite as Maid Marian, Basil Rathbone as the magnificent villain Sir Guy of Gisbourne, and Claude Rains as the weasel-like Prince John. The music delineates them all as it strides, bounces, and lilts along.

Its musical highlights include the rout of the Norman column in Sherwood Forest by Robin and his Merry Men, during which the music builds and builds and then releases as the men jump and swing out of the trees; the gaiety of the music for the banquet in the forest; the heraldic music for the archery tournament; the noble theme for King Richard when he reveals his identity to Robin; the gentle theme for Maid Marian when she understands Robin's purpose in being an outlaw; and the elaborately orchestrated march accompanying the outlaws, dressed as monks, as they make their way up the hill to the Abbey for the coronation. Altogether, like the film itself, the music is a never-ending delight.

Korngold's next three scores were for more massive historical subjects: *Juarez* (1939), *The Private Lives of Elizabeth and Essex* (1939), and *The Sea Hawk* (1940). Each called for, and received, lavish musical treatment. All of them were rich subjects for a composer of Korngold's leanings; had the dialogue been sung instead of spoken, each film might have been an opera.

Juarez appealed to him because of its story of the Hapsburgian monarch Maximilian and his devoted but tragic wife Carlotta, who lost her mind after her husband was executed by the Mexicans. The doomed pair loved the song "La Paloma," and Korngold treated it memorably in his score. He helped underline the nobility and the weakness of Maximilian, and made the rather austere Paul Muni image of Benito Juarez more appealing. Whenever ethnic music was needed, Korngold invented his own because he felt properly conceived dramatic music was more effective than the genuine material.

In speaking of his score for *Elizabeth and Essex*, he said:

> The loves and hates of the two main characters, the ideas expressed by the playwright generally, while taken from history, are symbolical. It is a play of eternally true principles and motives of love and ambition, as recurrent today as 300 years ago. The characters speak the English spoken today. Why then should the composer use "thou" and "thee" and "thine" if the dialogue doesn't?

The Sea Hawk was the last of the Korngold "historical romance" scores. From the first bar of the main title, it speaks of nautical adventure. The music captures the roll of the ocean and the splendor of fully rigged Spanish galleons and English privateers. Again, Flynn, the supreme celluloid cavalier, is supported in his amour and his heroics by suitably lush and dashing music. When, toward the end, he and his men escape the galleys of the galleon in which they have been imprisoned and take over the ship, they burst into a stirring operatic chorus, "Bound for the Shores of Dover." Ridiculous, of course, but so sweeping and rousing, why quibble?

Korngold's film music took a different turn with *The Sea Wolf* (1941), a fog-enshrouded filming of the Jack London story with Edward G. Robinson giving a masterly performance as Wolf Larsen. The scoring was dark, foreboding, and slightly dissonant. Less assertive and more subtle than his previous scores, the music for *The Sea Wolf* is more a favorite of other composers rather than Korngold's fans.

Then came *King's Row* (1942), the score that brought him his biggest response—one fan wrote to say he had seen the film sixty times, mostly with his eyes closed. The main title was especially arresting, a bold, almost heraldic statement that undergoes variations during the course of this story of life in a small Mid-western town, circa 1890. The town is rife with psychosis, love, hatred, bitter memories as well as tender memories, ambition and resolve. A field day for Korngold. Particularly memorable is the grandmother theme—a lovely melody stated by a cello for the diminutive, charming Russian actress Maria Ouspenskaya. The finale, with Robert Cummings declaiming Henley's "Invictus" to rouse legless Ronald Reagan from his lethargy, with a powerful choir breaking into the lines, "I am the master of my fate . . ." borders on the absurd, but it is beautifully operatic.

The Constant Nymph (1943) was another of Korngold's most generous scores. Margaret Kennedy's sentimental novel about a Belgian composer who marries a rich socialite instead of the young music student who adores him gave Korngold ample scope. He later adapted part of the score into a tone poem for soprano, choir, and orchestra, *Tomorrow, Opus 33*. This film represents the high-water mark of his career as a film composer, the films that followed were of lesser quality and far less successful with the public. *Devotion*, filmed in 1943 but not released until three years later, was a very romanticized and wildly distorted account of the Brontë sisters. The score is sumptuous but largely wasted. Particularly impressive was Korngold's darkly dramatic music for the Yorkshire Moors and the dream sequence in which a masked, mounted knight manifests himself and envelops Emily in his huge black cloak.

Korngold's next score (his favorite, even though the film was a failure) was *Between Two Worlds*, a Second World War setting of the play *Outward Bound*, in which a group of dead people are transported to the next world, their past and their characters revealed in the process. Since the leading character in this treatment was a Viennese concert pianist, Korngold had an opportunity to provide a little rhapsody for the piano, which he dubbed himself as Paul Henreid pretended to play.

After the disappointing reception to these two scores, Korngold began having doubts about film scoring as an art. He had been enormously lucky with his first dozen films; now the tide seemed to turn and his next job was a disaster. Warner Bros. decided to remake RKO's 1934 version of *Of Human Bondage* and star young Eleanor Parker in the Bette Davis role as Maugham's cold-hearted trollop and Paul Henreid as the medical student who loves her. Both were miscast, and the film was pedestrian and lackluster. For once, Korngold's music was obtrusive, much like an expensive suit hanging on a scarecrow.

Korngold was curious to see the previous version after he had finished scoring his own. Coming from the screening room, he happened to spot Bette Davis on the lot and called out to her. The two greeted each other warmly. Then he said, "I've just seen your *Bondage*, and you were wonderful. Of course, after ten years some of the scenes look a little ridiculous." Davis raised her eyebrows at this but before she could reply, Korngold added "But we, with our new version, are ten years ahead of time—we are already ridiculous."

Escape Me Never, made in 1946 and kept on the shelf for two years, was slightly less ridiculous but nonetheless pleasant and certainly easy to listen to. Errol Flynn appeared in his least-probable role, as a ballet composer, giving Korngold the opportunity to provide an original ballet and one song called "Love for Love," which had some popularity beyond the picture. Set in Venice, the Dolomites, and London during the Victorian era, the picture glows with music. Had the theaters been packed with millions of Korngold fans, Warner Bros. would have made a fortune. Unfortunately, people who go to films to listen to background scores are a distinct minority.

Korngold's last score was quite different from all the others in that it contained very little background music. *Deception* is an intellectual soap opera about a brilliant, modern composer-conductor, played to the bravura hilt by Claude Rains, his pianist mistress, Bette Davis, and her lover, Paul Henreid. Both melodramatic and highbrow, *Deception* is perhaps of interest mostly to music lovers. The score includes portions of Haydn's *Cello Concerto*, Chopin's *Prelude in E Major*, part of the second movement of Beethoven's *Seventh Symphony*, and the first movement of his *Appassionata Sonata*. Korngold supplied a new composition of his own, a short and brilliant cello concerto, which he later expanded into a complete concert work, his Opus 37. This film marked the end of his composing for films.

Dr. Julius Korngold died at his son's home in 1945. He had never been very pleased about his son's association with films and urged him to return to absolute composition and opera. In October 1946, when his Warner Bros. contract expired, Korngold refused to renew it. He said at the time, "I shall be fifty next May, and fifty is old for a child prodigy. I feel I have to make a decision now if I don't want to be a Hollywood composer the rest of my life." He also realized that the war had brought a change in public taste in films and those in which he had excelled were no longer in favor. His many jests about films masked his true feelings. When he first started scoring, he was enthusiastic about the possibility of reaching millions all over the world; in his last year, he quipped, "A film composer's immortality stretches all the way from the recording stage to the dubbing room." Just before he left Warner Bros., veteran producer Henry Blanke said to him, "Erich, when you first came to us, your music was so exciting and vibrant and soaring—now it doesn't seem to be quite the same." Korngold replied, "When I first came here, I couldn't understand the dialogue—now I can.

A favorite Korngold story in Hollywood music circles happened in his last year at Warner Bros. when he ran into Max Steiner, with whom he kept up a bantering friendship. Steiner needled him,

"Erich, I've been thinking. We've both been writing music for Warner Bros. for ten years, right?" Korngold nodded, wincing at the reminder. Steiner continued, "Well, it seems to me that in this time, my scores have got gradually better and yours have got gradually worse." Korngold beamed, "Maxie, my dear, you're absolutely right. And I'll tell you why—it's because I've been stealing from you and you've been stealing from me."

During the remaining ten years of Erich Korngold's life he composed a violin concerto, a symphony, a symphonic serenade, and several other works, mining his film scores for thematic material. The violin concerto, performed and recorded by Jascha Heifetz, is based almost entirely on film themes, as his father had advised him to do.

He returned to Vienna in 1949 with his wife and stayed for more than a year. He hoped he could revive his former activity and fame, but after a while it dawned upon him that what had happened twenty and thirty years before was irretrievable. His opera *Die Kathrin* was staged, finally, in Vienna in 1950 but withdrawn after only six performances, torn to shreds by the critics. *Die Tote Stadt* was slated for a Viennese performance but collapsed in a welter of complications during the rehearsals. It was not until ten years after his death that the opera was staged at the Vienna Opera House, warmly accepted by the public but denounced by the critics as "old-fashioned nonsense." However, *Die Tote Stadt* continues to be staged in European opera houses and will likely be one of the few enduring twentieth-century operas.

Korngold made one more contribution to the cinema. In 1954 he was asked by director-producer William Dieterle to arrange, conduct, and supervise the scoring of the Wagner biography *The Magic Fire*. Korngold told him, "I'll do it—if only to protect Wagner." The picture was made in Germany and turned out to be a disappointment, although for Wagner lovers it held much of interest.

Korngold made a remarkable three-and-a-half minute musical montage of the sixteen hours of Wagner's Ring cycle, and was later amazed when asked by Republic Studios (the U.S. distributor) if he could slice another twenty seconds out of it. The film was, in fact, cut by almost an hour for American release and butchered in the process. Korngold appeared briefly in the picture, as the famed conductor Hans Richter, and he was heard but not seen in two episodes as both Wagner and Liszt playing the piano. It was often said of him that he might have been a great concert pianist if he had devoted himself to the instrument. He said, "I play only two instruments—the piano and the orchestra, and the orchestra is such a nice instrument." Hugo Friedhofer recalls, "When Korngold played the piano, it sounded like an orchestra."

Korngold was an amiable man, vastly fortunate to be secure and confident and removed from the competitiveness that blemishes the film and music business. It was only in his later years that bitterness soured his good humor. He never fully accepted California as his home until the last years, when he realized there could never be a return, in the full sense, to Vienna. He spoke caustically about the atonal, anti-sentiment turns in modern composition. Many people regarded him as the last master melodist among the composers of this century, and he asked, "Should I deliberately become an ultra-modernist just because some critics would consider that an advance over what has gone before?" It was Korngold's conviction that the tonal system was inexhaustible, that there were endless melodic and harmonic combinations waiting to be discovered. He compared the process of artistic creativity with nature, a continually renewing source, but he would add with a twinkle in his eye, "Don't expect apples from an apricot tree."

As if abetting the decline of his career, ill health marked Korngold's last years and robbed him of his energy. He was only fifty when he suffered his first heart attack. In the winter of 1956 he suffered a stroke, and on November 29, 1957, age sixty, he collapsed from a heart seizure and died a few hours later at a hospital near his home, a mere half mile from the Warner Bros. studio. The next day, a black flag, the traditional Austrian mark of mourning, appeared over the Vienna Opera House. The city he loved, the city that had been the generous cradle of the famed Wunderkind but had been indifferent to his return, noted its loss. When told of the flag gesture, his widow stared silently for a few moments, and then said quietly, "It's a little late."

Korngold's widow lived for another five years, sadly not long enough to enjoy the upsurge of interest in her husband's music that came in the mid-seventies. That upsurge has so far resulted in recordings of three of his operas and most of his chamber and concert works. But not without a touch of irony. At the time of his death, Korngold believed that Hollywood had been the cause of the decline of his musical reputation. Instead, it was the recordings of the music he had written in Hollywood that sparked the new interest in his other compositions.

THE
PRICE OF
EXCELLENCE

K nowing the circumstances and conditions under which film composers work, we have every reason to be grateful that any good scores have been written. The film composers with the most musical intelligence and integrity often pay a price for their excellence—less fame than their more flashy colleagues and dwindling opportunities in a business that has become more and more commercial. Three American composers who fit into this odd but dignified niche are Bernard Herrmann, Hugo Friedhofer, and David Raksin.

Bernard Herrmann

Bernard Herrmann was the kind of composer somewhat feared in the Hollywood of years gone by. Young and brilliant, Herrmann excelled in every avenue of composition—symphonic, vocal, theatrical. He was modernistic, forceful, and very critical of film music. He may never have cracked the Hollywood barrier had it not been for Orson Welles, who insisted that Herrmann was the only man to score *Citizen Kane.* That celebrated picture launched several careers, but Herrmann might well have gone under had he not won an Academy Award for his next score, *All That Money Can Buy.* In the Hollywood of 1941, an Oscar was tantamount to the keys to the city.

For all that, Herrmann kept his distance and scored only one film a year at first while carrying on with his other musical activities. He scored no films between 1947 and 1950, but after that he averaged two or three a year. He might have done more, but he was very selective about his pictures and hardly endeared himself to the producers with his open contempt for their work. George Antheil referred to Herrmann as "my old squawking friend." Herrmann apparently insulted just about everyone in Hollywood and often stormed out of a projection room railing at the producer who wanted to hire him, "Why do you show me this garbage?"

Bernard Herrmann

Bernard Herrmann was born to a non-musical family in New York in 1911. While attending public schools he took music lessons from local teachers, and at the age of twelve won a prize for a song he had written. At New York University he studied composition and continued the study as a fellowship student at the Juilliard School of Music. By the age of eighteen, Herrmann was making a living as a musician; he had written a ballet for a Broadway show and he had formed and conducted a chamber orchestra to give concerts of avant-garde composers. In 1933 he was hired to compose and conduct music for the Columbia Broadcasting System and was

MUSIC FOR THE MOVIES

conspicuously successful in creating musical backgrounds for their dramatic and documentary programs as well as conducting his concert pieces with the CBS Orchestra. Herrmann became one of the leading figures in this heyday of American radio, which led to a profitable association with another young genius, Orson Welles. Herrmann scored many of the famous Welles broadcasts.

While he was an advocate of modern music and open to any style or school of musical thought, Herrmann never typed himself. "I count myself an individual. I hate all cults, fads, and circles. I believe that only music that springs out of genuine personal emotion and inspiration is alive and important." Herrmann qualified as the personification of what a composer should be—educated, knowledgeable, as respectful of old forms as he was interested in the new. All this in addition to being gifted with a great musical ability. Herrmann, somewhat like Richard Wagner, was a little difficult to accept on a personal level, often outspoken and unkind in his remarks about his peers. One of his close friends said, "With Benny for a friend, you hardly need a hair shirt." Those who knew him say that the rough manner of the man hid a warm heart, and that his depth of character was part of his skill in expressing himself in music. The quality of his music and the imagination and invention he brought to scoring set him apart from other film composers—where he no doubt preferred to be. Typical of Herrmann was his lack of interest in belonging to the Academy of Motion Picture Arts and Sciences, which he despised.

Bernard Herrmann's first film score (*Citizen Kane*) was an extremely interesting one. While scoring the picture he was present during the entire production and often made sketches during the shooting of the various scenes. His music accurately reflects the Welles and Mankiewicz story. The opening is sparse and ominous, and varies from faintly romantic to dry and dramatic as the character of Kane is revealed. Herrmann used music suggestive of the period—waltzes, ballet, opera, a newsreel episode, etc. It is interesting to note that Herrmann was the only major film composer in Hollywood to do his own orchestrations. He later adapted this score into an orchestral suite titled *Welles Raises Kane.*

For *All That Money Can Buy,* Herrmann wrote some superlative Americana, dexterously employing a number of New England folk melodies, creating a score full of charm and humor. Again Herrmann worked the material into a suite, *The Devil and Daniel Webster.*

Orson Welles called upon Herrmann to score *The Magnificent Ambersons,* but this time Welles had nowhere near the freedom he had enjoyed with *Citizen Kane* and, as a result, RKO edited and drastically cut the picture. It gave Herrmann scope for more turn-of-the-century Americana and allowed for his penchant for waltzes. The film's lack of success no doubt strengthened Herrmann's resolve not to become known as a film composer, and he returned to New York. Even when long established as one of the true craftsmen of film scoring, Herrmann bridled at the term "film composer." "America is the only country in the world with so-called 'film composers'—every other country has composers who sometimes do films."

In 1944, Bernard Herrmann was brought back to Hollywood by Twentieth Century-Fox to score *Jane Eyre,* yet another film with Orson Welles, although here Welles was merely an actor (Rochester) and not the writer-director-producer. Herrmann's music mirrored the somber tragic-romantic storylines with murmuring bass figures suggesting the malevolence and the mystery of Thornfield. Herrmann was, among other things, a fervent Anglophile and was attracted to most things English. His only opera is *Wuthering Heights,* and it contains many passages from *Jane Eyre,* along with themes from his score for *The Ghost and Mrs. Muir.*

Herrmann next scored the minor classic *Hangover Square* (1945), which starred the memorable Laird Cregar as a composer with intermittent amnesia. The film is especially interesting on the musical level because the composer is in the process of writing a piano concerto, and his drastically fluctuating state of mind affects his composition. The actual concerto, completed by the mad musician as his burning house falls about him, is one of the most interesting virtuoso pieces ever written for a film. Dark and dazzling, it was too cerebral a work to become widely popular.

Herrmann wrote sparingly for films in his first ten years in the medium, never more than one film a year. He was still active as a conductor for radio and concerts in New York, and it was only the attraction of a particular film that would bring him to California. He was also judicious in choosing subjects that were varied and could be scored in various ways. For *Anna and the King of Siam* (1946), Herrmann based his score on authentic Siamese scales and melodic fragments. "I tried to get the sound of Oriental music with our instruments. The music made no attempt to be a commentary on, or an emotional counterpart of, the drama but was intended to serve as musical scenery."

Herrmann considered his score for *The Ghost and Mrs. Muir* (1947) one of his best efforts, as well as his most romantic. It was an odd kind of love story between a young widow living in a seaside house and the ghost of a sea captain. It was obviously a story that appealed to Herrmann because his accompanying music was tender and charming. This from a man who in person appears anything but tender and charming, but as Aaron Copland once said, "If it's in the music, it's in the man."

In 1951, Herrmann scored one of the first major science-fiction films, *The Day the Earth Stood Still*. It was an experimental score, ahead of its time, in which he suggested electronic music without using electronic instruments. By this time, Herrmann was so well respected for his film composition to be unable to resist the increasing demands for his services and was producing two and three scores a year.

Among the more interesting are *The Snows of Kilimanjaro* (1953) and the films Herrmann scored for Alfred Hitchcock. *Kilimanjaro* was one of the few successful attempts to adapt Hemingway to the screen, and Herrmann's music had much to do with that success. His music commented on the African scenery and was especially effective in the flashback sequences where the hunter—played by Gregory Peck in an idealization of Hemingway—lies dying of an infected wound and muses on incidents in his life. The love theme was titled "The Memory Waltz," a delicate piece of music that Herrmann says is symbolic of Hemingway's recollections of his youth in Paris.

Herrmann's association with Alfred Hitchcock began in 1955, when the master of suspense and macabre asked him to score *The Trouble with Harry*, which was too short on suspense and overly macabre to find favor. Herrmann fared better the following year with the music for *The Man Who Knew Too Much*, although his score was somewhat overshadowed by Doris Day's singing of "Que Sera, Sera" and the finale of the film, a cantata called "Storm Clouds," written by Arthur Benjamin. The cantata was performed in London's Albert Hall and conducted by Herrmann himself—his only screen appearance. The music was integral to the story of the assassination of an international figure during a concert, with the assassin firing the lethal shot at the moment of a loud cymbal clash.

The Hitchcock film with which Herrmann is perhaps most identified is *Psycho* (1960). The bizarre, blood-curdling, bloody murders are accompanied by loud, high, bird-like shrieks made by violins, and they are probably the finest examples of music chilling an audience to the marrow. However, the best of the Herrmann-

Hitchcock scores is *Vertigo*, a landmark film score. This 1958 film, handsomely set in San Francisco, has James Stewart as detective Scottie Ferguson and Kim Novak as Madeleine, a woman of mystery. Page Cook, in his career profile of Bernard Herrmann for *Films in Review*, made this comment on the *Vertigo* score:

> The credit music, in an invention of major thirds, accompanies some dizzy optical effects, and the prelude begins with a huge basso ostinato upon which a solid horn figure startlingly appears. We then hear, for the first time, the melody, written in the key of D major, which is the clue to Madeleine's obsession about her dead grandmother. The melody's first use grows in intensity— the orchestration is quite bizarre—and achieves grim crescendo, which leads, after a harrowing drop, to a sustained note in the double bass. The harmonies are abstract but never cacophonic.
>
> For the chase at night over the rooftops, following the credits, there is a vibrant movement culminating in drum reverberations as the detective falls to his death. To depict Scottie Ferguson's acrophobia Herrmann uses a sharp discord based on an augmented triad. Madeleine's theme is first heard as Scottie spies her in a cocktail lounge, and, as she approaches him and then moves away, it grows and dims. There are no sounds on the soundtrack save this music. It's cinematic and extraordinarily effective. This theme is superbly used in the scene in which Madeleine pleadingly asks Scottie if he thinks she's insane.
>
> The key of the score, the note D, is somber when Madeleine gazes at the portrait of Carlotta, whose spirit, Madeleine believes, is slowly possessing her. The nightmare sequence—i.e., Scottie's dream of Madeleine and Carlotta—is scored for timbrels, castanets, and snare drums (Carlotta was of Spanish-Mexican descent). The entire movement grows into a fantastic array of orchestral timbres, which end as Scottie awakens.

The storyline in *Vertigo* is involved and mysterious, and

Herrmann's subtle score helps both the air of mystery and the final resolution. The excellence of this score paradoxically points to the problem that one viewing is not sufficient to really be able to appreciate what the composer has done. This certainly applies to Herrmann's intricate score for Hitchcock's *North by Northwest* (1959), music that should be part of any course about film scoring.

In 1958, Bernard Herrmann delved into another kind of film, the fantastic-exotic. He scored *The Seventh Voyage of Sinbad*, followed the next year by *Journey to the Center of the Earth*, and over the next few years *The Three Worlds of Gulliver*, *Mysterious Island*, and *Jason and the Argonauts*. All of these films allowed Herrmann rich orchestral palettes and scope for musical imagination. These scores called for a Rimsky-Korsakov feel or texture, which Herrmann gave them, along with wit and charm. He often said that the greatest inducement to writing film music (aside from the money involved) is the opportunity to experiment. However, composers, like actors, tend to become typecast, and after five fantasy films Herrmann decided he had fully explored that particular genre and declined similar offers. He reteamed with Hitchcock in 1964 to score the not-very-popular *Marnie*, writing another intriguing score for another story of a woman of mystery.

By the mid-sixties, Hollywood assignments became fewer for Herrmann, as they had for most of the veteran composers. In 1966, François Truffaut offered him the job of scoring his ambitious *Fahrenheit 451*. Herrmann was curious to know why Truffaut, whose circle of friends included many young jazz composers, would choose him instead of one of them. Said Truffaut, "Because they would give me music of the twentieth century; you'll give me the twenty-first." Herrmann scored the film somewhat differently than Truffaut specified, playing down the hard, emotionally dry futuristic concept of "things to come." *Fahrenheit 451* was a failure, but Truffaut was gracious enough to send the composer a note saying "Thank you for humanizing my picture."

Page Cook said that Herrmann was reticent with him at the time he was writing his *Films in Review* article, but that after publication the composer became somewhat more confiding. Herrmann has been called things much worse than reticent, but his idiosyncrasies were taken in stride by those who realized his musical genius. In his correspondence with Cook, Herrmann revealed his contempt for the direction film scoring was headed in the late sixties:

> Everybody's looking for a new sound, which means taking an old sound and jacking it up and amplifying it till it hurts your ears. There are no new sounds, only new ideas, and they don't come along very often. I've been extraordinarily lucky to have worked with men like Welles and Hitchcock. If I were starting now, I'd have no career in films.

Herrmann felt that if worthwhile scores were intelligently reviewed and assessed, it would have a beneficial effect on the medium.

> It's because there's no critical attention to movie music that it is left to producers—who are musical ignoramuses. I can't understand how a producer of a sophisticated film will pander in the score to the lowest common denominator. I am not interested in music, or any work of art, that fails to stimulate appreciation of life, and, more importantly, pride in life.

Bernard Herrmann left Hollywood in disgust to settle in London, which he claimed was his favorite city. Brian De Palma hired him for *Sisters* (1973) and *Obsession* (1976), and Martin Scorsese convinced him to return to Hollywood to score *Taxi Driver* (1976). Immediately after finishing the recording of the score at Universal, Herrmann returned to his hotel room, where he died in his sleep a few hours later, the morning of December 24, 1975.

Hugo Friedhofer

David Raksin said of his friend Hugo Friedhofer: "I think he had a better understanding of film music than any composer I know. He was the most learned of us all, the best schooled, and often the most subtle." This viewpoint is widespread in the Hollywood film community, yet Friedhofer's is a name that never caught the fancy of the moviegoing public despite the excellence of his work over a long period of time.

To explain this lack of fame, Raksin proffers the following.

> Virtue may be its own reward, but excellence seems to impose a penalty upon those who attain it. Composing something that isn't a repetition of what's been done before, cultivating differences from others, seeking out what is special, requires extra effort, extra time, and a little more indulgence from producers. Those who want scores "not good but by Thursday" often prefer to promote men whose qualification is that they deserve it less.

Hugo Friedhofer arrived in Hollywood in July 1929 and over the next forty-plus years scored some seventy feature films and contributed sections to the scores of at least as many more. Indeed, he worked as a collaborator, adapter, arranger, orchestrator, and utility composer on more films than he could remember. It's doubtful if any other composer had quite the degree of involvement with film

Hugo Friedhofer

music as Friedhofer. In the highly specialized field of orchestration he was regarded as "The Master." He orchestrated more than fifty of Max Steiner's scores and was the only man Erich Korngold fully trusted with his music—he orchestrated seventeen of Korngold's eighteen film scores.

The terms "adapter" and "arranger" tend to confuse, not unnaturally, since the terms often intertwine. To adapt is to tailor a piece of music composed for another purpose (e.g., a part of a symphony) to fit a scene. To arrange is to change the music—a sonata can be arranged into a concerto, or something written for certain instruments in a certain range can be arranged for other instruments in other ranges. Arranging often allows a musician more scope than adapting.

The skillful and imaginative work of Hollywood's best arrangers has never been fully appreciated. These men quite literally took the melodies of songwriters and built them into compositions. So many songwriters, gifted with melody though they be, are incapable of making even a respectable piano score, let alone an orchestration. As Friedhofer put it,

> Having been witness to what has been accomplished in the art of transmuting the baser metals into pure gold by such arrangers as Ray Heindorf, Conrad Salinger, Herbert Spencer, Eddie Powell, Earle Hagen, Maurice de Packh, Leonid Raab, and others, I can't help wondering if film musicals would ever have gotten off the ground without their blood, sweat, and tears.

Friedhofer was born in San Francisco on May 3, 1902. His father, also born in San Francisco, studied music in Dresden, and it was there he met his wife, who also was from a musical family. Friedhofer, whose early ambitions and education were in the classical arts, dropped out of school at the age of sixteen to work in the designing department of a lithograph firm while studying painting at the Mark Hopkins Institute at night.

Hugo's father had started him on the cello when he was thirteen, but it wasn't until five years later that his interest in music began to predominate his painting. Once he had chosen between the two, he studied seriously, and within two years he was able to earn his living as a musician—casual engagements at first, then steady work in movie theaters. In 1925, Friedhofer landed a berth with the orchestra of the Granada Theater, which he described as "one of that decade's most ornate film cathedrals."

It did not take Friedhofer long to realize that he had more interest in the other instruments collectively, i.e., orchestration, than as a performing cellist. And so he studied harmony, counterpoint, and composition with Domenico Brescia, a graduate of the Conservatory in Bologna. Brescia later became head of the music department at Mills College, a post he held until his death in 1937. Years later, Friedhofer picked up his studies of musical form with Schoenberg and composition with Ernst Toch. He also studied with Nadia Boulanger, the celebrated French teacher and musical mother to so many American composers, while she was living in Santa Barbara, California.

Friedhofer felt that a composer should never stop studying, although he cringed at the name-dropping of his famous teachers:

> I have an aversion to the types who try to impress you with the fact that they sat at the feet of this or that Great Master. I'm only interested in what they themselves have done. The woods are full of no-talent characters with degrees from this or that diploma mill. Ravel failed to win the Prix de Rome three times, despite the fact that his music was being performed and applauded concurrently with his bad status at the Conservatoire. Stravinsky, outside of a couple of years with Rimsky-Korsakov, was completely self-taught. In the last analysis, all a teacher can do is point out the road; after that you walk by yourself.

Friedhofer eventually was able to put aside his cello and pick up work as an arranger. George Lipschultz, a violinist friend, after becoming music director for Fox studios in Hollywood offered Friedhofer a job as an arranger. The first film on which he worked was the musical *Sunny Side Up*. He stayed with Fox for five years until he had a falling out with the new management after it merged with Twentieth Century.

Looking back on that busy period, Friedhofer reflected:

My activities as an arranger, composer, and orchestrator were so
intermingled that a catalog is out of the question—not that pos-
terity will be any the poorer as a result. Frankly, considering all
the work I've done in films it's a wonder I'm not blind or para-
lyzed or both. I give thanks for the stamina bequeathed me by
my peasant forebears.

In 1935, he was hired by Leo Forbstein, the head of music at
Warner Bros., as an orchestrator. Under Forbstein's astute command,
Warner Bros. maintained the most formidable music department
in the industry. Concurrent with Friedhofer's arrival at the studio
was the hiring of Max Steiner and Erich Korngold. Steiner's first
score for Warner Bros. was *The Charge of the Light Brigade*, and
Korngold's was *Captain Blood*. Both scores were mostly orchestrated
by Friedhofer, who performed the work so well that he became the
principal orchestrator for these two giants.

He had hoped that in joining the company he would become
one of the celebrated team of Warner Bros. composers, but in the
eleven years he spent at the studio he was assigned as composer to
only one picture, *Valley of the Giants* in 1938. Forbstein realized that
Friedhofer was a brilliant orchestrator and paid him well.

Friedhofer later reflected on his situation:

Forbstein was no musician to speak of, but he was an excellent
executive and a good businessman, and he organized that music
department so well it could practically run itself. We were all cogs
in his well-oiled machine. Forbstein had the complete confidence
of the Warner brothers, and it was the place for a musician to
work. We had a fifty-piece staff orchestra which we augmented
to seventy for the bigger scores, and Forbstein was fortunate in
not having individual budgets for the films, as was the case else-

where. The studio gave him an annual allotment of money, and he used it well. As for me—working conditions were good, and I suppressed my creative ego until I could do so no longer.

In between his Korngold and Steiner assignments, Friedhofer, with Forbstein's approval, was able to occasionally do a job for another studio. In 1937, on the advice of Alfred Newman, Samuel Goldwyn hired Friedhofer to score *The Adventures of Marco Polo.* His first full-length score is a fine piece of work and was well received, but it still didn't change Forbstein's mind. He already had superb composers on his staff. What he needed was the able orchestrator who serviced Korngold and Steiner so well. Steiner had himself been an orchestrator, and he knew the value of a good man in this laborious but essential aspect of scoring. He would indicate in his sketches the effects he wanted and leave it to Friedhofer to fill in. Steiner, in his first ten years at Warner Bros., averaged eight scores a year, and the success of this huge volume of work is at least partly attributable to Friedhofer. Friedhofer was one of several musicians who worked for Steiner while he was scoring *Gone With the Wind,* and sections of that long score were written by Friedhofer, developing Steiner material and interjecting a few fragments of his own.

The need for the orchestrator is obvious, and snobs who sneer that film composers are not able to orchestrate are being absurd. A composer like Korngold would hardly have used an orchestrator had there not been the matter of insufficient time. Steiner wrote almost three hours of music for *Gone With the Wind,* while at the same time writing the "Symphonie Moderne" for *Four Wives* in a twelve-week period. When Friedhofer wrote the score for *The Best Years of Our Lives* he employed an orchestrator and seldom afterward orchestrated his own scores.

Friedhofer claimed a musician either has a knack for orchestration or he hasn't. The same can be said for the art of film scoring. Friedhofer could look at a film and know immediately what it needed musically. He also had the ability to place himself musically in any environment, and without actually quoting local material, simulate the musical color of that environment. There's an Indian mode in his score for *The Rains of Ranchipur;* there's Native American music in his score for *Broken Arrow*, the tasteful and intelligent Western written and directed by Delmer Daves.

Friedhofer's score for *The Bandit of Sherwood Forest*, in which Cornel Wilde played the son of Robin Hood, came from a study of medieval English music.

> I knew I couldn't do anything like Korngold's *Robin Hood* and expect to get away with it. His approach had been rich and operatic, so I had to go the other way and be fairly austere and more historical. I used some old English melodies; one of them was the song "Brigg Fair," the same one Delius had used for his orchestral rhapsody. Of course, I got letters panning me for having stolen from Delius. One has to be philosophical about things like this. I tend to go along with Virgil Thomson's advice: "Never make the mistake of overestimating an audience's taste, but don't underestimate it either."

Friedhofer won an Academy Award (he was also nominated for eight other scores) for *The Best Years of Our Lives* (1946). The film was an intelligent treatment of American servicemen returning home after World War II and was done without so much of the cloying sentiment and patriotism that marred so many American films of this kind.

Said Friedhofer:

> I got the film because once again Sam Goldwyn called Al Newman and asked who should be the man for the job—I think Goldwyn still somehow thought Al was working for him. This

was years after Al had been head of music at Fox. Anyway, Goldwyn took his advice without question, and I got the job even though William Wyler and others didn't want me. Wyler was a very confused man about music—he was also hard of hearing. He had great trouble hearing the lower frequencies of music, and when he did hear them, he hated them. He obviously disliked my score very much—in fact, so did many people around the Goldwyn studio, and it wasn't until after I'd won an Oscar for it that they started talking to me again. It was a difficult score because of the three disparate story levels—disparate but connected, and I had to find a common denominator. Somehow I managed.

Managed is putting it modestly; *The Best Years of Our Lives* is a score that bears the closest examination.

Friedhofer's score for *The Young Lions* (1958) is as good as any ever written for a war film. The title music is especially impressive, a minute and a half of very business-like martial music. Melodic figures comprise the upper line, which is played by the brass, while the lower line is a relentless, repetitive rhythm played by a chorus of drums. It has that inexorable quality suggestive of the modern war machine moving like a juggernaut. In this and similar films, Friedhofer never indulged in flag-waving; what he says with the music is that war is ugly and non-glorious.

One of the themes in *The Young Lions* was written twenty-five years previously. It's the theme for May Britt, who played the wife of Marlon Brando's immediate superior. At the point in the story where Brando visits her in Berlin to tell her about her injured husband, he finds her more interested in him than the news about her husband. Friedhofer remembers:

> I racked my brain for something suitably decadent for this woman but with no luck. One night I awoke around three in the morn-

ing with this theme surfacing from my subconscious. It was something I had written in 1933 and discarded, knowing then that it was far too modernistic to be acceptable to the musically Neanderthal people for whom I was working. So, in the middle of the night, I searched frantically through old manuscripts, and after a couple of hours I found this thing. Miraculously, I didn't have to change a note—as originally conceived it was just the right length for this scene with Britt and Brando. All I did was hand it to the orchestrator. Eddie Powell looked at it and said, "Isn't this kind of way-out for 1942?" I reminded him, as gently as possible, that Strauss's *Salome* was written in 1905, and that by 1910 Schoenberg was doing things which made my little ditty sound like something out of *Carrie Jacobs Bond* by Charles Wakefield Cadman. He agreed. Moral: don't throw anything away, and, by God, I never do.

Friedhofer's most charming score was written for *The Bishop's Wife*, a 1948 Goldwyn picture in which Cary Grant appears as an angel and David Niven as a young bishop whose diligent efforts to raise money for a new cathedral are bringing him to the verge of an estrangement from his beautiful wife, Loretta Young. Grant, as Dudley, is a genial chap who performs all the required miracles but provokes jealousy in the bishop when the bishop's wife apparently falls in love with their angelic guest. Friedhofer's music is humorous and delightful. He uses a classical concerto grosso form for the opening and sparks it with the cheeky, earthy sounds of a saxophone for Dudley, the handsome, celestial visitor.

Completely the opposite of the music for *The Bishop's Wife* is Friedhofer's score for Billy Wilder's *Ace in the Hole* (1951), which the composer considered one of his most satisfying. The film was poorly reviewed, possibly because it put the Fourth Estate in a very poor light. Kirk Douglas plays a newspaperman who arrives in a small New Mexico town to work as a reporter, presumably having lost better jobs with better papers. He is assigned to cover a rattlesnake hunt, but when he discovers a man trapped in an old Indian excavation, rather than rescue him, he keeps him there in order to string out his exclusive reportage of the situation.

Says Friedhofer:

> It was a gutsy story and it got to me. I felt I could commentate on this miserable character, this exploitation of his, and the morbid curiosity of the people who traipsed to the scene, everybody cashing in on it. It had the kind of gallows humor that Billy Wilder is prone to, and which appeals to me. However, he was upset by the fact that I hadn't written a schmaltzy score, or at least something Wagnerian, since that's his favorite composer. When we were recording, he said, "It's a good score, but there isn't a note of melody in it." I replied, "Billy, you've had the courage to put on the screen a bunch of really reprehensible people. Did you want me to soften them?" He got the point. In general, you have to be careful with musical characterizations because the person on the screen—as in life—is not always what he seems, he may be smiling on the surface but snarling underneath. The music should point to the qualities behind the image.

Friedhofer's greatest technical achievement came with *The Sun Also Rises* (1957). He felt *en rapport* with the Hemingway story and was able to communicate musically the sense of turning the clock back a generation. His opening, in particular, has an enormous sense of nostalgia, the feeling of something lost. The problems come during the second half of the film, which takes place in Pamplona during the annual bullfight festival. What we see and hear is a mosaic of events—street parades, celebrations, carousing, bullfights—calling for a cascade of music. Friedhofer worked with composer-orchestrator Alexander Courage on these sequences.

Alex is an aficionado of Spanish bullfight and festival music, and we worked for two weeks on a sort of road map of themes, a layout of cross-fades. Very interesting and very difficult.

A film that gave Friedhofer unusual scope in instrumentation was *Boy on a Dolphin* (1957), a romantic, exotic story filmed in the Aegean Islands and beautifully photographed by Milton Krasner. The film contained footage that allowed for aural descriptions of mountains, a harbor, a monastery, the Acropolis, cafés, street scenes, and several long sequences of diving for ancient treasure:

> The nature of the film called for music written in an idiom which has been current for approximately fifty years. In other words, it is music essentially romantic and impressionistic in style. Anything in the nature of avant-garde experimentation would have been a shocking intrusion, completely out of harmony with the film itself. Some austere souls might even call it "lush," with no intention of using that adjective in a complimentary sense. I won't waste my time in vehement protestations. Southern Europe, and particularly the Mediterranean area, is hardly an Arctic wilderness.

Friedhofer's score for this film also incorporated Greek folk music with no attempt at absolute authenticity.

> The countries bordering the Mediterranean have been swapping cultures for centuries now, and to determine what is purely regional, and what has been borrowed, would take years of delving into the subject. With only ten weeks in which to write the music for *Boy on a Dolphin*, the best I could hope to achieve was a stylization which would be theatrically effective, rather than a completely truthful recreation, which might very well have turned out to be dull no matter how authentic.

Queried about his style, Friedhofer would squirm and deny he had striven consciously for a personal style. Some ears detect a certain Hindemithian quality, certain suggestions of linear dissonance. Friedhofer thought of himself in the mainstream of modern music, not "far out." He was schooled in the German masters, grew up in the jazz-impressed twenties, and was particularly fond of Spanish, Mexican and Latin music, although he did not know why. "Maybe there was a Phoenician in the woodpile away back. Or maybe I felt my flat-footed Teutonic genes could stand an infusion of Mediterranean sunshine."

Friedhofer's affinity for Mexican music was part of a larger interest in Mexico, where he hoped to retire once done with the Hollywood scene. This interest is apparent in his vigorous score for the Gary Cooper-Burt Lancaster romp *Vera Cruz* (1954). The score points to something Friedhofer felt keenly about—the frequent use of Spanish-type music in films about Mexico.

One of the few Max Steiner scores he disliked was *The Treasure of the Sierra Madre*, even though it is one of Steiner's most popular. He criticized it for not being truly Mexican:

Read Prescott and you'll quickly latch on to the idea that our neighbors south of the border aren't exactly enamored of Cortez and his crew. Actually, the folk music of Mexico has, to me at least, a strong aroma of Old Vienna, on which has been superimposed a curious rhythmic vitality. The Moorish influence, which is such a marked characteristic of Spanish music, is not at all noticeable in the Mexican folk-idiom. Art in Mexico is strongly nationalistic and largely derived from the pre-Hispanic heritage. Listen to Chavez's *Sinfonia India* and Revueltas' *Sensemaya*—Spanish flavored they are not. Furthermore, if you want to make yourself unpopular in Mexico, try speaking Spanish with the Castilian lisp on the sibilants. The natives will either laugh contemptuously or beat the hell out of you. The best film score by a North American in the Mexican idiom, for my money, is Alex North's *Viva Zapata!* Alex lived in Mexico for a while; consequently, he knows the difference. I found out the difference through research and through having been a resident there for nigh on four months while composing and recording the score for *Vera Cruz.*

Friedhofer felt that it was not the function of a film score to be wholly autonomous:

> In this respect it differs from music written for concert-hall presentation in much the same way that design for a stage setting differs from an easel painting. For example, a film score conceived with as much detail, or as richly textured as the Fourth Symphony of Brahms (we should live so long), would not be a good film score, regardless of its merits as music. Being inherently self-sufficient, it would be constantly drawing attention to itself at the expense of the drama it was intended to enhance.
>
> I don't mean to imply that music for a film should be as consistently bland and unobtrusive as the so-called "mood music" which accompanies the rattle of dishes and the buzz of small talk in a coffee shop. To the contrary, it is my belief that the ideal film score is one which, while at all times maintaining its own integrity of line, manages at the same time to coalesce with all the other filmic elements involved; sometimes as a frame, at other times as a sort of connective tissue, and in still other (although naturally rarer) instances, as the chief actor in the drama. Other than this, it would be foolhardy to make any sort of sweeping statement as to what film music should or should not be.
>
> The problems confronting the film composer are never the same twice and require in every instance another solution. Every film that comes along constitutes a problem and a challenge—unless one is completely bogged down in the morass of one's own clichés.

In the perpetual war between composers and producers, Friedhofer felt he fared fairly well and had less music scrapped than many of his colleagues. He sympathized with producers because their job requires them to be omniscient:

> The omniscience of producers isn't taxed as much in the fields of writing, photography, and acting as it is in music, which seems to be a closed shop to them. In many instances they are forced, in order to save face, to assume a profundity about music they don't possess.

Film music, claimed Friedhofer, must not be compared with concert music—its purpose and therefore its texture is different. Producers, like the public, are unmindful of this. On the other hand, he was not overly sympathetic to composers who complain about not having enough time.

> The composers of the baroque period also had to turn out scores whether they felt like it or not. They, too, had no time to second-guess. When Papa Haydn got another order from Count Esterhazy, he first knelt in prayer, then spat on his hands and wrote another masterpiece.

However, the film composer is much less likely to turn out a masterpiece because his music is determined by the nature of the film, and the technique obliges him to curtail material he might otherwise like to expand. Asked to explain his own modus operandi, Friedhofer said with characteristic bluntness: "I write 'em as I hear 'em. When I walk into the studio, I'm not an artist so much as a plumber."

Marlon Brando's *One Eyed Jacks* in 1960 was Hugo Friedhofer's last major score. He was hired only four times in the sixties, once in 1971, and for the last time in 1973. He was a meticulous composer who liked to take his time, often longer than allotted. Times had changed and he was not about to change. He lived his final years modestly in a small apartment in Hollywood, where he died on May 17, 1981. Producers had long since ceased to call, but many were the composers who dropped by to have him take a look at their work. A common piece of advice given to those studying film composition is still "Study Friedhofer."

David Raksin

David Raksin is a musician of substance—unfortunately, beyond the taste of many of the filmmakers for whom he has worked and over the heads of most moviegoers. He is thus caught in the valley between the peaks of ignorance and indifference. Raksin, however, is a man of forceful personality, neither reticent nor modest by nature, and is too creative to give way to despair. When not working on films, he writes and conducts concert works and contributes much of his time to music education. Raksin has for some years conducted a class in film music at the University of Southern California, and he has written scores for the theater workshop plays of that and other universities.

Raksin is an outspoken man, and it is likely that his honesty has injured his career:

> The stuff we do is sometimes good, sometimes bad, and sometimes lost. Sometimes you work on a picture that's worth doing; most of the time you don't. But at least you are composing all the time, and to me that's a marvelous thing. I get paid for doing what I'd be doing anyhow. And when we work for people of some sophistication and intelligence, who are not inclined to underestimate the public, we do work which amounts to something. All too often, the music is too good for the film. The frequency with which this happens is more an indictment of films than a compliment to composers.

David Raksin

In 1935 Raksin turned up in Hollywood—he was then twenty-three—with the specific ambition to become a film composer. Most of the musicians in the industry at that time had drifted into films from other musical avenues. Some, like Alfred Newman and Miklos Rozsa, had to be persuaded. Raksin had been indoctrinated at an early age; his father was for an extended period the music conductor for silent films at the Metropolitan Opera House in Philadelphia. The elder Raksin sometimes augmented the supplied scores with bits of his own composition, and on Saturdays he would take his son to the theater with him:

> I would sit alongside him in the orchestral pit as he conducted with a baton with a battery-lit tip on it. I was fascinated. I liked

the whole idea—even then I was impressed by the emotional effect of a film, and I was heard to say that was what I wanted to do when I grew up.

Raksin's father operated a music store, where David Raksin worked while attending Central High School in Philadelphia. He played in the school orchestra, edited the school magazine, and taught himself to play the organ and percussion instruments. He studied piano and learned about woodwinds from his father, an accomplished clarinetist. At twelve years old, Raksin organized his own dance band, which played at private parties around Philadelphia, and by fifteen he was a member of the musicians' union. Raksin earned his tuition to the University of Pennsylvania by playing in dance bands and the orchestra of WCAU, the CBS radio station in Philadelphia. At Penn he studied composition under Harl McDonald, then head of the music department, and participated in practically all the university's musical activities. He also compiled an extensive glossary of jazz terminology.

Twenty-one and armed with a degree in music, Raksin went to New York to play in and arrange for various dance bands, including Benny Goodman's. Conductor Al Goodman bought an arrangement of Gershwin's "I Got Rhythm" from Raksin, and when his pop concert orchestra played it on a radio broadcast, it brought more offers for arrangements and eventually a contract with Harms, one of the mightiest of the music publishing houses.

After two years with Harms, Eddie Powell and Herbert Spencer, two of Hollywood's top arrangers, recommended Raksin to Alfred Newman, who needed someone to work with Charlie Chaplin on the score for *Modern Times*. Newman would conduct the score but did not have the time to arrange Chaplin's music. Raksin's job was to make musical logic from the humming and whistling of Chaplin who fired him after ten days. Newman looked at the sketches for the score Raksin had concocted from Chaplin's ideas and persuaded Chaplin to take Raksin back.

Raksin reflected on the session with Chaplin:

> He was an instinctive musician. He had, partly based on his background in the English music halls, a certain conception of the way music should go in his films. He knew what he wanted, and he knew better than anyone else what was best for his films. But he couldn't write down the music that came to his mind because he had never learned how. Charlie and I would sometimes fight like tigers, but I felt his film was too good for anything but the best and he came to respect this. He is a man for whom I had the utmost personal and professional regard.

All through the late thirties and early forties, Raksin worked on a large number of films at various studios, sometimes as the composer, sometimes as an arranger and contributor to scores by other composers. *Laura* (1944) was not designed by Twentieth Century-Fox as one of their big pictures; that it turned out a minor classic was a happy accident primarily due to the flair of director Otto Preminger. Raksin was assigned to write the score, and it wasn't until the picture was in the theaters and requests by the thousands poured in asking for a recording that the studio and the publishers realized the value of the music.

The publishers quickly decided to add words to the theme and presented Raksin with an array of assorted lyrics, all of which he turned down. Recalls Raksin:

> They were aghast at my lack of appreciation. The conversation went something like this:
>
> Publisher: "Who are you to turn down these lyrics?"
> Raksin: "Who do you have to be?"
> Publisher: "You keep up that attitude and we may decide not to publish the thing at all."

Raksin: "Well, it could be worse."

Publisher: "How?"

Raksin: "You could publish it with those lyrics."

Anyway, I knew what I wanted and that was a lyric by Johnny Mercer, the Flying Wallenda of lyricists. I gave the melody to him and he went off to meditate, or whatever marvelous thing he did, and the rest is history.

"Laura" is among the half dozen most recorded songs; its popularity never seems to wane. In the film, the melody is a motif for the principal character, a girl who has been murdered by a jealous lover. A detective (Dana Andrews) is assigned to the case and gradually falls in love with the girl's image while staring at a beguiling portrait of her. By varying the theme, Raksin makes it speak for the detective's strange obsession—the image of the beautiful girl haunts him, irritates him, and moves him to anger and a determination to solve the crime. The Raksin score is one of the foremost examples of the power of music on film. Frequently asked if the melody came easily to him, he replies,

> It came quickly, once it came, but I had worried about whether such a melody would come at all. I had from Friday until Monday morning to turn up with something immortal, and after all, you don't do anything immortal every day.

Raksin's contributions to the art of scoring range from the melodic appeal of the theme in *The Bad and the Beautiful* (1952), one of the longest melodic lines ever invented for the screen, to the dry, dissonant lines of *Al Capone* (1959), a score full of subtly interrelated material. Possibly none but musicians actually hear the interrelationships, but the subliminal effect on the viewer is one of helping to tie together the disparate bits and pieces of the visual. Music can give a film a sense of unity, and there are scenes in *Al Capone* that would not have worked as well without the music. Raksin can be cerebral, as in *Force of Evil* (1949) and *Whirlpool* (1950), and he can be charming, as in *Forever Amber* (1947) and *The Unicorn in the Garden* (1953).

One of Raksin's treasures is a letter from James Thurber that reads in part:

> I am not a music maker, but I enjoyed your music for the unicorn and remember with affection the recorder that spoke up when the unicorn appeared. It sounded exactly right for unicorn.

Thurber was referring to Raksin's score for the delightful UPA cartoon *The Unicorn in the Garden*. The recorder mentioned is the English straight flute, which was an inspired choice to describe an animal as odd, whimsical, and forlorn as Thurber's unicorn.

The score for *Forever Amber*, which makes for enchanting listening, is an exercise and a study in period music.

> It was an absolute joy to do. Some people have said it sounds rather satirical—perhaps it is but it was a gentle satire because I love that period of music. The purists like to point out that it doesn't sound very English. I can only point out that the music of the court of Charles II was greatly influenced by the French. I aimed for a kind of mock-Lully, mock-Scarlatti sound, but again, a loving kind of mocking.

Raksin has had his share of poor pictures on which he was expected to work wonders. The capable professional is able to manufacture musical sounds appropriate to requirements, but as Raksin explains:

> Ersatz emotion is much harder to disguise than real music is to write. It's easier on one's conscience to be compassionate than to simulate compassion, and consequently, more practical. Many

films present in themselves challenges that arouse the composer, but when you cope with one that doesn't provide emotional or intellectual incentive, you must provide them for yourself. In *Forever Amber*, the Great Fire of London was presented almost as an interlude between beds; I tried to play it for the affliction it really was. I may experiment with musical forms and devices. In one film I used a twelve-tone row whose first five notes spelled out the name of the film's hero, which was otherwise not revealed until the last few seconds. The head of the music department asked what had prompted me to be so daring, and I replied that it was in the hope that the producer would come running out of the theater after the preview crying, "Fire that man, he gave away the secret of the picture in the main title."

Writing music for films is possibly more fraught with pitfalls and frustrations than most other professions. It needs a tough-minded man to survive the sometimes brutal decisions that affect the scoring. David Raksin recalls that while working on the score of *Carrie* (1952) he had a scene near the end of the film for which he wrote a piece six and a half minutes in length, a piece that carried the visual story. The producers decided to cut the scene to forty-six seconds.

There was another production decision on that film that was even harder for the composer to appreciate.

Carrie has left Hurstwood (Laurence Olivier) and goes her own way to fulfillment. Your reintroduction to Hurstwood—in the original print of the film—takes place in a horrid turn-of-the-century New York flophouse. We had a long dolly shot through the flophouse—all you hear are sounds of men who have awakened drunk, coughing, retching, spitting. The camera moves into this tiny cubicle in which you see this wreck of a man who was once so beautiful. Director William Wyler said he wanted the music for this scene to be "towering."

I said, "Willie, there's nothing I can do to approach the image you have on camera, and you know damn well that if I did, you'd have to squeeze the music down in order to hear all this coughing and spitting. What I have to do is think of something very meager. I don't know what but give me a little time."

Well, I thought about it and came up with an idea. When you first saw Hurstwood, he was the manager of a swank restaurant in Chicago and looked stunning in his morning coat and striped trousers. You saw him through Carrie's eyes and he was a sort of demi-God. Off screen there was a little orchestra playing a period waltz. I used this waltz as an association for Hurstwood and it made certain transformations in the film. Now I took a celeste and had them tape the bars, so that it would sound like a doll's piano. I played the waltz on this thing in a halting way, as a child would. The notes were dull and non-reverberating. It meant little when we recorded it, but when we put it in the film the effect was absolutely hair-raising—all of a sudden you felt as if your skin was crawling. Everyone thought it was a tour de force. But the producers decided the scene was too harrowing and the whole thing was cut.

Some years later, Raksin suffered an even keener disappointment when his score for *Separate Tables* (1958) was rejected by the producers as being too modernistic, too contemporary. Raksin simplified his score and incorporated, as he was ordered to do, a title song written by Harry Warren. He feels the change in the score weakened the film by altering the emphasis on the characters.

Raksin has used a scene from *Separate Tables* in his film composition class at the University of Southern California. He illustrates it in two ways—as it was heard in the released film and then as he had originally scored it. The scene involves Rita Hayworth attempting to inveigle the affection of her former husband, Burt Lancaster. The original scoring was contrapuntal, an "edgy" kind of music, to suggest the odd relationship between the characters on screen—the woman using her wiles on a proud man trying to resist. The producers insisted the scene be scored romantically. On one occasion in his classroom, Raksin asked his students for the comparative effects of the two pieces of scoring. One girl put up her hand and commented, "The second time, there were more close-ups." She had missed the device but got the message. The romantic scoring certainly matched the vamp image of Hayworth, but the more subtle music pointed up the uncomfortable intimacy of the scene.

Raksin has been unlucky with some of his assignments, not merely in scoring inferior pictures—that's the plight of composers in general—but scoring films that deserved much better reception than they received. Two cases in particular are *Too Late Blues* (1961) and *Will Penny* (1968). *Too Late Blues* is a story about jazz musicians made by John Cassavetes and which starred Bobby Darin and Stella Stevens. The failure of the film killed the proposed recording of the score, a great pity in view of the artistry involved. Raksin created a dozen pieces exploring various kinds of jazz, all tuneful and entertaining and played by the best musicians money could buy. The score is highly regarded among musicians, and producer Martin Poll requested Raksin to use several of the *Too Late Blues* pieces in his score for *Sylvia* (1964).

Will Penny is an unusual and exceptional Western. Beautifully photographed in color by Lucien Ballard, it is one of the few films to depict the cowboy as a working man who was often an illiterate and probably none-too-well adjusted, socially or personally, on a horse doing a rough, grimy, lonely job. Raksin had scored other Westerns; his music for *Smoky* (1946) and *Jubal* (1950) are tuneful but without the tinge of melancholy that is apparent in the *Will Penny* music.

Says Raksin:

There's something about the grandeur and the loneliness of the Western landscape that appeals to a composer's innards. Most composers like scoring Westerns because of the opportunity for descriptive music, and the opportunity for the music to be heard, due to the long, relatively silent sequences where it can assert itself. *Will Penny* required a special kind of expressive music to delineate the title character, an over-the-hill cowboy who knows there's nothing much left for him. I got the idea for a melody when I watched Charlton Heston doing a scene. I was suddenly struck by the poignancy of it. The theme emerged full blown in my head. Bill Stinson, the head of the music at Paramount, liked it and commented that it had a Slavic quality. I said, "Yes, I'm thinking of calling it 'On the Steppes of Central Utah.'"

Several scenes in *Will Penny* bear aural scrutiny. In particular, the scene where Donald Pleasence, as a mad, renegade, frontier preacher who has just had one of his sons killed in a gunfight with Penny, in a rage, delivers a series of biblical imprecations, "An eye for an eye," etc. The accompanying music is a set of variations on a twelve-tone row derived from the main theme. The music punctuates Pleasence's fearful speech, and its odd dissonance helps promote the impression of madness. At the end of the film, Penny, a basically warm-hearted but inexpressive man, realizes that he loves a widow and her son and that they want him, but he also realizes that it is too late in his life for him to adjust to such a change. In declining their love, he condemns himself to continued loneliness. Raksin scores this scene in a way that makes it both radiant and touching and articulates in a way the characters themselves cannot. The music says what is on their minds and in their hearts.

David Raksin is occasionally criticized for writing music that is too involved, and he would perhaps land more assignments if he were willing to simplify his scoring—in short, stress his gift for melody rather than his interest in subtle sonorities. But Raksin is a man not much prone to bending. In the late thirties and during the years of the Second World War, when Arnold Schoenberg was living in Los Angeles and available as a tutor, Raksin was among the composers who went to him:

> I wanted to learn from a man with such overall grasp of form in music, or larger form, which has always been a problem for me. I never believed that by filling in the cubes and other structures of a sonata form that I could compose music. There's a time in your life when you think there's some magic thing somebody can teach you that will let you bypass the sweating and suffering. There isn't. But a wise man can tell you when not to feel guilty.

Film music, Raksin feels, could and should occupy a kind of middle musical ground, between the poles of popular and serious music. As for the tired old dictum that film music is not supposed to be heard:

> That's like saying breathing is only useful when you don't know you're doing it. Film music is utilitarian, but so are a lot of things, and some of them are quite beautiful in their own right. A teapot is made for a purpose, but it can also be a work of art.

Raksin is long inured to the disdain some hold for Hollywood, and the peculiar kind of snobbism expressed toward the composing of film music.

> I've lived here so long that I've learned that the blanket indicters can't tell the difference between what is good and what isn't unless they're told. They lump people of talent and hacks together without bothering to discover the many different forms of aspiration and realization. I think they do themselves out of something.

AMERICANA
TO THE
FORE

The composers who found it most difficult to establish themselves in Hollywood during its so-called Golden Age were Americans who wrote what is generally regarded as classical music.

Hollywood film scores of this era, much like the music that was compiled earlier to accompany silent films, drew heavily upon the popular classics of European concert music, primarily late-nineteenth-century symphonic works, which were generally well received by audiences throughout the Western World. American concert music, regardless of its focus or inspiration, was usually not taken seriously or simply ignored.

Like most of the world, Hollywood's image of the distinctly American musical voice—the popular song-and-dance music that was inspired by and grew out of ragtime, spirituals, blues, etc. and rapidly spread around the globe after the First World War—was the work of Broadway's and Tin Pan Alley's tunesmiths, such composers as Harry Warren, George Gershwin, Irving Berlin, Cole Porter, Vincent Youmans, Arthur Schwartz, Sammy Fain, Jerome Kern, and Harold Arlen. (So, in effect, America's most identifiable musical style, which had great bearing on the music coming out of Hollywood, was set on the East Coast.) This music, recognized worldwide as the sound of America, recommended itself to Hollywood by its popularity, but did little to recommend American concert composers, even though many of them often dipped into that same well of musical Americana for their inspiration.

George Antheil

One of the few cerebral American composers of the thirties to establish himself in Hollywood was George Antheil, a real surprise since he had made his name writing quite iconoclastic music. Antheil was a darling of the Parisian intellectuals whose concerts drew packed audiences to the serious music salons of Paris. Jean Cocteau hailed him as a genius. In 1927 Antheil created a great deal of noise with his *Ballet mécanique*, a work scored for anvils, electric bells, car horns, sixteen player pianos, and an airplane propeller, plus orchestra. Said Antheil at the time, "My idea was to warn the age in which I was living of the simultaneous beauty and danger of its own unconscious mechanistic philosophy." Unfortunately, the notorious composition blemished his career when it became the one composition with which his name became identified.

Antheil grew more conservative with time, and his first major scoring job in Hollywood was Cecil B. DeMille's epic Western *The Plainsman* (1937). His music is much more modernistic than anything previously written for that kind of picture, but DeMille was intrigued by it and decided to give Antheil another historical pageant to score, *The Buccaneer* (1938). Antheil's music for *The Buccaneer* served the picture beautifully. It was clearly composed by someone of taste and skill. Yet, Antheil did what lesser composers strived to do—he wrote a score with good tunes and rousing emotions.

George Antheil

Insecure about entering the world of film scoring, Antheil felt at the time that he was on shaky ground. DeMille hired him to score *Union Pacific*, but when he came to the studio to play his themes, he found all the other Paramount composers and arrangers sitting with DeMille. Much as DeMille liked the music, he could be swayed, and Antheil knew from the dour expressions on the faces of the other composers that he was out. *Union Pacific* emerged with a patchwork score done by no less than four Paramount composers.

George Antheil left Hollywood in 1939, assuming his career scoring pictures had died an early death. However, he returned in 1946 to score *The Specter of the Rose*, an interesting and rather macabre movie that called for an original ballet sequence, and remained in California until he died in 1958. His once-brilliant reputation as a composer of symphonic, operatic, and chamber music had diminished, and the last decade of his life was spent in scoring films. He wrote interesting scores for several of the films Humphrey Bogart made for Columbia, notably *Knock on Any Door* and *In a Lonely Place* (1949). In 1952, Antheil became associated with Stanley Kramer, first scoring two of Kramer's lesser films, *The Sniper* (1952) and *The Juggler* (1953), and later the overblown spectacle *The Pride and the Passion* (1957).

Antheil, like most of the educated musicians who found themselves part of the glitter of Hollywood, was always critical of films and film music, but he once remarked, "I think this is one of the few so-called art colonies in the world that actually works." He also spoke for all film composers when he wrote in his autobiography, *Bad Boy of Music*, published in 1945:

> Hollywood music is very nearly a public communication, like radio. If you are a movie fan (and who isn't?), you may be in a movie theater three times a week listening to the symphonic background scores which Hollywood composers concoct. What happens? Your musical tastes become molded by these scores, heard without knowing it. You see love, and you hear it. Simultaneously. It makes sense. Music suddenly becomes a language for you, without your knowing it. You cannot see and hear such stuff week in and year out without forming some kind of taste

for it. You do not have to listen to a radio program of stupid, banal music. But you cannot see your movies without being compelled to listen.

In this special regard I sometimes wonder greatly at music critics. They take infinite pains with the molding of public taste, at least insofar as the concert hall and the symphonic radio program is concerned, but they absolutely ignore the most important thing of all, the background movie score.

In 1950, Lawrence Morton conducted a series of interviews with film composers for *Music from the Movies*, the long-running CBC Radio Network program produced in Toronto by Gerald Pratley. George Antheil was at that time working on his opera *Volpone* while also writing the score for the Humphrey Bogart film *Sirocco* at Columbia. Here is part of the Morton-Antheil interview:

MORTON: When you are working simultaneously on opera and film music, Mr. Antheil, do you find yourself leading a kind of Jekyll and Hyde existence? Do you have to keep your operatic right hand ignorant of what your left hand is doing in the studio?

ANTHEIL: No, not at all. I write all my music with my right hand, whether it's a film score or a symphony. Opera and film music, as a matter of fact, are very closely related, both being in the same category of theater music. They are far less separated from each other than they are from another large category—music for the concert hall. Of course all these categories intertwine, and their techniques and styles are transferable.

MORTON: Are there any specific film techniques that you can carry over into the field of opera?

ANTHEIL: Yes, there are several. One is the technique of underscoring. In the old operas the voice and the orchestra always go together, and even when they are musically "counterpointed" they are still, in a dramatic sense, presenting different aspects of the same pattern. This is not so in the films. The characters in a film drama never know what is going to happen to them, but the music always knows. Hence, an orchestral commentary is possible, but it can comment on the action without necessarily illustrating it. Film music can go against the voice—that is, against the dialogue—and also against the action. I did this in my early operas, and I was interested to notice that Menotti does it in *The Consul*, which I saw in New York recently. Much of Menotti's music is underscoring, and consequently it sounds a great deal like film music.

MORTON: One of the most characteristic techniques of film music is the montage where, in perhaps a minute of film, the accumulative action of days or years is reviewed in quick camera shots. Can this technique be used in opera?

ANTHEIL: Yes, I used it in my opera *Transatlantique* in 1927. It's more a staging problem than a musical one, however.

MORTON: Let's shift into reverse here. Can you use operatic techniques in the films—the aria form, for instance?

ANTHEIL: Well, in opera an aria is most often a way of letting a character express lyrically his feelings about a certain dramatic situation. We do this in films very often. We might write a string melody with an orchestral accompaniment, to be played behind dialogue or a long speech. If there is time enough, the music can take on the actual force of an aria.

MORTON: Yes, I can see how this is possible in a lyric scene. But what about a highly dramatic one requiring the kind of expressiveness in, say, the "Credo" in Otello, or "Vesti la giubba"?

ANTHEIL: That is also possible for the screen. In a recent score of mine, *Knock On Any Door*, there was just this kind of a scene. A boy is standing on a roof, watching on the street below the funeral of his sweetheart, who had committed suicide. He can't go to the funeral because he is hiding from the police. The music I wrote for the scene was a kind of aria—an aria of despair and hatred. Of course there was no dialogue here and the soundtrack was clear. It is in scenes like this that film music functions most effectively when it is doing something that neither speech nor photography is doing.

MORTON: Generally, Mr. Antheil, you have been highly critical of Hollywood music, though less so here tonight than in your book. Do you believe film music has a hopeful future?

ANTHEIL: Indeed I do. The problems of film music are very exciting. The composer is constantly challenged by dramatic situations which, however commonplace they may seem, all have their own peculiar and individual flavor. You have to have a real dramaturgical instinct. And there are purely musical problems, too, that keep a composer on his toes. Because there are so many short pieces in a film score, you have to find a way to make them stick together. There has to be cohesion, just as there is in any other music. The most difficult job of all is to make it sound like music, not sound effects. The very fact that there are problems in film music is what gives one hope for it. If there were no problems, the same thing would happen to film music as happened to old-fashioned opera. Opera died because composers had licked all the problems, and the whole form became a cliché. That is why composers today are trying to write operas of a new kind. Shows like *South Pacific* and operas like *The Consul* are tremendously important in the search for new operatic techniques. Films are very quick in taking up new trends in the entertainment world. And I believe that out of such trends there will eventually come a way of writing opera directly for the screen—with music in the driver's seat.

Virgil Thomson

Virgil Thomson (1896-1989) wrote only six film scores, and only one for a theatrical feature—*The Goddess*, made in Hollywood in 1958. Thomson's reputation rests upon his work for three documentaries: *The Plow that Broke the Plains*, *The River*, and *Louisiana Story*. He reworked all three scores into concert suites, and they have each been widely performed and recorded. Each is a monument of film music.

Thomson, born in Kansas City, Missouri, was a vital force in American music as a composer, author, and music critic. From 1940 to 1956 he was a music critic for the *New York Herald Tribune*, and his columns had considerable bearing on American musical matters.

In 1936 he was asked by the Resettlement Administration to score their documentary *The Plow that Broke the Plains*. Produced by Pare Lorentz, the film dealt powerfully with the glory and the desolation of the Great Plains. The narration begins: "This is a record of the land, of soil rather than people . . . the four hundred million acres of wind-swept grasslands that spread from the Texas Panhandle to Canada . . ."

The film outlines the history of the region, starting with the cattle empires, the coming of the railroad and the immigrants, and the evolution of the land into farms and vast fields of wheat. The story builds and builds, and then crashes with the stock market di-

Virgil Thomson, extreme right, at the recording of his *Louisiana Story* suite. To his left is recording engineer Robert Fine. Seated are Helen Van Dongen, conductor Eugene Ormandy, and producer Robert Flaherty.

saster of 1929 and the devastating drought of the mid-thirties. The ruined settlers of this immense man-made dust bowl fought their barren lands until their stock, their machinery, and their homes were finished. Then, like their ancestors, they packed up and moved West. Thomson's music for this documentary reflects the joy and the despair, the grandeur and the desolation in every frame. The score is epic Americana, involving hymnal passages, blues, and settings of folk melodies, in addition to descriptive passages for pastoral scenes and human activity.

A year later, Virgil Thomson was again approached by the government, this time the Farm Security Administration, to supply music for *The River*, another documentary produced by Pare Lorentz. The river in question was the Mississippi, and Thomson gave it a tonal setting that mixed original composition with folk themes. The concert suite derived from the score is in four movements and closely follows the progression of the music as it was used in the film.

There are four movements: The Old South, evocative of the area and its history; Industrial Expansion in the Mississippi Valley, describing scenes of new factories and the new way of life they bring; Erosion and Floods, poignant and slightly dissonant; and the Finale, bright and optimistic. The four movements constitute a symphony, and is a masterly example of the use of colorful scoring in a documentary of great scope and skillful construction. However, it's well to bear in mind that few films allow for that musical scope. It is easier to maintain musical forms in documentaries than in theatrical features because the former often allows for elongated lines and the latter usually does not.

Louisiana Story is even more of a musical subject than Thomson's previous vehicles. Made by Robert Flaherty in 1948, the film was shot in the Bayou region of Louisiana, among the French-speaking residents of the area, the Acadians, or "Cajuns" as they call themselves. *Louisiana Story* is much more atmospheric than dramatically narrative, and Thomson had ample opportunity to use music freely. Interestingly, and exceptionally, the recording of the musical track was made by forty-one members of the Philadelphia Orchestra conducted by Eugene Ormandy. The storyline tells of a young boy's adventures in the Bayou swamps, and his wonderment at the coming of modern machinery—an oil-well crew with drilling rigs and bulldozers—into his backwoods domain.

Thomson derived two orchestral suites from his score for *Louisiana Story*: one is a slightly expanded version of his original, descriptive music; the other is a group of his charming settings of melodies native to the region. The latter suite, the most popular of the two, is titled *Acadian Songs and Dances*. Thomson selected the tunes from Irene Therese Whitfield's collection of *Louisiana French Folk Songs*. The tunes in that collection were composed only of bare melodic lines, so Thomson could use his taste and skill to bring them to orchestral life. This he did not only deftly, but delightfully.

The other suite is divided into movements: Pastorale, the opening music of the film, describes the boy as he glides through the swamps in his little homemade canoe; later it describes the maneuvers of the amphibious oil-drilling buggies. Chorale is the music that accompanies the boy as he plays in a tree top with his pet raccoon, and then as he watches the oil barge approaching. Passacaglia Fugue is the chromatic music that accompanies the boy as he fights to land an alligator he has hooked with his fishing rod.

Thomson's score for *Louisiana Story* won him the Pulitzer Prize for Music in 1949. The music for the film succeeds on every level—as an outstanding composition, as skillful orchestration and as a fascinating treatment of indigenous musical material. Aside from their functional value, these three documentary scores by Thomson attain that utmost criterion of film music—the ability to stand by itself when divorced from the film.

Aaron Copland

Aaron Copland was a well-established and respected composer when he first turned his attention to film scoring. In 1939, he supplied the music for a documentary that was presented at the New York World's Fair, *The City*, a free-flowing impression of contemporary American life. Copland later extracted and rewrote two sections of this score for his concert suite *Music for Movies*. The titles given to the movements are self-explanatory, "New England Countryside" and "Sunday Traffic." The same suite also contains two movements from Copland's *Of Mice and Men*, his first score done in Hollywood. For *Of Mice and Men*, Copland wrote music that was suggestive of California ranch life. Some of the melodies have a simple, folksong-like character, the kind itinerant workers themselves might have whistled. The two sections of this score that Copland uses in his *Music for Movies* suite are "Barley Wagons" and "Threshing Machines." The first piece has a pastoral quality, as the wagons move across the fields, while the other is a fairly obvious piece of sound picturing done in a rhythmic, happy style.

Shortly after scoring *Of Mice and Men*, Copland was contracted to provide music for Thorton Wilder's *Our Town*, perhaps the definitive example of Americana. "Grover's Corner," the major theme of this score, was also included in *Music for Movies*. This theme

Aaron Copland

and other sections of the score were later fashioned into a short suite, much performed and several times recorded. The first five notes of the main theme make a melodic statement that beautifully pinpoints Wilder's story, while the whole score has a misty quality that delicately underlines the poignancy of the film. Copland evokes the atmosphere of the small town, the gentleness of life, the sadness, the remoteness. In short, Copland's score for *Our Town* is entirely appropriate to the visual.

Copland's next score was for a now almost-forgotten film called *The North Star*. Produced in 1943 by Samuel Goldwyn, it was one of Hollywood's rare cinematic tributes to the Russian war effort, which is the reason the film has virtually vanished. The film demanded more from Copland than any other film on which he worked, and it kept him busy for half a year. In addition to the background score, Copland wrote a number of songs and dances, which covered a huge emotional canvas of war, love, and comedy.

The chief problem was style:

> I wasn't sure how Russian the music should be. It was something of the same problem that Shostakovich would have had if he had been asked to supply a score for a movie set in the United States.

Copland wisely decided that since the American actors weren't speaking with Russian accents, he wouldn't overdo the Russian tone of his score. But the picture was not well received, and Copland realized that it is impractical to pour a great deal of time, hard work, and creativity into a dud film.

In 1945, Copland wrote the score for a documentary produced by the United States Office of War Information. *The Cummington Story* required that Copland once more underscore life in a rural New England town, but this time the theme was a contemporary one and made a plea for tolerance.

In 1949, Copland composed what is possibly his magnum opus film score, *The Red Pony*. The film was untypical for Republic Pictures since they specialized in purely program pictures, largely Westerns, and it is to the credit of the producers that they turned out a thoroughly good film. Having purchased the rights to a story by a master American writer, John Steinbeck, they decided to hire another American master to write the score. It was, however, no long-shot gamble since it depicts a rather idealized concept of Western American life—the young boy growing up on a horse ranch.

Shortly after completing the score for *The Red Pony* Copland decided to adapt it into a concert suite, and it has become one of his most popular pieces.

> Steinbeck's *The Red Pony* is a series of vignettes concerning a ten-year-old boy called Jody and his life in a California ranch setting. The story gets its warmth and sensitive quality from the

character studies of the boy, his grandfather, the cowhand Billy Buck, and Jody's parents. The kind of emotions that Steinbeck evokes in his story are basically musical ones since they deal so much with the unexpressed feelings of daily living. In shaping the suite I recast much of the material so that, although all the music may be heard in the film, it has been reorganized as to continuity for concert purposes.

The suite from *The Red Pony* has six movements. "Morning on the Ranch" suggests daybreak and the simplicity of country life. "The Gift" depicts the boy's surprise when his father gives him a pony. "Dream March" and "Circus Music" describe the boy's day-dreams—his imagined adventures as a knight in silver armor and as a ringmaster. "Walk to the Bunkhouse" points up the boy's admiration for Billy Buck, " . . . a fine hand with horses." "Grandfather's Story" underlines an old man's reminiscences about his days as a young man and his bitterness over the disappearance of the spirit of the Old West. "Happy Ending" restates the gentle folk-like themes of the score's opening in a bolder and happier vein.

Aaron Copland won an Oscar for his score for *The Heiress* (1949); the award, in this case, carried a marvelous ironic twist with it. After Copland had recorded the score and returned to New York, the front office at Paramount (producer-director William Wyler must have been the main voice) decided to remove Copland's title music from the picture and replace it with an arrangement of the song "Plaisir d'Amour," which was also featured in the course of the storytelling. Copland wrote to the press disclaiming responsibility for that part of the score. Just how much this damaged the picture is hard to tell; certainly it ruined Copland's intentions of setting the tone and character of the story. Copland's original title over-ture sets a marked tragic-dramatic mood, suggestive of the compli-cated life of the young woman who is thwarted by a domineering father and cheated by a shallow lover. The title music in any film is the one spot in the score where a composer can employ strictly musical form to summarize the content of the film. Copland in this instance, like the heiress herself, was thus badly cheated. It was a brutal professional insult, yet one with a strange rebound when it became the only occasion when a composer won the coveted gold statuette of the Academy of Motion Picture Arts and Sciences for a score minus its title overture, which is usually the only part of a score the majority of filmgoers ever consciously hear.

Copland's music for *The Heiress* is especially interesting in that it reveals his research into music that was current in New York in 1850. He chose several pieces of the period, including Gossec's "Gavotte," Ketterer's "Queen of the Flowers," and several little dance pieces of unknown authorship. To this he added a number of his own compositions cast in the same genre.

The score has two levels—foreground music and background, with both helping to tell the story. It is also the only Copland film score in which he has used the operatic device of giving the principal characters a musical motif and then varying it according to the shifts of revelation in the story. Copland mostly disapproves of the leitmotif device in film scoring but felt it was necessary in *The Heiress* since the story is a series of character studies, principally the main character of the woman whose personality moves from innocence and timidity through love and disappointment to bitterness and reclusiveness. Copland declined to concertize the score, feeling that, eloquent though it might be in the picture, it didn't lend itself to divorcement.

The fact that Copland had won an Oscar and was quite clearly the foremost American composer made little impression upon the Hollywood producers. Copland never again worked in Hollywood after *The Heiress*, and it was fifteen years before he scored another film. This was a film made in New York by Jack Garfein, starring his then-wife, Carroll Baker. It's title—*Something Wild*—fairly describes this not-very-successful picture about a young girl raped in a Brooklyn park and then imprisoned by a brute of a garage mechanic. A none-too-convincing "beauty and the beast" story, the most interesting aspects of *Something Wild* are the glimpses of New York and Copland's musical accompaniment. Rather than allow the score to pass into oblivion along with the film, Copland wisely rewrote it into the compelling symphonic suite *Music for a Great City*.

Copland was frequently asked about writing film music, the implication being that it is somewhat degrading for a serious composer to be thus employed—a composer of stature writes for films only for the high pay. Copland squashed this argument immediately:

> I would do it even if it were less well paid and moreover, I think most composers would, principally because film music constitutes a new musical medium that exerts a fascination of its own. Actually, it is a new form of dramatic composition and it opens up unexplored possibilities, or should.

What bothered Copland about writing for films was its being taken so much for granted by most moviegoers:

> Five minutes after the termination of the picture they couldn't tell you whether they had heard music or not. What is lacking here is a proper attitude. One's appreciation of a work of art is partly determined by the amount of preparation one brings to it, and since they should be encouraged not to ignore the music; on the contrary, I would hope to convince them that by taking it in they will enrich both their musical and their cinema experience. Hopefully, some day the term "movie music" will clearly define a specific musical genre and will not have, as it does have nowadays, a pejorative meaning.

Alex North

Another serious American composer highly respected by the Hollywood music community was Alex North. This mild-mannered, soft-spoken, and completely unpretentious man was referred to by the younger composers as The Boss. North, who received an Oscar nomination for his first score, *A Streetcar Named Desire* (1951), was a composer of depth and substance whose music is less obvious than most. He went on to score films as varied as *The Member of the Wedding* (1953), *Spartacus* (1960), *The Rose Tattoo* (1955), *Cleopatra* (1963), *Who's Afraid of Virginia Woolf?* (1966), and *The Agony and the Ecstasy* (1965).

Alex North was born in Philadelphia in 1910 of Russian parents. As a youngster in a poor family, North won a scholarship to study piano at the Curtis Institute of Music, which led to his winning another scholarship to the Juilliard School of Music in New York. It was a four-year course in composition:

> To support myself I learned to be a telegraph operator, and I worked from six in the evening until two in the morning, and then went to Juilliard during the day. After three and a half years of this my health descended to the breaking point.

Alex North (photo by David Kraft)

In his desperation, North hit upon a wild idea: at the time (1934), the Russian government was in dire need of skilled artisans, and they were openly inviting engineers, scientists, technicians, and doctors to work in the Soviet Union, all expenses paid. North went to the Soviet agency in New York and allowed them to assume that he was a telegraphic engineer:

> I wanted to go somewhere where my musical education could be subsidized. I was attracted to the idea of studying in Russia, partly because I idolized Prokofiev. The Russians probably thought I would rework their telegraphic system for them, but after a couple of weeks in Moscow I was put to sorting nuts and bolts. They were about to send me home, but they were intrigued when I said I was a composer and wanted to study music in Russia. They auditioned me at the Conservatory and I got in. I was there for almost two years; I had picked up a little Russian from my parents, who were born in Odessa, but I had an interpreter who came to the classes with me. But I gradually got home-

sick for American music. I remember one night playing a re-
cording of Duke Ellington's "Mood Indigo" and breaking into
tears. As a kid working in Atlantic City, I used to go to the
Steel Pier to listen to Paul Whiteman, Coon Sanders and Ted
Weems. I soaked up all kinds of jazz, and suddenly it hit me in
Moscow: I had to go home.

Back in New York in 1936, North studied with Ernst Toch, a
refugee from Germany. When Toch went to Hollywood to score
films he encouraged North to send his compositions to him. "He
was a beautiful man. He would comment on my music, correct
things, and send them back. It was a great help."

North also came into contact with Aaron Copland, who was
helpful in getting North work writing music for contemporary
American ballet companies.

> My first functional music was for modern dance. I wrote for
> Martha Graham, among others, and I joined the Federal The-
> ater Project, along with many other unemployed artists. I wrote
> music for their plays and this led to offers to score documentary
> films for commercial companies. Some years later I got to scor-
> ing films for the government, for the State Department, the
> Health Department, the Agriculture Department, etc. All in all
> about eighty such films, and it was hard going because these
> things, running from fifteen to thirty minutes, called for wall-
> to-wall scores—you started at the beginning and went nonstop
> to the end. It was a lot of experience.

North got to Hollywood through the influence of Elia Kazan.
He had been working in New York with Kazan and Arthur Miller
writing incidental music for the play *Death of a Salesman*. When
Kazan went to Hollywood to do the film *A Streetcar Named Desire*
at Warner Bros., he plugged for North to do the score. Kazan wielded

some power at that time and got the New York composer into that august music department.

North's score for *A Streetcar Named Desire* is a landmark in the history of Hollywood music because it was the first major jazz-oriented score, and its impact was instantaneous. Richly colored with the sound of New Orleans jazz, the music wailed and stung—it pointed up Brando's coarse Kowalski and tinged the delusion and despair of Vivien Leigh's Blanche.

Alex North felt that jazz has been abused by "pop" musicians and sadly neglected by most serious contemporary American composers:

> I tried to simulate jazz, to get its essence rhythmically and harmonically and apply it to drama. It was tailored. Some years previously I had done a similar thing when Benny Goodman commissioned me to write him a jazz concerto for clarinet and orchestra. It was introduced by Leonard Bernstein at New York City Center. The object was the same—to simulate jazz in a classical structure.
>
> Jazz is by far a more authentic indigenous ingredient of American music than the folk music which is expressed in mountain ballads and cowboy songs, which are, for the most part, of English and Scottish derivation. True, jazz has become commercialized to the degree where it has lost its freshness and spontaneity, but the jazz form should not be snubbed by composers because of its occasional maudlin wanderings into Tin Pan Alley. An attempt should rather be made to extract the essence and spirit of jazz and to project it with all the resources of craftsmanship at one's command to produce an end product which will have artistic integrity as well as emotional impact.

North's next major score, also with Kazan, was another with which he felt musically comfortable, a film in which he could use his own musical interests. This was *Viva Zapata!*, the story of the Mexican patriot Emilio Zapata.

I went to Mexico in 1939 when the Federal Theater Project folded. I went there with Anna Zololow and her ballet company. I stayed there two years and I was able to sop up their music. I met and studied with Silvestre Revueltas, to my mind the top Mexican composer, more interesting than Carlos Chavez because his roots were more indigenous to Mexico. He had a more earthy personality than Chavez; he would conduct in a blue denim shirt whereas Chavez would appear in full evening dress— I'm not knocking Chavez, he was a more social man and had to be in order to hold his position as Mexico's foremost conductor. But Revueltas was a marvelous person. I would go to his classes, and he might take his four or five students and go to a bistro and hold the class there. What I learned from him was invaluable when it came time to score *Viva Zapata!* because it's important when you write music based on the elements of another country's music to be able to feel it. I was also very fortunate with this film because Kazan hired me from the start of the production. He and I often wandered around our Mexican locations together, going from village to village. I would jot down little tunes I heard peasants humming or singing. This really was a luxury, this is ideal for a composer because you can work directly with the director and get to know exactly how he feels about the story. It doesn't happen very often.

Viva Zapata! contains some excellent musical moments. One occurs in the sequence where Zapata is arrested by four mounted policemen and led out of his village with a rope around his neck. As this happens, a man picks up two stones and taps them together, and other men in the village pick up stones and tap them in acknowledgment. A simple musical statement arises from this cadence of tapping stones. A group of villagers follow Zapata and the policemen and, as the group moves across the fields and into the hills, small groups of men trickle into a growing stream of men silently and passively walking alongside and behind Zapata. The music grows in scale and intensity as the number of men increase, and it reflects their purpose and their pride. Eventually it becomes a full statement as both the men and the policemen realize the situation. The music stops as the chief policeman halts his men, dismounts, and takes the rope from Zapata's neck. The sequence to this point has been devoid of dialogue; its long pictorial sequence is impressive in itself but made magnificent by the use of music.

Another of the musical highlights of *Viva Zapata!* came about through the insistence of Kazan:

> In the scene near the end where Zapata is to be assassinated, the sound effects men prepared their track, the sounds of horses and soldiers, but when Kazan heard the music for the scene he told them to hold back, that he didn't want to hear horses or footsteps, that he wanted the music to carry the scene up to the point where the massive fusillade of shots cuts Zapata to pieces. This was unusual because the emphasis is almost always placed on realism in terms of sound in films. Music and sound effects are too often in conflict, with the music losing. I prefer to have one thing or the other. I have sometimes suggested that sounds be used in favor of music, but the attitude of producers seems to be that they are paying you to write music, so go ahead and write it—it can always be thrown out later. This attitude results in many films being over-scored, and this is unfair to the composer because he has, or should have, a knowledge of what is dramatically right.

Alex North's musical preference in films is for small subjects, those that are intimate and personal. For all that, he has been assigned some of Hollywood's weightiest epics—*Spartacus, Cleopatra, The Agony and the Ecstasy,* and *The Shoes of the Fisherman.*

> What I try to do in these cases is to personalize the films as much as possible, to concentrate on the character relationships; *Cleopatra* was interesting because I was working for Joe Mankiewicz, who is a musically sensitive man. This was another exceptional experience because I was able to go to Rome and watch them shoot. Usually the composer is brought in at the end of the picture so that they don't have to pay him from the start. Mankiewicz felt differently; he wanted me to be there and amalgamate my ideas. I was able to do some research on music of the period, and I tried to simulate the musical sounds of what I thought might have prevailed at the time.

Mankiewicz was pleased with North's score for *Cleopatra.* Alluding to one point in the film, he remarked, "As the muted trumpets scream, in Antony's name, for honorable death, they scream an anguish that cannot be written, in a voice no actor can project."

North felt that writing for huge spectacles was difficult for him because he likes to identify with the film and its characters:

> Spectacles call for writing that is objective in character. I prefer to be subjective. I like to say something that has to do with myself personally and mold it so it fits the content of the film. I write best when I can empathize. When you can't do that, then you have to fall back on technique and write programmatic music. Each picture calls for its own solution. I remember being stunned when I looked at *The Agony and the Ecstasy.* It was so pictorially vast. How can you illustrate with music anything so magnificently illustrative as the ceiling of the Sistine Chapel? I did a lot of research into music of the Renaissance period, particularly Gabrieli. I listened and I listened and I arrived at a concept. I

decided to stay close to that style and interject my own manner of writing.

North had to return to more or less the same location some years later to score *The Shoes of the Fisherman* (1968), an expensive, earnest, but ultimately unsuccessful picture. This film also demanded a broad palette, calling for a musical depiction of modern Rome and, in contrast, melodic ideas in modal style for the more intimate moments of the Pope and his loneliness. The theme for the Pope posed a problem for North because the producer insisted on a Russian theme, in as much as the Pope in this story was Russian:

> I resisted this; the dramatic theme of the picture seemed to me to be much broader—it had to do with a possible clash between Russia and China, the possible devastation of the world. But the composer is an employee, and I did write a Russian theme for the Pope. I thought it was wrong and I still do. I don't think it means much dramatically when you see the Pope when he is alone and troubled and you hear a simple Russian theme. However, your own ideas don't always prevail, you must compromise.

A favorite score of North's was the one he wrote for *The Rose Tattoo*. Although set in the South, the principal character is a Neapolitan woman, played to the hilt by Anna Magnani.

> This is what I mean by an intimate story. A woman of great personality. I could color the music in a Neapolitan fashion and the performance allowed for humor, lightness, and pathos. It gave me a great range musically to say what I had to say. Another film I enjoyed scoring was John Ford's *Cheyenne Autumn* (1965), unfortunately a flop but a film with admirable intentions. It dealt with the tragic migration of Indians and their hardships. I felt great sympathy with the story—I had an emotional reaction to it. That's one of the joys of writing functional

music, if you can identify with your subject. This was especially interesting because it allowed me to study Indian music. It's not a case of using the music per se, it's a matter of letting it seep into the recesses of your mind so that when you sit down to write, the subconscious is permeated with the sound and the style of that music.

One of Alex North's finest scores was for Mike Nichols' excellent screen version of *Who's Afraid of Virginia Woolf?*, with Elizabeth Taylor and Richard Burton giving full force to Ernest Lehman's scenario based on the Edward Albee play. North was a rather diffident man by nature, and his initial reaction to many films is one of self-doubt. This is uncommon among Hollywood composers, especially in a man with such command of interpretive music. He told Nichols that the picture was so intense and so full of brilliant dialogue that it hardly needed music. Nichols didn't agree and hounded North to come up with a musical solution.

I thought I would try a jazz approach, but I was soon unhappy with that and threw out the idea. Maybe a twelve-tone score would work? No, that was too abstract for so personal a story. The solution came from my own rather romantic concept of the man-woman relationship, and I decided on a quasi-baroque feeling, one that would play against the picture and suggest that these people basically had something going for them despite the fact they were haggling and fighting—a common problem in society today. The obvious thing to have done was to write *schrecklich* (cruel, fierce) music to go along with the hysteria and the violent situations, but I thought something rather pure would work. I wanted to get to the soul of these people and suggest they were really meant for each other. Frenetic music would have tipped the scales too much in one direction. You have to let the scenes play themselves.

Scoring films was never easy for Alex North. It was serious work, and he always sought to provide music that delved into the character of the film. He was meticulous and painstaking—and he paid a price for it. In 1968 North was deeply hurt when Stanley Kubrick decided not to use his score for *2001: A Space Odyssey* and opted instead to use recordings of classical pieces. North put the music away and declined to let anyone hear it. However, a few months before his death in 1991, he agreed to a recording. This was done two years later with Jerry Goldsmith conducting London's National Philharmonic Orchestra. The consensus is that the score is a remarkable composition and would have made an impressive film even more impressive. The music is noble, elegant, and richly original. Says Goldsmith, "I was deeply touched and honored when Alex asked me if I would conduct it. My respect for him was more than musical. He was a rare blend of creative talent, compassion, and humanity."

Elmer Bernstein

The most dynamic and productive film composer to emerge in the 1950s was Elmer Bernstein, a man of enormous energy and vitality whose good fortune was to be gifted with a strong sense of theater and a seemingly endless pool of melodies.

Some of Bernstein's themes, particularly those for *The Man with the Golden Arm* (1955), *Walk on the Wild Side* (1962), *The Magnificent Seven* (1960), *To Kill a Mockingbird* (1963), and *The Great Escape* (1963), are among the most familiar examples of film music. The criticism that his overall output is somewhat uneven is true of all film composers who write for a vast number of pictures. This was true of Steiner and Tiomkin; the strain of writing four and five major scores a year is possibly too much for any composer. Bernstein, given worthy vehicles like *Summer and Smoke* (1961) and *Hawaii* (1966) has proven himself to be a master of the medium.

Bernstein's interest in composition grew from his study of the piano. His affinity for the piano was apparent at an early age, and by the time he was twelve he wanted to be a concert pianist. His piano teacher noticed that the boy was always improvising, and rather than discourage the tendency, as some piano teachers are wont to do, this teacher was wise enough to seek a qualified opinion. Bernstein, at thirteen, was taken to see Aaron Copland, who was sufficiently impressed to send the boy to one of his own pupils, Israel Sitkowitz. Bernstein's teenage years were spent in a formal study of composition, while maintaining the study of the piano. He later studied piano with Henrietta Michelson at the Juilliard School of Music and composition with Stefan Wolpe and Roger Sessions. His budding career as a concert pianist was interrupted when he was inducted into the Army in 1943.

It was during his military service that Bernstein was introduced to the art of scoring incidental music. Bernstein was assigned to write orchestral arrangements of folk songs like "Blue Tail Fly" and "Sweet Betsy from Pike" for Major Glenn Miller and the Army Air Force Band. From this came the chance to score a dramatic radio program for the Armed Forces Radio Service. That was the hook. By the time Bernstein got out of the service he had written nearly eighty scores for radio.

After the war, he resumed his career as a concert pianist. As a result of his experience with the Armed Forces Radio Service, in 1949 Bernstein was asked to write the music for a United Nations Radio documentary about the armistice the UN had effected in Israel. Henry Fonda was the narrator and the program was carried by NBC. From this came an offer from writer-producer Norman Corwin to score one of his impressive radio programs, which in turn brought an offer from Hollywood.

Elmer Bernstein began his Hollywood career in 1951 by scoring two undistinguished films for Columbia, *Saturday's Hero* and *Boots Malone*. By his third score, *Sudden Fear* (1952), it was obvious to the composer and those who employed him that he had found a natural niche. His music for *Sudden Fear*, a Joan Crawford melodrama, revealed characteristics that would mark his work in this medium—the use of some of the more exotic instruments; the use of solo instruments, like the piano and the flute; and the use of

Elmer Bernstein receiving the 1988 Career Achievement Award of the Society for the Preservation of Film Music, with the previous year's recipient, George Duning, presenting the award.

smaller instrumental groupings, a thinning out of the concerted form that was prevalent at that time.

Bernstein is, among other things, one of the most articulate of film composers. What follows is the text of an interview conducted by the author with Bernstein for the Canadian Broadcasting Company. The author's questions are in italics.

How did the musical atmosphere of Hollywood in the early fifties appeal to you?

Greatly. It was exciting and intriguing. Bear in mind that the veterans were still operative—Steiner, Tiomkin, Newman, Herrmann and John Green were here and highly productive, Alex North had made a big impression, Franz Waxman was in full flower, so to speak. It was a kind of Golden Age, a Golden Age Plus. I say "plus" because we could look to the future with great hope at that time. Film music was a burgeoning art.

What attracted you to picture scoring?

I found it very exciting to be given a musical problem, solve the problem, and then hear the results almost instantly. In the past, writing symphonies was a long, laborious process, and even if the composer was lucky enough to get a performance, he might not ever hear the piece again. With film music you can write something and quickly find out if it functions in the situation. You know immediately if you've won or lost, and I've always found that very stimulating. People continually refer to the limitations of writing film music; actually, the limitations are not that severe. Every form has its limitations; if you write opera you are limited by the range of the human voice; if you accept the challenge of writing a three-part fugue you have to keep within the framework of a three-part fugue. Most composers become annoyed at this harping on the so-called limitations of writing film music. You could hardly call Prokofiev's score for *Alexander Nevsky* a limited composition, or Vaughan Williams' for *Scott of the Antarctic.* I don't hear much limitation in Korngold's music for *The Adventures of Robin Hood.*

But I can understand why people nowadays might think this way because there has been a change, largely for the worse, in scoring due to commercialization, promotion, the record business, etc. Let us say that theoretically film scoring is an open form of composition, and that it has done, occasionally still does, and always should give a capable composer ample opportunity. The film is a marvelous medium of composition. Composers have done things in films they couldn't get away with in any other medium. For a while, in that Golden Age, the best film composers were a kind of vanguard. Leonard Rosenman's twelve-tone score for *The Cobweb* in 1958 comes to mind. Millions of people heard the music and were affected by it, yet how many of them would have wittingly gone to hear a twelve-tone composition in a concert hall?

Are you concerned about the snobbism displayed by so many critics and music lovers toward film scoring? The stigma that seems to go with the job?

There is a stigma, yes. It's because we're attached to big business and an industry whose morals are, rightfully, suspect. That's a problem and you learn to live with it. Haydn was attached to the Esterhazy Court—that was his problem. As for the critics, you have to realize that they themselves are basically entertainers and they are writing to amuse rather than to analyze. I enjoy reading them. What we have to bear in mind is that few of us are qualified to criticize anything.

Why is it that the Hollywood composer comes in for heavier criticism than film composers from other places?

Simply because this is, or was, the major center of film production, turning out an enormous amount of product, and it was possible for a composer to work here and make a very good living without having to write for any other medium. This was not the case in London, Paris, or Moscow, where working composers worked for the theater, the stage, the concert hall and occasionally the film studios. Once a composer had established himself in Hollywood, especially if he was contracted to a studio, he hadn't time for much else but composing film music. It was therefore easier to draw a bead of criticism on him, but what the critics often overlooked was that such a composer had distinguished himself elsewhere before he took to the road to Hollywood.

Don't you also have to come to terms with the public? You can write a splendid score, but it's likely to be only that simple four-bar theme that they will remember.

That's a sore point. Yes, it's true and the composer has to learn to respect this because it is his job to communicate and if he can reach out and touch them with a four-bar theme, provided it is in keeping with the character of the film, so much the better. There are, of course, composers who look down their noses at this, but they most often are the ones who can't come up with an attractive four-bar theme. But here again, you must be careful. Sometimes music in a picture can do its emotional thing best when you don't have a melody. It's a tricky business—a melody can call attention to itself.

You have to be careful how you use melody in film scoring; the melody must be an absolute extension of what is taking place on the screen. For example, in *The Man with the Golden Arm* the main character, Frankie, was a man who wanted to be a jazz drummer, so I there tried to make that broad jazzy theme speak for his ambition, and by giving it a sad quality it also implied his frustration. He was a tormented man, a narcotics addict, and there are sounds in jazz-blues—wails, trumpet screeches—that are perfect for expressing anguish. The truly fascinating thing about scoring films is that it allows for any kind of music.

What are your views on the use of jazz in film scoring? The Man with the Golden Arm *is considered a landmark in jazz scoring, and you've used that kind of music in pictures like* The Rat Race *and* Walk on the Wild Side.

Out of respect for the field of jazz and the many gifted people who work in that field, I must say I've never considered myself to have written a jazz score. I've written scores that have used certain elements of jazz. In the case of *The Man with the Golden Arm*, I used the rhythmic elements, I used certain of the harmonic limitations that are inherent in jazz, but I never gave that free rein to the players, which is the thing that becomes jazz. So it was really a score that used jazz to color it. It's extremely difficult for jazz in the pure sense to become a film score because one of its greatest assets is its improvisatory quality, whereas a film score is one that must be very carefully thought out. However, there are times in scoring pictures when the kind of primitive excitement that is created by jazz can indeed be an asset.

It's odd how jazz is used mostly in films with connotations of sleaziness—crime, juvenile delinquency, drug addiction, etc. It hardly speaks well for jazz.

It doesn't speak well for jazz at all. One of our great problems is divesting ourselves of prejudices. We're born into a society that has inherited all sorts of prejudices—racial, religious, and even musical—and this one concerning jazz, like most prejudices, has its roots in truth or reality at some point. There's no question that at the time of the origin of jazz it was something that grew up in a rather sleazy atmosphere. But that was a long time ago and the prejudice has no relevance in contemporary terms. However, it is a subtle prejudice, and I find myself fighting it within myself. The times I've used jazz to color my music have been in films with sleazy atmospheres: *The Man with the Golden Arm* was about narcotics, *Sweet Smell of Success* dealt with some very unsavory characters in New York, and *Walk on the Wild Side* was largely set in a New Orleans house of ill repute. So I'm guilty, although I don't think it's necessary to use jazz in this way. It's simply something that is very difficult to avoid.

Let's talk about another kind of Americana, the turn-of-the-century, small Southern town milieu that Tennessee Williams conjured up in Summer and Smoke. *Was that much of a musical problem for you?*

Summer and Smoke posed great problems in composition because it was a story with very delicate balances. It's the story of a minister's daughter who is afraid of love and life in general, and her love for a young doctor who has lived a worldly life. The music had to reflect the effect they have on each other—she converting him to the realization that there is something within all human beings beside their own pleasures, and he opens up the door for her in the sense that she realizes she is a woman. But it was something that happened too late for her. Obviously, the emotional balances of a thing of this sort are very delicate, and the problem of the music was to portray something of the inner turmoil of these characters without stepping on the delicacy of the film or overshadowing it. I tried to write tenuous, shimmering music for the relationship of the two main characters within the broader framework of the period and the Southern locale, with the overall music tinged with a folksong-like quality. Again, it's a matter of coloring your music.

You revisited the South some years later with To Kill a Mockingbird, *although it was a very different kind of story, this one being mostly about a young boy and girl growing up in a small town. Your title melody was a simple piano statement, to my ears a very wistful kind of Americana.*

I remember that very well because it was difficult to do. The biggest problem was to make the initial decision about the musical evaluation of the picture. You have to decide what the music must do. Sometimes it's obvious. It was easy with *The Magnificent Seven* because the image was active and muscular. But *Mockingbird* was a more complicated story. Here you had two children with a father but no mother in a rather isolated community that is suffering from a racial disturbance. The father is a respected attorney. And there is also an eccentric neighbor of whom the children are afraid. What was the element to be discussed in the music? I decided to focus on the kind of particular and peculiar magic that is the imaginative world of a child. There's an unsophisticated mysticism about a child's imagination and it's a marvelous thing. Simplicity was the keynote. The score starts with just the right hand playing a simple melody, and I tried to orchestrate simply, with bell-like, harp-like sounds.

I was turned on immediately when I heard that melody.

Well, it sounds egocentric to say it, but I think you reacted that way because the music was right. It was one of those cases where I was fortunate enough to hit on exactly the right thing to do. And if you do something in any art form that is exactly right, everybody knows it instantly. It's very hard to fool people. They can be confused, but if something feels nice and right, they react to it instantly.

Isn't that the secret of film scoring—appropriateness?

Yes, but the roads to appropriateness, like the roads to hell, are paved with good intentions. Also, stylistically, what is appropriate changes from time to time. For instance, in the thirties and forties the writing of symbolic music was very popular—music that immediately tells you where you are, so to speak. And it was something at which Max Steiner had no peers. These are things that you would not do today because people want more sophisticated ways to create the same effect. And, of course, we are living through an anti-feeling period. It's a cool age, people don't want to be that emotionally involved, to be touched. Today a love scene scored with a beautiful melody for strings is likely to be scoffed at.

How about another film music problem—scoring pictures of scenic magnificence? How do you approach so pictorial a subject as Hawaii?

That was an interesting problem of another kind. I knew that part of the problem was to create something of the euphoric feeling we associate with the South Seas, although the real problem was that the music we associate with Hawaii is strictly twentieth century. What we now know as Hawaiian music isn't really Hawaiian at all, and it certainly had nothing to do with Hawaii of the nineteenth century. I recall a similar problem working on *The Ten Commandments*, in particular working the music for an Egyptian dance. We know what instruments they used, but Lord knows what they played on them. In doing my research for *Hawaii*, I found that the Hawaiians of the period had no melodic instruments at all, except for a little nose flute that would produce about three notes. They had a lot of percussion instruments like gourds and small drums, and they had chants, basic two- or three-note chants rocking back and forth between those notes. I used that characteristic in the score; in fact, the overture starts that way on the bass marimba. Well, from those meager resources I had to create a whole cloth, and it was almost pure invention. I must say it's one of the scores of which I'm proud, and I was especially pleased to have Hawaiians tell me it sounded Hawaiian to them. I'm very fond of Hawaii, and I suppose I was able to get that feeling across in the music.

Isn't it the composer's job to sympathize with a subject? To make some kind of appeal?

The job of the composer is really very varied. You must use your art to heighten the emotional aspects of the film; music can tell the story in purely emotional terms and the film by itself cannot. The reason it can't is that it's a visual language and basically intellectual. You look at an image and you then have to interpret what it means, whereas if you listen to something or someone and you understand what you hear—that's an emotional process. Music is particularly emotional—if you are affected by it, you don't have to ask what it means.

Film music is almost an idealization of the visual image?

Yes, even with a subject as kinetic as *The Magnificent Seven,* the moment you translate into music the scene of horsemen riding over the plains it becomes an emotional accompaniment to the action. That's part of the fun of being a film composer, that you are reaching people at a subliminal level, where they are relatively defenseless. That's an exciting thing because you can make people feel a certain way, even though they may not understand why they feel that way. Film music does its job best when it deals with what is implicit in the picture, not what is explicit. And this calls for a special attitude from the composer toward the concept of listening on the part of the audience—he must expect them to listen to music in a different way than if he were writing for the concert hall. However, being musically implicit presupposes that you have a film with certain depths. Sometimes a film is so simple-minded that nothing is implicit, it's all explicit—and that's the hardest kind of film to score because you find yourself being so straightforward that you have to strain to avoid being dull.

Suppose this was a classroom of film music students: how would you illustrate, from your own work, this business of writing music that is implicit?

I would pick a score I wrote in 1956 for a film called *Men in War*. This posed a fascinating problem. It was a simple story of a beleaguered platoon in Korea; they can't get back to their lines; they're moving through enemy territory; the men are tired, nervous, etc. It was a good picture but yet another war film. What was there to say? Then something struck me: the men were moving through beautiful wooded countryside with death and danger on every side. Nothing I could write could make the danger any more obvious than it already was on film. What I decided to do was comment on the beauty of the surroundings, the hidden beauty of the woods, the birds, the pastoral feeling . . .

You wrote against the picture.

Right. I wrote what was implicit, and something you might not have noticed without the music. That to me is the best use of music in a film because it gives another dimension, something it might not otherwise have had. If you can allude to something more than is seen on the screen, you can make a valuable contribution to a film.

This is something that doesn't seem too obvious to many film producers. Isn't there a gulf between producers and composers?

You can't live in this community and work at writing music for films without realizing that the accent is definitely on the "pop" song and not on the art of scoring. One has to censor oneself, to watch out for the tendency to please the producer rather than produce a good score. It's to be hoped that there are enough serious producers—those who are dedicated to making fine pictures—who will eschew the easy way out of looking for the hit song, the supposed easy way out. The reason I say supposed is that with all the best intentions in the world, that is probably the most difficult thing to do.

In 1972 you wrote an article for High Fidelity *entitled "Whatever Happened to Great Movie Music?" Is that question still relevant today?*

I think it's more relevant today than it was at the time I wrote the article. I said then that the art of scoring was being strangled by the search for effects, for new sounds. It still is. It seems unfortunate that in some pictures today interpretive music is not even called for. Films are more tracked than scored. Music is an adjunct rather than a part of the texture of the picture.

It's just very difficult to maintain principles in this society—moral principles, ethical principles, any type of principles. I think that the tide running against good music is so strong that none of us who care are surprised or outraged any more when we hear dumb music accompanying a film. We've become inured to it. Film has become, with some exceptions, a special effects medium. Films reflect the generally shoddy standards of present-day society. It's a junk culture, and people buy junk. Every once in a while you will encounter a truly stunning director, such as Steven Spielberg, who really understands the use of cinema and the function of music as one of its most important components. But generally speaking, film has not advanced in terms of taste and intelligence, and that makes it tough for music.

George Duning

Any account of American film music that did not include George Duning would be remiss. While lacking the distinct individuality of an Alex North, or the recognizable vitality of an Elmer Bernstein, his forty years in film scoring represent a perfect example of a composer doing an expert job while never calling a great deal of attention to his work. Or expecting attention. An affable and modest man, Duning is a personification of the old studio-system professional. By the time Duning retired in 1983 he had scored more than a hundred films. His five Academy Award nominations merely hint at the range of his accomplishments. Two were for musicals, *Jolson Sings Again* (1949) and *The Eddy Duchin Story* (1956), and three for dramas, *No Sad Songs for Me* (1950), *From Here to Eternity* (1952), and *Picnic* (1954).

Born in 1908, Duning never considered any career other than music. He majored in theory at the Cincinnati Conservatory of Music, where he excelled as a trumpeter. After playing with various jazz and dance bands, he turned to arranging. Duning's skill as a fast and inventive arranger won him the job as musical director for *Kay Kyser's Kollege of Musical Knowledge*, a post he held for eight years. It was with Kyser that Duning gained entry into the movie business. Kyser was under contract to RKO for a series of films

George Duning at Columbia in 1961

starting with *That's Right, You're Wrong* in 1939. The last of the Kyser musicals, *Carolina Blues*, was made at Columbia in 1943 and resulted in that studio putting Duning under contract as an arranger. However, within weeks he was inducted into the Navy for wartime service and spent the next three years arranging and conducting programs for the Armed Forces Radio Service.

After his discharge, Duning rejoined Columbia, where he gradually managed to move from orchestration into original composition. His first scoring assignment was for *Johnny O'Clock* (1947). For the next fifteen years, Duning, virtually Columbia's house composer, scored an average of a half dozen movies each year, scoring every conceivable kind of film.

> It was a wonderful job, and I had the great good fortune to work under a superb boss, Morris Stoloff, who was classically trained, in fact he had been a child-prodigy violinist, and who ran Columbia's music department the way he wanted it run. We conferred with directors and producers, but we didn't have them telling us what to do, which is too much the ways things are today. Young composers these days miss out on the kind of in-house training I was lucky enough to get.

Among the many Westerns scored by Duning, two merit study: *3:10 to Yuma* (1957) and *Cowboy* (1958), both written and directed by Delmer Daves, who, in all his Westerns, was more concerned with character than myth.

3:10 to Yuma is a story of conflict between an outlaw (Glenn Ford) and a family man (Van Heflin) who, badly in need of money, accepts the job of escorting the outlaw to jail. Duning, at Daves' behest, underlined the tension and the basic sadness of the story. For *Cowboy*, a lusty account of a trail drive, Duning wrote a lively score, basing much of it on traditional western songs.

Duning's background as a jazz and dance-band arranger was used to full advantage in *Bell, Book and Candle* (1958). This romantic comedy dealing with witchcraft allowed Duning a wide range of expression pointing up the antics of a gorgeous witch (Kim Novak), a befuddled publisher (James Stewart) with whom she falls in love, her wacky jazz-musician brother (Jack Lemmon), and her Siamese cat, Pyewacket:

It was an interesting challenge. It needed a strong central theme as well as shorter ones for the cat and the brother, and I also used some electronic trickery for the occult comedy. I recorded sounds on tape and speeded them up by using a variable mixer to alter the pitch. For the jazz sequences I was able to call upon some of the best musicians in town, including John Williams, who was at that time a pianist. Not all movies are fun to score. This one was.

The World of Suzie Wong (1960) was another challenge for Duning since it required a blending of mystic, exotic Oriental music with modern American themes, in addition to a goodly amount of jazz and dance music for the Hong Kong saloon settings. Duning deftly interpolates touches of the Chinese pentatonic scale into his love theme for the American (William Holden) and the sensuous, quixotic, and doomed bar girl (Nancy Kwan).

Duning scored another film dealing with emotionally clouded relationships—*Toys in the Attic* (1963), Lillian Hellman's tale of a pair of spinsters (Geraldine Page and Wendy Hiller) and their over-attachment to their wastrel young brother (Dean Martin). The sultry Southern atmosphere of New Orleans and the seething relationship between the characters was, as Duning puts it:

> . . . catnip for a composer. It offered an enormous range of musical expression, and for the main title I was able to come up with a lengthy, sensuous, blues-like melody, which I think set the tone for the piece.

It does indeed, and had not *Toys in the Attic* been a box-office flop, that theme would be more widely quoted as one of the most conspicuous examples of a purely American musical sound in film scoring.

The Indiana-born composer was honored on November 6, 1993, when it was declared George Duning Day at the Festival of Indiana Music held in Indianapolis. Selections from some of his film scores were performed, as well as the première performance of a new work for clarinet and chamber ensemble called *Clariflections*. The comment was made that it was the work of a composer who deserved to be much better known than he is, a comment that gets a general nod of approval in Hollywood.

Arthur Morton, who has for many years been Jerry Goldsmith's principle orchestrator, orchestrated most of Duning's scores during the Columbia years:

> Lest it seem strange to the layman that a man with George's ability as an orchestrator should himself use an orchestrator, it can be explained simply as a matter of time. The volume of composition in those days was great and George never took any easy means. And composition being the lonely job it is, I'm sure he found it a help to have a colleague. He has always had a shrewd sense of what would and wouldn't work in scoring films, of what you could and couldn't do. George is a first-class musician, and working with him was a pleasure.

HENRY MANCINI AND OTHERS

It was said of Arnold Schoenberg that the worst thing about him was the misguided enthusiasm of his disciples. A similar thing might be said of Henry Mancini. Mancini brought a fresh sound to film scoring in the late fifties, a sound more in tune with the times, which took advantage of new instrumentation and modern recording techniques. Mancini's deft sense of orchestration and his enviable gift for melody quickly made him the most sought-after musician in Hollywood. Unfortunately, his success persuaded all too many producers that the modern, "pop" sound was what films now needed—a persuasion heavily endorsed by the music publishers and record companies.

As Mancini saw it, there was nothing wrong with finding new ways of scoring provided they are appropriate. By 1970, the use of popular songs and rock music had become prevalent and, for the most part, inappropriate:

> We've become a nation of followers when it comes to fashionable trends. Scoring *The Graduate* with a string of songs by Simon and Garfunkel was an excellent device for that particular film, but it set off repercussions, just as I did myself with the use of jazz in *Peter Gunn*. For years after that, jazz was used in films for which it wasn't suited. As for integrity, we have the music departments thinking about the record album even before the picture is scored! It's the kind of thing where the tail is wagging the dog. I don't think the craft of film scoring is being furthered by this particular development.

Mancini was among the most adroit instrumentalists ever to work in films. His book *Sounds and Scores* is a widely used course in orchestration. His own instrument was the flute, an affinity that is apparent in his film scores. The Mancini recording orchestra always called for piccolo, flute, alto flute, and bass flute. He used the bass flutes effectively in dramatic segments of *Peter Gunn*. In *Mr. Lucky*, the TV series that followed *Peter Gunn*, Mancini often used the Hammond organ as the principal voice against a string section. In the opening scene of *Breakfast at Tiffany's* (1961), an amplified harmonica plays the "Moon River" melody as Audrey Hepburn gazes into Tiffany's windows. The combination of the instrument and the lonely image of the fragile beauty of Hepburn was incongruous, but it worked perfectly.

This imaginative use of instrumentation was perhaps Mancini's major contribution to scoring. In *Experiment in Terror* (1982), he employed two autoharps, one strumming the background for the other, which picked out the notes of the theme. This odd effect was used chillingly for each appearance of the film's asthmatic villain, played by Ross Martin.

Henry Mancini

In scoring the African adventure romp *Hatari!* (1961), Mancini had the studio piano slightly retuned in order to give an eerie quality to those sections of the score pertaining to the mysteries of the strange landscape. In the same picture, Mancini came up with one of his most popular themes, the one for the baby elephants. In the scene where Elsa Martinelli takes three little pachyderms to the lake to give them a bath, Mancini has a calliope play a boogie-woogie rhythm as a high E-flat clarinet plays a perky tune. The music is very much "foreground," and being aware of it makes the scene more enjoyable:

> I don't believe in this theory of music in films not being no-
> ticed—it must be noticed in its place. In this elephant sequence,
> as in the opening of *Breakfast at Tiffany's*, if I hadn't made my-
> self felt, I wouldn't have been serving the picture. You have to
> be felt at certain points. Where there is no dialogue, no sounds,

just the visual—you'd better say something interesting. I don't know who started this theory of the best film music being that which you don't notice, but it isn't true.

Mancini's concern with orchestration marked his film scores. In 1970, he produced two scores of widely different natures. For *The Hawaiians*, a sequel to *Hawaii*, Mancini, as had Elmer Bernstein beforehand, had to deal with the fact that there was barely any native Hawaiian music. However, this section of the epic story dealt with the Oriental influence on the islands, and this was the theme Mancini seized upon. To get an authentic, ethnic flavor he used a number of ancient Chinese and Japanese instruments and hired several experts to play them. Included in the score were extended passages for the cheng (a Chinese zither known to have been in existence for five centuries), the hsun (a Chinese ocarina), the hichiriki (the Japanese oboe), the santure (an oriental cymbalum), plus kotos and the Chinese flute. The score is possibly the most interesting thing about *The Hawaiians*.

Mancini next went to England to record his music for *Salem Come to Supper* (*The Night Visitor*), a thriller shot in Denmark in the dead of winter. He used an orchestra of only seventeen pieces: twelve woodwinds in threes, and five keyboards—an organ, two pianos and two harpsichords, with one piano and one harpsichord tuned a quarter-note flat. Mancini felt this was good for establishing the mysterious atmosphere, the winter scene, and the chilling characters in the film. A large orchestra was unnecessary.

The assumption might be that a man as abundantly endowed with music as Henry Mancini might have been born humming, and crawling to the piano while still in diapers. The assumption would be false:

> I was forced into music by my father. He started me on the piccolo when I was eight, and I was later railroaded into the Sons of Italy band in my hometown—Aliquippa, Pennsylvania. It was

always Dad's prodding and persistence that made me practice. He and my mother were Italian immigrants. At the time he came over, the American Dream was still "on the charts" so to speak— I don't know where it is now. But he was enamored of the idea that his son wouldn't have to go into the steel mills and work as he did. He loved music and played the flute, and he made many sacrifices to send me to teachers and schools. I would never have had any interest without him, and I didn't start to enjoy music until I became interested in arranging. I then studied with Max Adkins, the conductor and arranger at the Stanley Theater in Pittsburgh, and a new world opened up for me. After graduating from the Aliquippa High School in 1942, I enrolled at the Juilliard School of Music in New York, but after a year there, Uncle Sam nabbed me for the service.

Mancini spent three years in uniform. With his release, he joined Tex Beneke's newly formed "Glenn Miller" styled orchestra as a pianist-arranger. Out of this job came Mancini's meeting with the woman who became Mrs. Mancini, singer Ginny O'Connor, then a member of the Meltones, Mel Tormé's group.

It was through Ginny that I started with film music. She and a singing group were hired to appear in a short film at Universal, and I was offered the job of arranging the music for it. I hit it off with Joe Gershenson, the director of music at Universal, and he asked me to do some work on an Abbott and Costello picture called *Lost in Alaska*. It was supposed to be a two-week job, but I ended up spending the next six years at Universal. That was where I served my apprenticeship: I worked on everything from Francis the Mule and Bonzo the Chimp to *The Glenn Miller Story* and *The Benny Goodman Story*. The best thing I did was the score for Orson Welles's *Touch of Evil*. I must have worked, in some capacity or other, on about 100 pictures. I had no control over what I did. I learned all the stock situations. I did all the cliché things and got them out of my system.

The six years Mancini spent at Universal was an apprentice-ship of enormous value, the like of which is no longer available. The lack of similar training is something to regret. Scoring is a delicate and intricate job, and the studios cannot provide the train-ing since they no longer support large musical staffs. Sadly, this situation also applies to many other areas of the entertainment in-dustry, where fledgling artisans have fewer outlets in which to learn while working.

During his years at Universal, Mancini studied composition with famous European exiles Mario Castelnuovo-Tedesco and Ernst Krenek, but:

> I found that for what I wanted to do, there was no real training other than actually doing it. I feel sorry for the young compos-ers coming into the business now because they are expected to be good immediately.

Mancini's stint at Universal came to an abrupt end—he was laid off. Unemployment was a new experience for him and turned out to be the turning point in his career. Producer Blake Edwards had a television idea, about an elegant private detective, and he needed a composer who could accept the budget limitations of the show to score it. Coming out of a barber shop, Edwards ran into Mancini and casually asked him if the job appealed to him. It did. *Peter Gunn* launched both Edwards and Mancini into the upper echelons of their respective trades.

Mancini's treatment of the *Peter Gunn* score was heralded as a new sound in film music, although he claimed he was unaware at the time that he was breaking new ground. He was too busy to notice.

> I had to make do with an eleven-man orchestra—that's all we could afford. That's how the unusual instrumentation came about, the use of the bass flutes, etc. I had to pull away from the old

string tremolo business. There's a certain direction movie music must take in order to stay alive; the large orchestra playing all the time is outmoded, and I was forced into this realization by doing *Peter Gunn*. The melodic approach is still valid, the Tchaikovsky-like melody is still wanted and needed, but the treatment of that melody has to be different, it has to be in keeping with our times. And we can do much more now, we have a vast instrumental world at our disposal and constantly evolving recording techniques.

According to Mancini, the Hollywood studios brought about their own downfall by turning out too many of the same kind of pictures, draining ideas and talents:

In my years at Universal, the studio was packaging around fifty films a year, mostly made for the same people. Musically there tended to be a sameness. Your thoughts became molded into thinking that the thirty-five-piece studio orchestra was the only means of scoring. Only occasionally would you go beyond that concept, and that was to increase the orchestra, not to decrease it. The general musical concept was one of bigness, lushness. The large orchestra was always used as a canvas. I think one of the reasons the *Peter Gunn* music caught the ear was its sparseness, the economy of the scoring. Up until then, economy had not been a major factor in filmmaking in California. It had been a super-rich industry, it was a mentality geared to abundance.

The Mancini experience also points to something that is not generally known about the Hollywood studios: they were behind the times. By the late fifties the methods of filmmaking were already becoming old-fashioned and much of the equipment was ancient, although kept in excellent running order. This was largely due to the impact of television on the film industry. The fifties were years of decline, years in which the television habit replaced the theater-going habit. With income down, the movie chieftains flailed around for ways to increase profits, to the extent that they created their own toughest competition by selling their old films to television and renting their facilities to television production companies. All the studios were abundantly equipped, but little thought was given to technological progress. Recalled Mancini,

> The quality of the recording in the film studios was way behind the quality in the studios of the various recording companies in Hollywood. There was a lethargy in the studio music departments. The record companies were using jazz men and guys coming off the road from dance bands. The film studios used jazz musicians with great reluctance, only if they had a score that called for jazz. They had the idea these men couldn't read music, they thought they would be lost when faced with classical pieces. Well, they eventually found out the classical pieces were the easiest for these fellows—they read anything, play anything. Most of the men I used scoring *Peter Gunn* were formerly with the great bands, and if it can be said that I had any influence, I think it was using good musicians to give personality to the music and having those musicians well-recorded. Initially, this was a great problem. We recorded *Peter Gunn* at Universal, and when I told the engineers I wanted a microphone put on the drums, one on the piano, and another on the bass, they looked at me as if I was crazy. This was 1958 and they still thought in terms of a single mike hung over the orchestra. I wanted people to be aware of musical detail in scoring. I didn't consider this exactly revolutionary because the record companies had already created a fresh, "alive" sound. But it took the film studios years to catch up.

Peter Gunn definitely had an effect on the use of music in other TV and feature films, but Mancini shied away from overstressing the importance of his influence.

There's a horrible tendency to pick upon one man and brand him as a trendmaker. These things get all out of proportion. For example, the Beatles weren't aware they were doing anything vastly different. I think they got more of a kick out of reading about what they were supposed to be doing than they did in doing it. I did a hundred segments of *Peter Gunn,* and all I could think about was getting the stuff done, getting it on, and getting to the next one. You do what you have to do and the discussion comes later.

I'm strong in the belief that a person has to have a point of view, a conviction. I'm convinced of the value of music on film, but my point of view is that it's only one part of a group effort. The legitimate composer has to answer only to himself; the film composer is a different animal—he must know where he fits in the scheme of filmic things. I'm constantly asked about what it takes to be a film composer, and I reply, "A sense of drama." I can't stress that too much, it's as important as the ability to compose. The ability to become part of something—to be able to help the picture and not get in its way. I know there's a lot of talk about film being an art. Actually, what we have here are a number of crafts having the ability to create art. We are craftsman, and we become artists if what we do is good enough. But I confess I feel that art has been attained rarely on the screen.

Filmmaking, especially in Hollywood, is fraught with an evil called "typecasting." This is apparent in the case of many popular actors, but it also applies to composers. Mancini had to fight against his own success in writing light and amusing music. Many of his films were purely entertainment assignments—comedies and romantic romps.

Occasionally Mancini showed the deeper side of his talent with such pictures as *The Days of Wine and Roses* (1962) and *Wait Until Dark* (1967). During 1969 and 1970, Mancini scored three big-budget vehicles, each calling for a wide range of composition: *The Molly Maguires, Sunflower,* and *The Hawaiians.* Unfortunately for him, all three were box-office disappointments. He felt, as do many, that *The Molly Maguires* was one of his best scores. Aside from the romanticism and the humor that is generally apparent in his music, there was also a hint of sadness noticeable in *The Molly Maguires.* The story is a tragedy set in the Pennsylvania coal fields in the 1870s. Mancini's score is a perfect complement to the imaginative photography of James Wong Howe, a genius with lighting and shading. The atmosphere is one of ugly beauty, and Mancini's main theme, played by an accordion, immediately speaks of remoteness and a wistful sadness.

Mancini's image as a composer of entertaining music was fostered by his secondary career as a recording artist. He was by far the foremost Hollywood composer-conductor active in the record world, recording a large portion of the music he wrote for films as well as the music of other composers. Mancini was an affable and modest man, little afflicted with the competitiveness that marked many musicians. Mancini's association with director-producer Blake Edwards evolved into something quite remarkable—Edwards had Mancini score twenty-two of his films, with *Victor/Victoria* (1982) a major success for both. Says Edwards, "I love going to scoring sessions and hearing what he has done. There are times when I feel he's embellished the effectiveness of the scenes by fifty percent, he's made them come more alive than I had imagined. A lot of my success is due to his scoring."

Henry Mancini wrote music for films for forty years, enjoying both success and popularity. His highly productive career came to a sudden end in early 1994 when he was diagnosed as having pancreatic cancer. He died on June 14th, only two months after his seventieth birthday.

Leonard Rosenman

Despite the increasing use of light, commercially oriented music in Hollywood films, several young composers of a more avant-garde persuasion managed to invade the colony with considerable success, in particular Leonard Rosenman, Jerry Goldsmith, and Lalo Schifrin. Their success tends to negate the decline of serious music in film scoring, although it is obvious that they would survive in any musical environment because they are about as knowledgeable about jazz and electronic music as they are the more cerebral contemporary forms of concert composition. If film scoring has a future, as it must, in spite of the epic ignorance and bad taste that swamps the industry, it will lie in the hands of this kind of composer.

Leonard Rosenman's entrée into the film world came at the behest of Elia Kazan, and he doubts he would have gained recognition without this invitation. Rosenman, born in New York in 1924, studied composition with Roger Sessions, Luigi Dallapiccola, and Ernst Bloch, with his musical sights set on the concert stage. He did some theater music in New York and was a resident composer at the Tanglewood festivals, where his chamber works were performed. Rosenman received a Koussevitsky commission to write an opera,

Leonard Rosenman

and, as with almost all serious modern composers, his income from composing had to be supplemented by teaching. One of his piano pupils was the young actor James Dean. When Dean was chosen to star in *East of Eden*, he suggested to Kazan, the director, that Rosenman might be the man to compose the score. A rapport was quickly established between the director and the composer when Rosenman asked that he be present during the entire filming, since he knew nothing about filmmaking and would prefer to make his sketches during the filming rather than afterward. Kazan then explained that he considered this the preferable way of working.

Rosenman's score for *East of Eden* (1955) was pleasing to the ear of the audience, but the tone is sparse and close in style to Alban Berg. The theme for Dean is spoken by woodwinds—two bassoons and two clarinets—and clearly conveys the loneliness of the Steinbeck character. The final scene of the picture—the death of the father—is one of the longest musical cues ever recorded, running almost ten minutes. All the main characters come together in this scene and Rosenman uses it as a musical chart, with the main themes in counterpoint as a comment on the conflicting characters. He said later,

> Kazan and I worked together to fit the music to the film. This is not the general practice because it's too expensive—and the studios don't care about music anyway. But I couldn't have done the job otherwise because I hadn't learned enough. I was very green. I remember going up to a little man at a desk in the music building at Warner Bros. and asking him, "Do you know what a click track is?" He said, "Yes, I invented it." The little man was Max Steiner.

Flushed with the success of his initial score, Rosenman chose to be even more daring on his next project, *The Cobweb* (1955).

> The film was directed by Vincente Minnelli, a man of taste and imagination, and produced by the very literate John Houseman. I told John I wanted to go all out and do a piece in my own style, and he gave his consent. The setting of the picture is a Midwest psychiatric clinic, where the staff seem almost as psychotic as the patients. The place is thrown into a tizzy over a seemingly trivial incident, the hanging of new drapes in the clinic's library, which initiates a mess of conflicts and jealousies. Those of us working on the film came to call them "the drapes of wrath." What I wrote was the first twelve-tone film score, non-thematic except for one main motif to denote the madness of the place.

To my surprise the score was liked by the MGM music department and actually recorded. I was beginning to think everything
I'd heard about Hollywood was untrue.

Rosenman and Alex North did more to bring the sound of serious mid-twentieth-century music to Hollywood than any other
composers, although Rosenman's success has not matched North's.
Their new techniques helped the development of scoring, although
as Picasso once said, "Every time somebody innovates something,
somebody comes along and does it prettier." The important thing
is that an innovator does occasionally manage to squeeze through
the Hollywood gates.

The enthusiasm for the Rosenman scores is something less than
widespread, although they never lack for musical interest. For John
Frankenheimer's first film, *The Young Stranger* (1957), Rosenman
sought a romantic musical approach, so he studied the songs of Hugo
Wolf rather than apply the usual Tchaikovsky tinge, seeking to give
the score a slightly different flavor. For *Pork Chop Hill* (1959), Lewis
Milestone's stark film about the Korean War, Rosenman unearthed
a 2000-year-old Chinese lullaby and adapted it into an oddly harmonized march in a score that was otherwise non-martial. For *Fantastic Voyage* (1966), he talked the producer out of using jazz and
suggested instead that the first few reels be scored only with electronic sounds, with music introduced only after the miniaturized
scientists arrive inside the human body and discover its wonders.

In 1970, Leonard Rosenman produced scores for two films of
strange and different characters: *Beneath the Planet of the Apes* and
A Man Called Horse. The picture about the apes has a rather ca-
cophonous sound, with piercing brass chords over shrill strings, all
suggestive of a nightmarish world. At one point Rosenman sup-
plies a march for a gorilla army that is a satiric comment on the

moronic, cruel mentality of the animals. He parodies the mutated humans with mocking distortions of the hymn "All Things Bright and Beautiful."

For *A Man Called Horse*, Rosenman not only used genuine Indian music, he adapted it for a choir from the Rosebud Sioux of South Dakota. The score is rife with rattles, whistles, drums, and chants, and is possibly a little too authentic for most moviegoing ears. Certainly, no one interested in the culture of North American Indians could fail to be impressed by the sincerity of the film or the composer's rather odd amalgam of avant-garde techniques with primitive music.

Rosenman is not at all sentimental about film music.

It has all the attributes of music—melody, harmony, counterpoint—but it is something less than music because its motivating pulsation is literary and not musical. Unlike other mixed-media forms, such as opera, the composer has no control over the text, over the *mise en scène*; he is writing to a circumscribed form. The challenge for me is extra-filmic, it's a question of dramaturgic talent. Either a person is talented dramaturgically or he isn't—you can have a marvelous composer write a score and it might not fit. You're dealing with two arts that are very similar—sight and sound—both move in time and both require memory for the perception of organization. For instance, you may feel the reemergence of the theme in Beethoven's *Eroica* is thrilling, but that's because you remember what it is at the beginning. If you conceive of the *Eroica* as a series of isolated musical events, it isn't thrilling. The same thing in film—if the villain finally gets punched in the nose, it's thrilling because this is reel twelve and he's had it coming since reel five.

The film composer has to bear in mind that we are a visually oriented society. In fact, it's biological: more of our brain is given over to vision than to hearing. Film music must be an analog to the action of the film, and likewise, the film should become an analog of the dramatic action of the music. This is the value of a director and a composer working together in the construction of the film.

Rosenman has continued his career as a composer of absolute music, although while working in films he has found it more difficult to get performances in the concert hall. This is doubly irritating because he has generally been regarded in Hollywood as something of an interloper. He is, or tries to be, totally schizophrenic about his concert music and his film music, although he candidly admits that he uses the cinema as a musical laboratory:

> I think Mozart and Beethoven would have given their eye teeth to write for films, because of the opportunity it gives to write something and hear it played the next day by fifty or sixty crack musicians. These are the optimal conditions in which to study orchestration and to try out musical ideas.

Rosenman looks upon the musical ignorance of filmmakers as both good and bad, good in that they are not qualified to interfere and bad in that they do not understand the functions of music.

> They tend to think of music in literary terms. When I was scoring for the TV series *The Defenders*, the producer said: "I want music that describes the law." That's a literary idea—music can't describe law. Richard Strauss came as close as any composer in being able to communicate pictures, but five people listen to *Ein Heldenleben,* and if they have no idea what it's about, you'll get five different stories.

Since composers remain a mystery to many producers, they too often become convenient repositories of blame. One of the most common cries in Hollywood is heard from an incompetent producer claiming that a composer has ruined his film, although this cry never seems to arise from well-made pictures.

> I was asked by a producer at Universal to rescore the opening episode of their TV series *The Survivors*. One of my colleagues had done a good job, but it was a terrible film, impossible. The producer felt that my changing the musical concept would improve the film. When a picture is really bad, no composer can save it.

Rosenman has an optimistic nature, and he is grateful to have worked in films, although he has some regrets.

> Unfortunately, in America we have the opinion that if a composer works in film, he can't write good music. This isn't true in other countries. I'm a better composer now than I was before I started film scoring, yet before I started in films I had less trouble from the critics than I do now. Recently, a chamber piece of mine was performed at a concert, a quite serious composition, and a critic said, "It sounds like Alfred Newman." Everyone's entitled to be a snob, but this man must either have fallen asleep or been deaf. All you can say to these people is what Brahms said to Hanslick when that august critic told him his first symphony sounded like Beethoven's Tenth—"Anybody can see that." However, I think this kind of snobbism will disappear in a generation. Film art is growing fast. This is the technical mythology of the twentieth century, and the kids taking film courses today seem to have—pray to God—open minds.

Jerry Goldsmith

The career of Jerry Goldsmith is perhaps the most remarkable of all the composers who came to prominence in the 1960s, a decade often regarded as the dark age in American film music. It was a time when the European-born giants were eased aside as producers brought in jazz, rock, and folk musicians to spruce up their films, invariably with dismal results.

Goldsmith, rare among film composers in that he was actually born in Los Angeles, majored in music at the University of Southern California and studied with pianist Jakob Gimpel. In 1950 he took a job with the music department of the CBS West Coast headquarters in Los Angeles, not as a musician but as a clerk-typist. Goldsmith did his first chores as a composer and conductor for CBS radio programs. By the late fifties he was well ensconced as a composer of television scores. By the age of thirty, Goldsmith had established a reputation as inventive and imaginative as well as fast and dependable, a combination of qualities no film studio could overlook in a bright, new composer. He had written dozens of scores for *Playhouse 90*, *The Twilight Zone*, *Gunsmoke*, and *Climax*; his work for *Thriller* and *The Man from U.N.C.L.E.* had brought him Emmy nominations, and his theme for *Dr. Kildare* was a popular hit.

Jerry Goldsmith conducting the National Philharmonic Orchestra of London
in the Varèse Sarabande recording of Alex North's legendary unused score for
2001: A Space Odyssey (photo by Matthew Peak).

The first Goldsmith film score to receive critical attention was
Lonely Are the Brave (1962), itself a remarkable film. With a script by
Dalton Trumbo and a convincing performance from Kirk Douglas
as a contemporary cowboy out of place in the modern world, Goldsmith underscored the picture gently and discreetly. His sensitive
orchestration pointed up the poignancy of a stubborn, free-spirited
man unable or unwilling to conform to the twentieth century. Even
a barroom brawl was lightly scored with percussive instruments. Certainly, the musical touch was different, and very welcome. The film

was not widely successful when first released, but over the years it has come to be recognized as a minor American classic.

Goldsmith also wrote a similarly quiet and subtle score for John Houston's *Freud* (1962), but the film's failure to win public approval failed to bring the composer the recognition he deserved for scoring a difficult and convoluted subject. The first wide recognition of Goldsmith came not long after when he scored *Lilies of the Field* (1963), a minutely budgeted film shot in a few weeks on location in Arizona. The picture was the longshot winner producers dream about, and it made a star of Sidney Poitier, whose winning performance as a good-hearted drifter was greatly aided by Goldsmith's infectious use of an old "clap hands" spiritual.

Mickey-mousing (i.e., a man slips on a banana skin and the music slips with him), a film-music style that had long been prevalent, has been almost totally avoided by Goldsmith. His scoring tends to be subjective, and he says,

> The function of a score is to enlarge the scope of a film. I try for emotional penetration, not complementing the action. To me, the important thing about music in film is statement. I can't describe how I arrive at the decision to make a statement—I simply feel it and react to it. But I do know you have to be very careful with what look like obvious moments for music. It's easy to be wrong, and a scene can be changed by the weight of music, which is something many filmmakers still don't seem to understand.

Goldsmith gives the impression of being diffident. He seems to take little pleasure in discussing his scores, a few of which he refuses to discuss at all. If pressed to reveal those that he liked, he will usually mention *A Patch of Blue* (1965). He feels his music made a contribution, which is a modest evaluation. The film was a touching story of a blind girl desperately in need of human contact, and her friendship with a black man. Everything the girl can't say or can't see is conveyed by the music, and the scene in which the girl and Poitier playfully thread beads is a masterpiece of scoring; as the beads drop in ones and twos, Goldsmith delicately places little percussive noises in the light orchestration of piano and bass strings to coincide with the beads falling on the thread. Even Goldsmith allows, this was "pretty good."

John Frankenheimer's *Seconds* (1966) is a bizarre and terrifying picture. It is a futuristic story of a man undergoing plastic surgery in order to continue with a second life. Goldsmith treated a disturbing visual in an opposing manner, and while writing an orderly and almost serene score, somehow came up with a perfect counterpoint. The music was everything the film wasn't, and only an imaginative composer could make such a method work.

Most Hollywood composers speak freely, and sometimes volubly, about their work, but Goldsmith is the kind of composer who manages to do brilliant things yet finds it difficult to explain why or how he did them. His comments on the lack of appreciation for his line of work are likely to be terse:

> The fact that certain composers have been able to create first-class music within the medium of film proves that film music can be as good as the composer is gifted.

Goldsmith is especially irritated by the lack of response from responsible critics.

> You read reviews by top reviewers of films that not only had remarkably interesting scores but films whose effectiveness was absolutely enhanced, and frequently created by the music, yet the reviewers seem unaware that their emotions and their nervous reactions to the films have been affected by the scoring. This is a serious flaw. Any film reviewer owes it to himself, and the public, to take every element of the film into account.

Goldsmith also feels that films could do with much less music, but rightfully and tastefully placed. His own score for the almost three hours of *Patton* (1970) totals only thirty-five minutes, but the judicious placing of it seems to suggest a much wider musical coverage.

Goldsmith takes advantage of the newer recording technology; having worked in films since the advent of stereo and multi-track methods, he utilizes isolated musical sounds, fades, reverberations, delayed sounds, and reversed sounds. Part of Goldsmith's success as a film composer comes from his keen interest in sound. In his studio he constantly experiments with sounds, with electronic instruments and reproductive equipment, all used as an adjunct to his creating process as he strives for new ways to express music in film. In *Planet of the Apes* (1968), arid-sounding string scales flutter across the screen when the astronauts first come upon the Forbidden Zone, and later when the gorillas attack, blood-curdling trumpeting spits out from the soundtrack, instantly communicating the fear and confusion of the astronauts.

In *Sebastian* (1968), Goldsmith deftly counterpoints the ancient against the modern. The story has Dirk Bogarde as a crack British cryptographer, working amid banks of fantastic computers and decoding machines; yet he is also a man "turned on" by Bach, which gave Goldsmith opportunities to use Bachian fugal passages with contemporary rhythm accompaniments. In short, baroque form in discotheque style. The score for this "mod" picture also uses some of the newer musical instruments, such as the varitone trumpet which can actually play in two octaves at the same time.

Another interesting Goldsmith score is *The Blue Max* (1966). The film is a rather long-winded account of a German aviator's rise and fall set during the First World War. Goldsmith went to London to score the film, where he found the producers had pre-tracked the film with Richard Strauss's *Also Sprach Zarathustra* to give him an idea of what they wanted.

> I admit it worked fairly well, but my first reaction was to get up and walk away from the job, but I couldn't. Once you've heard music like that with the picture, it makes your own scoring more difficult to arrive at, it clouds your thinking. Later, as an inside joke, I included a snippet of the Strauss in the score, and some critic pounced on me for stealing. You can't win.

Page Cook, in his review of *The Blue Max* score for *Films in Review*, made this analysis:

> The opening music begins as Bruno Stachel (George Peppard), in the trenches, enviously watches a squadron of planes pass over him. A solitary horn for this leads into the film's main theme, which alerts our mind to Stachel's aspirations. This theme is natural material, full of conflict within a relatively simple outline. It's developed with some stunning orchestral effects that simulate the sensations of being airborne. Stachel's nature is perfectly caught in Goldsmith's music for Stachel's first "kill." It's an exciting reworking of the main theme, with brilliant woodwind coloring. There's ordinary music for Stachel's affair with a countess (Ursula Andress), but earlier, when she tries a cat-and-mouse seduction, the main theme is used as a waltz—mockingly. The grim side of war is effectively indicated by the fine passacaglia which accompanies the retreat of the German army. The final scenes are heightened by tense music, first as Count von Klugermann (James Mason) asks Stachel to take up the experimental plane, and when Stachel is performing stunts in the air, unaware of his inevitable crack-up. The finale music, though far from subtle, is a grand finish.

One of the most highly regarded Goldsmith scores is *Patton*. The film is one of the most incisive examinations of warfare, particularly on the command level, brilliantly photographed and directed, with a stunning and deeply perceptive performance from George C. Scott as the famous, controversial American general. Patton was a complicated and contradictory man—proud and profane, ferocious and religious—a medieval warrior in the twentieth century, who believed in reincarnation. Goldsmith captures the man in music; the jaunty main theme, a catchy tune in breezy martial tempo, denotes this soldier's joy of battle, his absolute belief in himself. As Patton looks across the scene of an ancient battleground in Africa and says, "I was here," the sound of archaic trumpets cry out in triplets and fade away, as if passing through the man's mind. The *Patton* score bears close examination.

Goldsmith's prolific output amazes all who work with him. If there is any valid criticism of him, it lies in the opinion that he has lent his talents to films that have not merited them. Among the films he has made considerable contributions to: *Papillon* (1973), *Chinatown* (1974), *The Wind and the Lion* (1975), *The Omen* (1976), for which he won an Oscar, *Alien* (1979), *Star Trek* (1979), *Gremlins* (1984), *Legend* (1985), *Lionheart* (1987), and *Basic Instinct* (1992). He also scored the epic mini-series *Masada* (1981), which is generally regarded as his finest work for television. As of this writing, there have been 130 Goldsmith film scores, an amazing body of work.

As Goldsmith sees it, the real problem of film music is blending art with commerce. The composer who can't come to terms and realize that he is part of a big-business enterprise had best avoid the medium. As for the limitations and restrictions people assume to be the bane of the film composers life:

Working to timings and synchronizing your musical thoughts with the film can be stimulating rather than restrictive. Scoring is a limitation, but like any limitation it can be made to work for you. Verdi, except for a handful of pieces, worked best when he was "turned on" by a libretto. The most difficult problem in music is form, and in a film you already have this problem solved for you. You are presented with a basic structure, a blueprint, and provided the film has been well put-together, well edited, it often suggests its own rhythms and tempo. The quality of the music is strictly up to the composer. Many people seem to assume that because film music serves the visual it must be something of secondary value. Well, the function of any art is to serve a purpose in society. For many years, music and painting served religion. The thing to bear in mind is that film is the youngest of the arts, and that scoring is the youngest of the music arts. We have a great deal of development ahead of us.

Lalo Schifrin

Lalo Schifrin is a student of film. He studied film at a university in his native Buenos Aires. He conceives of a film as a kind of human body:

> The producer is its lungs, the director is its brains, the cameraman is its eyes, and the composer is its ears, and we should not be aware of any one detail too much. The music shouldn't overplay any more than an actor should overact, but neither should it be so subtle it is almost nonexistent.

Lalo Schifrin is typical of the futuristically minded composer in that his musical modus operandi includes a thorough classical education, a love of jazz and all kinds of improvisation, and the ability to understand and use electronic instruments and technology. This enviable combination of skills made Schifrin the Hollywood composer most in demand by the late sixties, especially for television scoring, where producers are always looking for spectacular and distinct musical cues to grab attention to their credit titles and opening sequences. This particular ability is highly sought-after in the keenly competitive world of commercial television programming. Among the TV series that have been aided by Schifrin's inventiveness are *Mission: Impossible*, *Mannix*, *The Young Lawyers*, and

Lalo Schifrin

Medical Center. In all these TV scores, Schifrin cleverly combines sound effects with music. All these series are contemporary in their settings, and since noise is a part of everyday life, he utilizes it in his scoring, including even a musical motif arising from a sound effect. In the main title of *Medical Center*, for example, Schifrin used a Moog synthesizer to imitate the sound of a wailing ambulance siren, which increases in pitch and moves in harmony right through the orchestration.

Schifrin's father was for thirty years the concertmaster of the Buenos Aires Symphony Orchestra, and his uncle was the first cellist.

> I was steeped in classical music. Buenos Aires is spiritually a European city, and the repertoire of our orchestra was basically the same as those of London or Paris. Only occasionally did they play a Latin American composition. My father was very academic in his thinking—I remember string quartets being played in our house on the weekends—my early musical training was of this kind, and I was almost asphyxiated by it. This was "the establishment" to me and I rebelled against it. When I was sixteen I discovered modern American jazz and became addicted to it, especially the work of Thelonius Monk, Charlie Parker and Dizzy Gillespie. Jazz was the strongest influence on me because it was my own discovery, it helped me find myself. My early musical training was very severe, and jazz helped me to realize that music is alive. Later on, when I matured, I discovered that there wasn't all that much incompatibility between classical music and jazz. Jazz is very old technically, and the more I studied it, the more I wanted to play well. To really understand jazz, you have to understand harmony and counterpoint—which brings you back to the classics.

Born in 1932 into a totally musical milieu, Schifrin finds it difficult to pinpoint his beginnings as a composer.

> I wasn't aware of the difference between composing and arranging or orchestrating and playing music—it was all part of the same thing to me, although I do remember writing a sonatine for piano when I was about fourteen.

He began his formal study of composition in his late teens with Argentinean modernist Juan Carlos Paz, and later he studied at the

Paris Conservatory with Olivier Messiaen. Upon returning to Buenos Aires at the age of twenty, Schifrin started to write music for the theater and television. His first film score was for an Argentinean art short, which he modestly scored for one violin, one viola, one cello, two saxophones, and one timpani.

Schifrin's other major interest as a young man was film:

> I was a member of cinema societies, and we studied all the classics, all the works of the masters, and all the good new films from everywhere. Being musically inclined, I became aware of the use of music in film, and I would sometimes go three or four times to a film to hear the score. I did this with *Viva Zapata!* and was amazed at Alex North's music. I liked Georges Auric's scores, and Prokofiev's *Alexander Nevsky* was one of the strongest influences on me. I thought, and still do, that Rozsa's *Ben-Hur* was great. Kaper's score for *Lord Jim* is incredible.

The turning point in Lalo Schifrin's young life came with the arrival of Dizzy Gillespie in Argentina on a U.S. State Department tour in 1957. Schifrin went to meet his idol, and when Gillespie heard the young man's music, he offered him a job. Once he had cleared the hurdles of immigration, Schifrin proceeded to the United States and joined Gillespie as an arranger. His reputation grew during the Gillespie tenure, especially with his arrangements for Jazz at the Philharmonic, which included his *Suite for Trumpet and Brass Orchestra (Gillespiana)*.

Schifrin went on to do similar work for Count Basie, Stan Getz, Jimmy Smith, and Sarah Vaughn, but over a period of time tired of all the traveling this work involved. What he wanted was a base from which to work. He decided on Hollywood, where, with his shining recommendations from some of the world's greatest jazz musicians, he had little difficulty finding work. Schifrin owes his entry into the Hollywood music world—a world populated by the brightest talent money can buy—to the late Stanley Wilson, then head of TV music at Universal.

> I started scoring segments of *The Alfred Hitchcock Show*, *The Kraft Theater*, and *The Virginian*. There were all kinds of shows—comedy, mystery, Western. It let me get used to the methods of synchronization and the very sophisticated technology of scoring. It was a paid apprenticeship.

Schifrin scored two low-budget feature films during the time he was working in television: *Rhino* (1963) and *Joy House* (1964), neither of which were memorable, but they were useful when the time came for his first major film assignment, *The Cincinnati Kid* (1965). The film studios, ever cautious about using composers from TV, were more inclined to hire Schifrin when they learned he had scored a few features. *The Cincinnati Kid* marked the real start of Schifrin's career as a film scorer. With this and several other films dealing with the American scene, his knowledge of jazz and the roots of American music gave him a definite edge on other composers. Schifrin's study of "bluegrass" music came in especially handy when he was assigned to score *Cool Hand Luke* (1967), a story of convicts in the South of a few decades ago.

Concerning his method and his manner of scoring films, Schifrin says,

> I follow my instincts. When I try to rationalize, I cannot arrive at decisions. In general terms, I think that which is acoustical is a counterpoint to that which is visual, the *cantus firmus* concept: what is seen is tenor and what is heard is bass. My own taste runs to linear scoring, like a Japanese design, in which things are not told but suggested, implied. I admire the use of music in the Kabuki theater in Japan, where the drama is punctuated by

music. This is also similar to the traditional use of the chorus in Greek drama.

Schifrin's film scores are characterized by sparse, modernistic lines. In *The Fox* (1967) he used an orchestra of ten instruments of differing timbres, and managed to convey the bleak Canadian winter landscape and the odd relationship between the two women living together and the tension aroused by a young male interloper. In *Cool Hand Luke*, Schifrin wrote a guitar theme for Paul Newman, the existential hero, a silent man. Sparingly used, the theme had to mean something when it spoke for Newman and his contempt for the prison, his rebellion, and his strength. At those times, the music was foreground, not background. Dexterously used, a musical theme can sometimes become almost a character in the film.

Three of Schifrin's most interesting scores have been in films that met with little response from the public, *Che* (1968), *The Brotherhood* (1968), and *Hell in the Pacific* (1968). Schifrin claims that the first script of the Che Guevara story was primarily an action vehicle that was spoiled by attempts at political philosophizing. The most vital part of the film, visually and musically, is the opening title sequence, which, with split-screen projection, tells the story of the finding of Che's body and transporting it by helicopter to an army base:

> Che came from Argentina and he died in Bolivia. Coincidentally, the music of northern Argentina, Bolivia, and Peru is from Inca sources. For the main title I used a dirge and scored it for drums and wooden flutes from the Andes, which have a piercing quality. I wanted these Bolivian scenes to have a primitive feeling, one of despair, in contrast to the Cuban scenes.
>
> In scoring *The Brotherhood*, I also considered it necessary to give a genuine ethnic feeling to the music because this was a

story of an ancient Sicilian tradition, the Mafia. I went into re-search on Sicilian music, and I think this helped convey the strange, medieval code of the main characters. The jew's harp came in useful in this score.

With *Hell in the Pacific*, I didn't want to be ethnic. This was about two men marooned on a South Pacific island in the Sec-ond World War—a Japanese and an American with neither of them able to speak the language of the other. You didn't need to comment on the fact that they were Japanese or American, only that they were afraid and suspicious and hostile. There was no dialogue, just snatches of monologue, so the music had to speak for them. The music doesn't have to be loud—what we see is the loneliness, the solitude, the sexual misery of these two men. Under these conditions, a flute can have the impact of an or-chestra—an orchestra would be overpowering. I believe single instruments can be very communicative.

Lalo Schifrin was approached by the music department of the University of California, Los Angeles, to conduct a class in film composition. UCLA's rival, The University of Southern Califor-nia, had a long-established, excellent course in film composition, first under Miklos Rozsa and then under David Raksin. Schifrin was puzzled by the request:

I told them I had no teaching experience, and they said, "It doesn't matter, just go ahead and do it." I quickly devised a method. My first assignment to the students was "write a musical de-scription of the color orange, and do it with just one sound." They all came up with different solutions. Next, write a descrip-tion of a still photograph of a scene or a landscape. Afterwards came my requests for descriptions of an abstract painting; a pho-tograph with human beings in it; and then a musical illustration of a comic strip. This seemed to me a functional way of teach-ing. Writing film music is a very personal form of composition.

In addition to the understanding of drama, I want to encourage the students' sensitivity to audio-visual counterpoint.

Apart from his film scores, Schifrin has written a dramatic cantata based on his score for the TV film *The Rise and Fall of the Third Reich*; an orchestral study called *The Ritual of Sound*; a trumpet concerto; a piano concerto; *A Jazz Suite on the Mass Texts*; and a piece for chamber orchestra, *Variants on a Madrigal by Gesualdo*. Some of these scores look like the blueprints for computing systems.

The assumption that Lalo Schifrin might take a disdainful view of the film music written by an earlier Hollywood generation is false:

> I am far from denying the past in any part. We owe to Max Steiner and Alfred Newman and the others all the things we do now—it is easier to improve upon something than it is to discover it. History is a continuity. Beethoven was a development of Mozart and Haydn, and Brahms was a development of Beethoven. Avant-garde music is not a negation of the musical past—it's an extension of it. When Schoenberg was young, he wrote in the style of Mahler, and Mahler was a continuation of Wagner. You might say that the Prelude of *Tristan and Isolde* was the beginning of contemporary music because it's so chromatic it's one step from atonality.

In 1968, Schifrin's score for *Bullitt*, with Steve McQueen zipping up and down the hills of San Francisco, led to similar assignments. It was followed by *Coogan's Bluff* (1968), with Clint Eastwood as an Arizona cop zipping around New York, which in turn led to a string of similar Eastwood adventures, including *Dirty Harry* (1972), *Magnum Force* (1973), *Sudden Impact* (1983), and *The Dead Pool* (1988).

> It's always been a problem in Hollywood that if you prove you're good at something, they keep asking you to do it again. But there

are only so many ways you can score a car chase, and I'm not looking to do any more.

Vastly different in tone and style are his scores for such movies as the rollicking *The Four Musketeers* (1975), the tragic *Voyage of the Damned* (1976), the war adventure *The Eagle Has Landed* (1977), and the spoof on the rich and famous, *The Beverly Hillbillies* (1993). Schifrin has scored close to 200 theatrical and television films. However, he does not expect to add a great many more titles to the list.

In 1989, Lalo Schifrin accepted the position as music director and conductor of the Glendale Symphony Orchestra, whose members are among the elite musicians who play in major film-scoring sessions. In addition, he guest-conducts symphony orchestras in Europe and South America. (Schifrin is noted for promoting the works of composers from South America's musical world.) As busy as his conducting schedule is, Schifrin is still always interested in composing for films, "provided they don't involve any car chases."

MORE RECENTLY

More than twenty years have elapsed since the first publication of *Music for the Movies*. What has happened with
the art and craft of film music in that time? The answer is, aside
from the ever-evolving technology, nothing is very different. Films
still need music and they always will—not only feature films but
cartoons, documentaries, and television shows, including commer-
cials. The amount of music written and performed in Southern California is immense, possibly more than in the rest of the world combined. Hollywood is the source of much of the world's filmed entertainment; a smash-hit movie in America is a smash hit globally,
and so the opportunities for composers would seem to be richer
than ever before. But are they? Composers still complain about not
being given enough time to write; producers and directors will spend
endless amounts of time shooting a film and then expect the com-

poser to come up with an hour of original music within a month. The complaints from composers working for people with little comprehension of music are more bitter than ever.

Says Elmer Bernstein:

> I've done nearly 150 films and much television, and there were probably not more than half a dozen directors that it would be safe to trust insofar as they have any knowledge of music and its function in motion pictures.

Hollywood has always had to deal with the conflict between art and commerce, with the latter understandably dominant. Today, with the average film production costs running into the tens of millions of dollars, Hollywood is even more attuned to commerce. Movie producers are also aware that although they are not married to record producers, they are, so to speak, living together and playing to the same public. The ears of that public are far more in touch with popular music than serious music, and it is not unreasonable for movie producers to be aware of that fact. Thus, the old war between producers and composers goes on and on, the producer thinking in terms of the musically obvious and the composer thinking in terms of the more subtle and subliminal ways of affecting the audience (while at the same time agreeing that it would not hurt to come up with a theme that turns into a hit record).

Hollywood, like life itself, is full of contradictions. While movie music has tended more toward the popular taste over the past couple of decades, the fact is that the two most successful composers, John Williams and Jerry Goldsmith, have scored their biggest successes with full symphonic orchestras. The same can be said for four other composers whose scores over the past twenty years have given them solid reputations: John Scott, David Shire, Bruce Broughton, and Basil Poledouris.

John Scott

John Scott, a gentlemanly Englishman born in Bristol in 1930, maintains homes in both London and Los Angeles. The son of a military musician, at the age of fourteen he joined the British Army as a boy musician (he had studied the clarinet as a child) with the Royal Artillery and underwent four years of training. The orchestra of that regiment had the reputation as the best of its kind, and after fulfilling their military service, its members usually went on to positions with top dance bands and orchestras, Scott among them.

Giving up the clarinet in favor of the flute and saxophone, Scott found constant employment:

> My big break came when I was invited to join the Ted Heath Orchestra, which was then at the pinnacle of the British dance bands. I also started to arrange music for the band, which led to an offer from EMI (Electrical Musical Industries, the leading British recording company) to arrange and conduct for popular artists like Tom Jones and Cilla Black. I had also formed a jazz group and we did dates and broadcasts, with me playing flute and saxophone, while at the same time I also played flute with the various symphony orchestras in London. All of this led to me being hired for film scoring sessions, and my entry into the film business, something had I never thought about previously.

John Scott

Scott played for the British film composers and for Henry Mancini on his London sessions. He gradually became fascinated with the scoring business, and after a while a thought took root:

I one day said to myself, "I can do this." It took a while to get going, but I started with small documentaries, which proved I could compose as well as play, and then in 1965 I was hired to score *A Study in Terror*, a Sherlock Holmes picture. All of a sudden I was a film composer, although one who had not studied composition. I then went to the esteemed composer Leslie Bridgewater to study form, theory, and technique, all the things I should have studied years before had I known I would become a composer.

After a number of forgettable movies, in 1971 Scott scored *Outback*, an Australian film that finally brought him favorable critical attention. The critics remarked that his music helped capture the heat and desolation of the Aussie interior, as well as the plight of the main character, a man trapped in a desperate situation. Two years later he scored the Shakespearean tragedy *Antony and Cleopatra*, followed by *England Made Me*, a Graham Greene story set in Germany between the two world wars, allowing for both dramatic orchestral comment and period dance music.

Scott got his first Hollywood job in 1979, with the football comedy *North Dallas Forty*, followed by an entirely different form, the drama *The Final Countdown* (1980). In 1984, John Scott scored the film for which he is best known, *Greystoke*, with Christopher Lambert as Tarzan and Sir Ralph Richardson, in his final work, as Lord Greystoke. Beautifully filmed in Africa and England, the score is richly romantic and full-blooded.

> There were special demands made on the music throughout the first part of the film because there is no spoken language and the music has to communicate with the audience, although they might not be aware of it. We see Tarzan in the process of growing up, his fight for supremacy in the jungle, his baffling encounter with civilization when he is brought to England and becomes part of high society, then his rejection of that society and his return to the jungle. As a composer I enjoy having a big canvas on which to paint, but I also like films that have an "in the mind" quality that allows for conveying thought and emotion. This one gave me both. It was an interesting experience

because they had previously scored the film with the music of Gustav Holst, Maurice Ravel, and other great composers. I saw the film with that score, and it was interesting because it didn't work—it had the effect of pushing the audience away, which is the opposite of what a score is supposed to do. My object was to pull the audience in, to involve them, and I think I did.

Like all film composers, Scott has written for good films that for reasons difficult to understand, simply did not go over well with the public. Among them are *The Shooting Party* (1984), a study of English high society just prior to the first World War, and *Winter People* (1989), which is set in rural North Carolina during the Great Depression and deals with a deadly feud between two families. Another film that quickly disappeared was *Ruby* (1992), with Danny Aiello giving a touching performance as Jack Ruby, the man who killed Lee Harvey Oswald. It came just after Oliver Stone's *JFK* and found almost no audience, a disappointment for Scott, whose music underlined the sorrow of Ruby's actions and the sleazy background in which he operated.

> It was not a difficult score to write because the film worked so well and inspired the music. But it was a typical Hollywood assignment in terms of time. I got the green light on December 18th, 1991, with recording dates set for the following January 14th and 15th, so I said goodbye to Christmas, New Year's and a lot of sleep.

Scott's longest association with a filmmaker is with the celebrated French oceanographer Jacques Cousteau. He has scored dozens of hours of Cousteau adventures, films dealing with the Amazon, the Great Barrier Reef of Australia, the British Channel Islands, the Saint Lawrence Seaway of Canada, Cape Horn, and any number of underwater locations.

I was very lucky to work for Cousteau because he is a musician himself and could discuss what he wanted. That is rare. He was encouraging but he never interfered. We would get together in the dubbing room and go through the score, so I always knew what he wanted. Again, it isn't often that a composer has that kind of understanding from a producer or director.

Like most composers today, Scott knows how to use electronic instruments, but he is not happy about the effect of modern technology:

The film business has changed a great deal with the advent of computers and synthesizers. This has brought a new group of composers, some with very little musical ability. The orchestrator has always been one of the most important elements in film scoring but he is even more important for those who compose by humming or playing something by ear on a synthesizer and relying on a computer to print it out. In that sense it's easier to be a composer than it was before. If such a composer is lucky enough to write for a successful picture, then he, too, is a success. But success on those terms is not really what music composition is all about. Also, so much of filmmaking today, every aspect of it, is done by committee decision—and nothing is worse for music than a committee decision.

David Shire

Among Hollywood composers, David Shire is unusual in that he is one of the few who seems equally at home in both the legitimate theater and the movies. Born in Buffalo, New York, in 1937, Shire is the son of a man who was both a band musician and a piano teacher, and his early introduction to music was more popular than classical.

I grew up with what was then standard pop songs, especially those written for Broadway, and when I went to Yale, where I started as an English major and then switched to music, I got into writing shows for the Yale Dramatic Association. I graduated in 1959, after which I did a few months of graduate work in composition at Brandeis University. I then put in half a year with the Army Reserve Program. I had long studied the piano, and my earliest ambition was to be a concert pianist, but when I went to New York after leaving the Army, the first work I could find was as a rehearsal pianist for musicals and recording artists. By then I was interested in composing but for the stage rather than films. I thought I might be able to do films between stage shows, but it's turned out to be the other way around.

Shire was working as a pianist, arranger, and conductor for various stage and nightclub productions at the time Barbra Streisand was emerging as a major artist. He took two of his songs, "Autumn" and "No More Songs for Me," to her and she recorded them. Her pianist at the time she was starring in *Funny Girl* on Broadway asked Shire to take over for him, as both pianist and assistant conductor. Streisand did a TV special, *Color Me Barbra*, and asked Shire to be involved as assistant arranger and accompanist. Two more TV specials with her, and a few more of his songs recorded by her, and Shire was on the way to bigger things.

In 1967, he wrote background scores for the series *CBS Playhouse*, which led him to Hollywood.

> I came to Los Angeles with a stage musical I had written but after six weeks of tryouts it folded. By now I was getting a little tired of the uncertainty of life in the theater. I knew Billy Goldenberg, who was one of Universal's top television composers—still a top composer—and he introduced me to Stanley Wilson, the head of the music department at the studio. I played him some of my *CBS Playhouse* tapes and he put me to work, starting with a few episodes of *The Virginian*, then *McCloud*. My first feature film was a dreadful Western called *One More Train to Rob*.

Dreadful or not, other films were immediately offered him, such as *The Skin Game* (1971), a comedy set in the post-Civil War South with James Garner and Lou Gossett, Jr. After several lesser films, he did an impressive score for *The Conversation* (1974) in which he used only a piano.

> One of the things that makes scoring films so much fun is the opportunity to constantly write for orchestras of all sizes and shapes, and to write only as much music as a film really needs. The most economical score is often the best one, just as the simplest solution is often the most effective. But it always depends on the picture. If next week I get one that calls for ninety minutes of orchestral scoring, then that's what I'll give it, but *The Conversation* required very little. In that film, about a surveil-

lance expert whose obsessive nature gets him involved with a case that causes him to lose his mind, I used a synthesizer to modulate the texture of the piano cues to give a weird, unsettling effect to underscore the man's dilemma. It's opportunities like this that make film scoring a fascinating business.

In 1975, David Shire scored two films that brought him praise, *Farewell, My Lovely* and *The Hindenberg*. The former has Robert Mitchum as Raymond Chandler's classic private detective Philip Marlowe, with a story set in the sleazier parts of Los Angeles. Shire uses a saxophone as the lead instrument in the main title, giving a bluesy, languid, and vaguely uncomfortable feeling to the visual. In the scene where Marlowe is doped, he uses an electronic tuba in a low register to communicate the man's dizziness as he struggles to maintain his sanity.

Music of an entirely different nature was required for *The Hindenberg*, a film about the doomed German dirigible that crashed in Lakehurst, New Jersey, in 1937. The score took into account the popular music of the period, but in the main it stressed the German romanticism of a Richard Strauss, particularly in the main title.

I wrote the main title theme as a vocalise for soprano, trumpet obbligato, and large orchestra. But when the picture previewed, a Universal executive complained to director Robert Wise that he couldn't hear the lyrics. When informed that there weren't any to hear, he said that this would be confusing to an audience and asked to have the problem cleared up. I then had the onerous task of turning the main title into an instrumental, giving the vocal line to the trumpet and the trumpet obbligato to a handful of woodwinds. People said they liked it, but it wasn't the effect I had wanted. Along with the benefits of film scoring you also have the limitations forced on you by the people for whom you work. This was a very disappointing experience.

David Shire (photo by Andrew D. Bernstein)

For *All the President's Men* (1976), Shire wrote another sparse score, one he had to be persuaded to write.

When the director, Alan J. Pakula, asked me to do it, I said I thought it didn't need any music. This was the story of the investigation of the Watergate break-in. Pakula explained that he needed only a little music, that it was a tense story and that the music would come like breathing points in the action. He reminded me that it was a story about people and emotions and he wanted me to underline those points. This was a case where a director had a better grasp of what music could do for a film than a composer. That doesn't happen very often.

Shire's career shows a good balance between the use of popular music and dramatic composition, such as in two 1977 films, *Saturday Night Fever* and *Raid on Entebbe*. And his ability as a song writer has not gone unused in Hollywood: for *Norma Rae* (1979), he wrote the song "It Goes Like it Goes" (lyrics by Norman Gimbel) and won an Oscar for it. He was nominated for an Oscar for "I'll Never Say Goodbye" (lyrics by Marilyn and Alan Bergman), written for *The Promise* (1979). As a composer for stage musicals, Shire has been successful with *Baby* (1983), *Closer Than Ever* (1989), and, particularly, *Starting Here, Starting Now* (1975), which, with a cast of three, is almost always in production somewhere. In television, he received Emmy nominations for the mini-series *The Kennedys of Massachusetts* (1990) and *Sarah, Plain and Tall* (1991).

David Shire's magnum opus as a film composer is, in his opinion, *Return to Oz* (1985). Unfortunately, it was a major flop at the box office and soon disappeared. The film is a lavish, effects-filled fantasy that is rather dark of spirit and much closer to the Frank Baum original than the beloved MGM musical. However, the Judy Garland concept is the one the public loves, and they showed no interest in this version.

But I was glad to have the opportunity to write an extensive, symphonic score for a major orchestra—the London Symphony—a score with a great number of themes. I've done a lot of films that didn't require a great deal of music—I call them my brain-surgery scores, where you have to walk on eggs and work hard to keep the music out of the way most of the time and work, for the most part, on a subliminal level. So I was happy when director Walter Murch said that he wanted a lot of music. I wrote the major themes as extended pieces in addition to their function in the picture. I wanted the score to hold together somewhat along the lines of *Pictures at an Exhibition* or *Peter and the Wolf.* I felt this would give the picture a coherence musically and make for a recording that would really tell the story of the picture. This is one of those rare occasions when the score turns out to be more popular than the film for which it was written.

Not many of Shire's film scores are available as recordings. This is not something that bothers him.

As recordings of film music proliferate at a seemingly exponential rate, it's sometimes easy to lose sight of the fact that its primary function is to increase the dramatic effectiveness of the films it underscores. A lot of great underscoring, judged purely as such, makes for some rather boring listening away from the picture. Such music needs the film as much as the film needs the music. But like most film composers, I've always relished those scoring opportunities when I could write music that, without compromising its primary purpose, is worthy of a life of its own. I hasten to add that one shouldn't always take this approach. Less independently potent music often better serves a movie's dramatic intent. My job as a composer is to serve the picture, to service the drama. If the score can later become a nice concert suite so much the better. But basically the rule has to be to service what's there, and that can be like night and day from one movie to another. Each movie has its own problems, and there aren't any pat solutions.

A problem faced by today's Hollywood composer is having a score rejected. This has happened to even the best of them. Alfred

Hitchcock rejected Bernard Herrmann's score for *Torn Curtain* and Henry Mancini's for *Frenzy*. Composers as prestigious as Elmer Bernstein and Jerry Goldsmith have suffered the same indignity. In 1993, it happened to David Shire when the Disney Studio decided not to use his music for *Homeward Bound: The Incredible Journey*.

I have no idea why, other than their decision to take what they described as a "new approach," which included changing the actors. What made it even harder to understand was that they then brought in Bruce Broughton to write the score—and Bruce, whom I admire very much, writes pretty much in the same style as myself, especially for a Disney picture calling for traditional, upbeat, romantic descriptive music, and especially since they had been raving about how much they liked what I had written for them. However, there's no point in trying to apply logic to life in Hollywood.

Bruce
Broughton

Bruce Broughton's score for *Homeward Bound* is, like so much of his work, propelled by a melodic surge and an optimistic disposition. Broughton can be as dramatic and introspective as any of his peers, but he seems to be fully at home leading an orchestra in the lilting main theme of *Silverado* (1985) or the flight theme in *The Boy Who Could Fly* (1986).

For *Homeward Bound*, the story of two dogs and a cat making their way across rough country back to their human family, he begins with a soft guitar theme for the pup narrator (with human voice), then brings in strings to underline the warm family setting. Sassy the cat has a theme to match the name, and the older dog that leads is marked by a dignified, heroic theme. The conflicts with wild animals and wild rivers give plenty of scope for musical comment. In short, it is the kind of film that needs music almost as much as it needs photography. But it has to be intelligent music, not maudlin and sentimental.

Broughton was born in Los Angeles in 1945 but grew up in other cities because both parents were Salvation Army officers whose assignments kept them moving. Music came into his life at an early age:

Music is very much a part of life in the Salvation Army, and everyone is encouraged to play an instrument, especially brass. I picked up most of the brass instruments, but my main study was piano. I was pretty good and I found I could write little pieces, but I never had any ambition to be a composer. In my teens, I wanted to be a film animator, but I got tired explaining to people what that was. Eventually, I settled on a career as a composer because it was the only thing I knew how to do. And it's only been in recent years that I've enjoyed being a composer. It's hard work, and I think a lot of us tend not to like the process very much, but when the music is right for the picture, it can be exciting to see what it does. Then it gets to be like a drug—you want to do more of it.

Broughton returned to Los Angeles in 1962. Two years later, he enrolled at the University of Southern California, where he studied composition with David Raksin, whom Broughton credits with steering him the direction of film composition.

I studied technique and learned that there was a world of difference between concert and film music. Raksin was the best kind of teacher because he was encouraging. He told me what he expected from me, he convinced me of my ability.

After graduation, Broughton joined CBS as a music supervisor but a year later he was drafted and spent two years in the Army, playing French horn in a band. After his discharge, CBS took him back and he was with them until 1977, scoring programs, at first with library music, and then with pieces of his own.

He scored episodes of *Dallas*, *Quincy*, *Hawaii Five-O*, and *How the West Was Won*, and ended up winning five Emmys for his work. His scores for two television feature films, *The Blue and the Grey* (1982) and *The Master of Ballantrae* (1984), drew the attention of writer-director Lawrence Kasdan, who was planning *Silverado* and wanted a full-blooded musical score. The resultant score, generally considered the best of its kind since Jerome Moross' *The Big Country* (1958), was nominated for an Oscar but lost to John Barry's *Out of Africa*.

> Since there was nothing emotionally understated in the film, I felt that the music should be the same. I geared the orchestration toward power and energy. I think Kasdan intended this as a Western for those who had never seen one. Except for Indians, it had just about every element of the genre. It also had a lot of humor, but mostly it was the story of the friendship between four larger-than-life men, so I felt the music should stress that, with a theme that was heroically lyrical and rambunctiously rhythmic. It was filmed in New Mexico, with scenery that goes on forever, and I felt the music should reflect that, too. You can do that in epic Westerns—the music sort of fills up the spaces. When I was writing it, I said to Kasdan, "If I'm making a mistake here it's in overdoing it!" He replied, "That's alright. Just don't underdo it."

Soon after *Silverado*, Broughton had another opportunity for expansive scoring with *Young Sherlock Holmes*, a fantasy adventure initiated by Stephen Spielberg and directed by Barry Levinson. A wildly imaginative concept of what Holmes and John Watson might have been like as university students and filmed with a big budget in England, the film failed to find an audience. It has the kind of slam-bang action sequences that Spielberg worked to advantage in his Indiana Jones pictures, but here little is convincing as the two boys tackle master criminals in Victorian London. Broughton was brought in after the film was completed and encouraged by both Spielberg and Levinson to write a lot of music in sweepingly symphonic style.

Bruce Broughton (photo by Dana Ross)

It's almost a wall-to-wall score, and looking at the film now, I think there's too much music. But it was Levinson's picture, and my job was to give him what he wanted. From a purely musical point of view, it was a great project to work on, especially recording it in London, but it proved to me what I had heard many composers say, that music can never save a film that doesn't please or interest the public.

Some of Broughton's other films include Alan Alda's comedy about making a period movie on location, *Sweet Liberty* (1986); *Harry and the Hendersons* (1987), the story of a sweet-natured monster imposing himself on a family; and, among his best work, the television film of Ernest Hemingway's *The Old Man and the Sea* (1990), starring Anthony Quinn. It is regarded among his peers as superior to the score Tiomkin wrote for the 1958 Spencer Tracy film, being more lyrical and pensive.

Also lyrical and pensive is Broughton's score for the "Hallmark Hall of Fame" television production *O Pioneers* (1991), with Jessica Lange as Alexandra, the heroine of Willa Cather's story of a farm family in the Midwest. Clearly influenced by the works of Aaron Copland in style, with a broad, hymn-like main theme for Alexandra, a strong woman with a passion for the land. It is quintessential Americana, and it appears to be a style in which Broughton is at ease.

Broughton claims to lean in no particular direction in terms of the kinds of films he likes to score.

> I like variety. I want to expand my dramatic and musical abilities, to try other modes and other areas of music and drama and be challenged by whatever problems they offer.

The variety of his work includes the dramatic *The Presidio* (1988), the comedic *Honey I Blew Up the Kids* (1992) and the romantic *For Love or Money* (1993). However, with *Silverado* being the score most associated with his name, it was only a matter of time before he scored another epic Western.

Tombstone (1993) is nothing if not epic. It might be subtitled *The Ring of the Nibelungen Out West*, such is its searingly dramatic gunplay, its grandiose concept of the city of Tombstone, sweeping photography, and flamboyant characters. It is almost choreographic, the kind of film that desperately needs music to match the mythology come to life. Broughton was an obvious choice—in fact the producers had tracked the edited film with parts of his *Silverado* score to give him an idea of what they had in mind.

> This was a big problem for me because it didn't call for that kind of music. It was also a problem because they had also tracked parts of it with Jerry Goldsmith's *The Wild Rovers* (1971). Jerry happens to be my own idol among film composers. In fact, if I can admit to being influenced by anyone, it is him. But *The Wild*

Rovers approach was also wrong. It seemed to me that *Tombstone* needed music that stressed the drama and the romance, that it shouldn't be western in character, and because of that I avoided such typical Western instruments as the guitar and the harmonica. I opted instead for instruments with ethnic color, such as the Hungarian cimbalom, the Irish tin whistle and bhodran, and the French contrabass sarrusophone. The brass sections include the massive contrabass trombone, along with tenor and bass trombones. When we were recording these sections, I was reminded of what Bernard Herrmann once said to his orchestra: "The highest note here is middle C."

Anyone believing that there are no new ways to score Westerns should consider *Tombstone*. The film has no main title music; instead, the music gradually appears with the antics of the fierce band of outlaws known as The Cowboys. A relentless, dark motif of metal percussion, low strings, and contrabass underlines these mean spirits, contrasted to the gentle music noting the arrival of Wyatt Earp, his two brothers, and their wives. The score comments on the violence, the saloon life, and the sleazy nature of the characters, as well as pointing up the romantic elements of the film.

Historically correct, the end of the film shows Earp as a widower locating the actress (Dana Delany) and declaring his love. With snow on the ground, the pair lapse into a waltz, giving *Tombstone* the distinction of being the only epic Western to conclude with a lilting, symphonic waltz. As bizarre and florid as *Tombstone* might be, it is an extraordinary Western, and Broughton's score has much to do with its appeal and its effectiveness. And it does it without sounding at all like a typical Western score.

Bruce Broughton knows that there is no standing still in the film industry and that change, reasonable or mercurial, is part of its nature.

Styles and tastes change and you can't allow yourself to get stuck. I listen to everybody, even composers I don't like all that much. I may be influenced by Bartók for one reason and Stravinsky for another, Rachmaninoff for this and Mozart for that, and Wagner for many reasons. It amazes me that Wagner still has such a grip on us. Even with composers who don't charm me, like the minimalists, there is always something to learn. I listen to current pop and ethnic music. I heard something the other day by a Japanese composer that set my mind going in a whole new direction. The thing about composing for films is that you do so much work that you develop technique very fast, but you have to be careful that you don't write yourself out. You may not like all the music you hear, but you may find you can learn something from it, it might give you some technique, something you can incorporate or assimilate. As a film composer you must keep your mind open.

Basil Poledouris

Of all the composers to emerge in the 1970s, none has a better film education than Basil Poledouris, who graduated from the University of Southern California with a Bachelor of Arts degree in Cinema. Whereas in previous times film composers were likely to be men who did not set out with the idea of writing for films, the contemporary film composer is more often than not someone who has taken film courses in college. In that sense, Poledouris personifies the new school.

Born in Kansas City, Missouri, in 1945, Poledouris was taken to California as an infant and describes himself as essentially Californian. He is a dedicated surfer and sailboat sailor, enthusiasms that he has actually been able to express in some of his film scores. Both parents were amateur musicians and encouraged his obvious talent. He could play the piano by the age of five and as a teenager won several competitions, leading him to consider a career as a concert pianist. Poledouris won a music scholarship to Long Beach State, which led to him enrolling a year later in the School of Music at USC.

> By this time I was also interested in film. I'd long been a photography buff and I liked to put together shows of my slides, for which I composed musical accompaniment. This is what got me hooked on film composition. One of my reasons for going to

USC was that Miklos Rozsa was teaching a course in film composition. He left just as I joined, but David Raksin took his place, and from him I learned a lot.

After a year, Poledouris became disenchanted with music studies at USC. He had grown up with classical music, and he found the school's proclivity toward ultra-modern composition not to his liking. He switched his major to Cinema, where he excelled in editing and directing and won the George Cukor Academy of Arts and Sciences Award. He was also given the Edward Dmytryk Directing Scholarship, which facilitated his graduate studies.

By now, I decided I wanted to be a filmmaker—this seemed to be the art and craft of my generation. But I didn't give up on music because I was scoring not only my own pictures but those of other students. By the time I graduated I was agonizing about giving up music in order to find work in the film business in editing or some form of production. My music-loving parents were very upset that I didn't seem to want to make a living as a musician.

Poledouris found a job as an editor with a company that produced industrial and educational films. He worked on more than a hundred of these productions, for most of which he also provided the music scores, doing it at no extra salary.

It was a great opportunity because it helped me understand the use of music in films and how to use various instruments, the parts of the orchestra, what's possible and what isn't.

Still more interested in being a filmmaker than a composer, Poledouris, sponsored by director Larry Turman, became the first American Film Institute intern, resulting in a six-month contract for him with Twentieth Century-Fox in 1969.

Basil Poledouris (photo by Breeze)

It was there I made the decision to go with music. This was the Big League, and the more I saw of film production on that level, the more I realized I was best suited for the kind of anonymity and solitude I enjoy as a composer, especially when George Lucas took me aside one day and said, "Basil, you're a much better composer than you are a director."

With credits that included more than a hundred student, industrial, and educational films, Poledouris began scoring television films in 1971. Seven years later came *Big Wednesday*, which can be regarded as the first distinctly Poledouris score. It was made by his friend and fellow USC graduate John Milius and dealt with a subject close to both their hearts—surfing.

In college we had a piano in our fraternity house. Some evenings John would sit by the piano and tell stories and I would invent music to go along with them. We did it then as a pastime, but now we found ourselves doing it and getting paid. *Big Wednesday* is still one of my favorite films, largely because of the working relationship with Milius and our shared interests. We both admired the scoring of Goldsmith and Morricone, and we both loved surfing. For the score, I drew upon the style of Hawaiian music because surfing was the sport of Hawaiian kings, that's where it started.

We also agreed on the philosophical concept of the film. We shared the same mythological notions about surfing. John saw it as the ultimate end of American westward expansion. So do I, in fact I consider this my first Western score. As a writer and director he likes to take things back to their original elements. I like that concept. I try to approach everything in terms of myth, and I see mythology as anything people believe to be true. Beyond that, Milius was a big influence on my concept of film. He introduced me to the work of Akira Kurosawa and the other Japanese masters, this at a time when everybody else was worshiping Antonioni, Fellini, and Kubrick. This had great bearing, both visually and musically, when we did *Conan the Barbarian* in 1982. George Lucas was also with us at USC, and John introduced him to Kurosawa. I see a lot of that influence in *Star Wars*. To me the Jedi Knights are very Samurai.

The Blue Lagoon (1980) gave Poledouris another opportunity to indulge his love of nautical settings with an unabashedly romantic score. However, it was *Conan the Barbarian* that put Poledouris on the film scoring map. John Milius scripted and directed this fantasy adventure set in some unspecified past historical age, with the spectacularly muscular Arnold Schwarzenegger as a superman warrior. Since dialogue was not a key factor in the film, Milius thought in terms of a fusion of image and music and asked Poledouris to write sections of the score before and during the production. This is a luxury seldom afforded a composer.

> *Conan* is an unusual film because it's a music drama and Milius involved me with concept all through the filming. It called for almost continuous music and a huge orchestra and chorus, all of which we recorded in Rome.

The film offered its composer the richest of orchestral palettes in illustrating this lavish tale of sorcery and savagery. Massive brass, strings, and percussion announce the hero; the arch villain Thulsa Doom (James Earl Jones) is underscored with energetic choral passages. It was Milius who suggested to Poledouris that something like Carl Orff's *Carmina Burana* might be suitable for the pagan villain. Poledouris agreed but came up with his own text, adding to it the famous Gregorian chant "Dies Irae," in order to communicate the tragic aspects of the cruelty wrought by Thulsa Doom.

Two years later came the sequel, *Conan the Destroyer*, but neither the film nor the score made the same impact as *Barbarian*. The first one seemed to say it all. Next, Poledouris was again required to turn medieval for Dutch director Paul Verhoeven's *Flesh and Blood*, with Rutger Hauer as a sword-wielding crusader. This time the composer opted to stress the romance and heroism rather than the barbarism.

Verhoeven then called upon Poledouris for *RoboCop* (1987), a futuristic fantasy overflowing with graphic violence, about a Detroit policeman who turns into a machine.

> What I tried to do here was hint at what that experience might be like. I blended electronic and acoustic music with the orchestral to try to capture that feeling. There are two main themes, the first being a fight theme for his conflicts and then a "home" theme

to deal with his humanity in flashbacks to his former life with his wife and child.

Poledouris was not available for the sequel, *RoboCop 2*, but he did agree to score *RoboCop 3*.

I found this interesting because the character had regained some of his humanity. He knows who he is, and he isn't so disturbed. With the character more resolved, I didn't feel the need to use electronics extensively. The score is more grounded in human emotions. This is the approach I prefer. I like stories that have to do with people, I like to write for human relationships. I like the intimate rather than the violent.

Poledouris has scored two major television series, the fourteen-hour *Amerika* (1987) and *Lonesome Dove* (1989). The former failed to make the hoped-for impact, dealing as it does with a Russian invasion of America. *Lonesome Dove,* on the other hand, was a conspicuous success, with a quintessentially Western main theme that has gained popularity in concert form.

What made this interesting for me is that it isn't just a Western, it's a character story about two men, wonderfully played by Robert Duvall and Tommy Lee Jones, and their rigidly strong personalities, especially their moral integrity. Character is the predominant issue in *Lonesome Dove*, and that's the kind of challenge I welcome.

Having scored both *Amerika* and *Red Dawn* (1984), John Milius's fantasy of war between America and Russia, Poledouris was an obvious choice to write the music for *The Hunt for Red October*. The film, released in early 1990, suffered from the changing political climate.

At the outset, I was thinking in terms of Rachmaninoff-goes-to-sea. There's a little of that in the score, but as the emphasis changed from political statement to mystery, I thought more of the kind of music Bernard Herrmann might have written, with a Russian twist. The director, John McTiernan, asked me if I could use a Russian folk song for male chorus in the main title. I agreed with the concept but chose to invent my own song, one from which the thematic material for the rest of the score could be drawn.

This score, regarded by his peers as one of his best, was later adapted by Poledouris into a Suite for Symphonic Band and Chorus.

The only film Poledouris has asked to score is *Wind* (1992), which deals with a subject dear to the heart of the composer—the America's Cup yacht race. Filmed mostly in Australian waters with spectacular photography of the yachts in furious competition, *Wind* was a box-office dud, mostly because the story away from the water was trite and dull:

> But it was a joy to score those sea sequences. The director, Carroll Ballard, came up with shots of those boats and those races that are absolutely fabulous. It gave me a chance to use my banks of synthesizers and multiple keyboards and electronic gadgetry. I thought that the effects you can get with all this stuff—the pounding and surging and the almost illusory feeling you get with that kind of action on the water—was the right way to go with those sequences. But you have to be very careful about the use of electronic music in film scoring. You can do all kinds of wonderful things with these modern computer systems, but you can never duplicate the feeling you can get with real instruments played by humans. You must never lose sight of the difference.

Poledouris was again able to indulge his nautical tendencies when he was hired to score *Free Willy* (1993), the story of a boy's fight to save the life of an orca whale. The lyrical, emotionally based score is the kind that seems closest to his heart but for which there is little demand.

His ability to score visual, action-filled stories filled with Conans and RoboCops keeps him, according to his agents, highly marketable. He began 1994 scoring *On Deadly Ground*, with Steven Seagal as an oil-fire fighter in Alaska. Filled with frantic action, explosions, and violence, the film is Seagal's first as a director—and another challenge for Basil Poledouris to somehow humanize it all.

> Frankly, I was a little scared at the start because of Seagal's image as a tough action hero. He not only turned out to be a sensitive director but a man with a love of music—in fact, he can actually read music. We could discuss the use of music in his film, and he gave me ideas that I accepted. Working with such a director makes all the difference for me. I think composers should be hired by directors, since they have to work so closely on the concept and texture of the film. More often than not, directors and composers get stuck with each other. Both directing and composing are rather subjective arts, and it helps the film when you have someone with whom you have an understanding. For example, one of the problems in scoring films is that it's easy to be misled by the personalities of the actors. It helps if you have a director who can point out that it's the characters about whom you should be writing.

• • • • •

Film music is in a constant state of development, as are all the arts, but it can no longer be regarded as the new kid on the block. After all, it was in 1908 that Camille Saint-Saëns scored *The Assassination of the Duke de Guise,* and there have been thousands of film scores since then. A lot of mediocre music has been written for films, but there is also an abundance of excellent music. It is a form that is a constant challenge to those who have the talent, the imagination, the inventiveness, and the tenacity to score films—provided, of course, that they are hired by people who understand the functions of music in films.

That there were fine composers in Hollywood's past is obvious; but what about now and what about the future? There is no shortage of talent among the many fine young composers who have already proven their ability: Randy Edelman, John Morgan, Joel McNeely, Hans Zimmer, Christopher Young, Mark Isham, Cliff Eidelman, Brad Fiedel, Carter Burwell, James Newton Howard, Marc Shaiman, Howard Shore, and the two sons of the legendary Alfred Newman—David and Thomas.

But what, you may ask, about women composers? In what had formerly been a male-dominated craft there are now many excellent women composers, including Shirley Walker, Nan Miskin, Rachel Portman, and Angela Morley.

Much has been said about the use of music in films, and much will continue to be said. There are no absolute theories, nor should there be. But most people feel that movies need music. Burt Lancaster, an actor who loved music and was noted for his support of the arts, made a movie in 1947 called *I Walk Alone*, about which he related the following:

> My father was making his first visit to Hollywood from New York and I took him to a screening of the picture at the studio. This was before it was scored. I hated it. I thought I was bad and the picture was awful. I was embarrassed and angry. As we were coming out of the screening room, my father asked me what was wrong, and I told him. He just smiled and said, "Don't worry, son, it'll be alright when they put the music to it."